Advertisers at Work

Tracy Tuten

Apress

Advertisers at Work

ISBN-13 (pbk): 978-1-4302-3828-7

ISBN-13 (electronic): 978-1-4302-3829-4

President and Publisher: Paul Manning
Lead Editor: Jeff Olson
Editorial Board: Steve Anglin, Mark Beckner, Ewan Buckingham, Gary Cornell,
    Louise Corrigan, Morgan Ertel, Jonathan Gennick, Jonathan Hassell,
    Robert Hutchinson, Michelle Lowman, James Markham, Matthew Moodie, Jeff Olson,
    Jeffrey Pepper, Douglas Pundick, Ben Renow-Clarke, Dominic Shakeshaft,
    Gwenan Spearing, Matt Wade, Tom Welsh
Coordinating Editor: Rita Fernando
Copy Editor: Kimberly Burton-Weisman
Compositor: SPi Global
Indexer: SPi Global
Cover Designer: Anna Ishchenko

Distributed to the book trade worldwide by Springer Science+Business Media New York, 233 Spring Street, 6th Floor, New York, NY 10013. Phone 1-800-SPRINGER, fax (201) 348-4505, e-mail orders-ny@springer-sbm.com, or visit www.springeronline.com.

For information on translations, please e-mail rights@apress.com, or visit www.apress.com.

Apress and friends of ED books may be purchased in bulk for academic, corporate, or promotional use. eBook versions and licenses are also available for most titles. For more information, reference our Special Bulk Sales–eBook Licensing web page at www.apress.com/bulk-sales.

Any source code or other supplementary materials referenced by the author in this text is available to readers at www.apress.com. For detailed information about how to locate your book's source code, go to www.apress.com/source-code/.

For David

Contents

Foreword

I went to the Cannes Advertising Festival last year, and as I was walking up the red carpet with the stairs lined with photographers and half the ad people in tuxes and gowns, I started thinking that Scorsese and Almodóvar walked up these same steps a few weeks back at the Cannes Film festival. Maybe they deserve the press and glamour and all that, but this crowd? No. At the end of the day I sell candy. I'm also a satellite TV salesman and a travel agent. The people I walked up the red carpet with at the Grand Palais were car salespeople and hawkers of sugar water.

So keep that in mind. In the advertising world, words like "legendary" and "genius" are thrown around a lot, but at the end of the day the only legendary thing these people did was design a nice computer store and sell a lot of milk.

The people in this book aren't strangers to fancy accolades, but I don't think they would ever use the word "genius" to describe themselves. What they would say is they work harder than most, they are always learning, and they are always in search of the "new." And working harder and never being satisfied, regardless of how I make it sound, is quite admirable even if you are just looking for a new way to sell deodorant.

The hard working people Tracy Tuten interviewed for this book are the types of people you want to learn from. I know this because I have personally learned a lot from them. I have a long past with many of them. There are a few people in this book that I have worked for. There are some that I wanted to work for but they didn't want to work with me. There is one that I did get to work for but then they fired me. There are also a few who worked for me and are quickly getting to the point where I will one day be working for them.

And what will you learn? Work harder than everyone else, create something that has never existed before, and be very wary of tuxedos.

Gerry Graf

Founder/Creative Director

Barton F. Graf 9000, LLC

About the Author

Dr. Tracy Tuten is an associate professor of marketing at East Carolina University, where she teaches advertising and social media marketing. Tuten is the author of *Advertising 2.0: Social Media Marketing in a Web 2.0 World* (Praeger, 2008) and coauthor of the textbook *Social Media Marketing* (Prentice Hall, 2013). Frequently quoted in the press, including in the *New York Times, Brandweek,* and the *Washington Post,* she is a leading contributor to industry views on branding. An award-winning scholar, her research has appeared in such journals as *Psychology & Marketing,* and the *Journal of Business Research,* among others.

Acknowledgments

This book would not be possible without the complete willingness and openness of the eighteen people who participated as interviewees. They made this book what it is. Every aspect of value a reader may experience from the book is tied to their experiences, stories, opinions, and advice, and above all else, their willingness to share all of that with those they've never met.

Many of these advertising greats were supported and, yes, even gate kept, by agency professionals. I relied heavily on these professionals for their organizational skills and helpfulness.

I thank Bart Cummings, who provided an example of excellence for me to use as a benchmark and as inspiration.

I thank Gerry Graf, who wrote the Foreword, and John Sweeney and Mark Tungate, both of whom contributed their reviews and endorsements.

I thank Jeff Olson, who developed the concept based on the Apress "At Work" series and believed in me as the person who could see the concept through to its final form. He provided me with the greatest fun I've known in my role as a professor of advertising.

Rita Fernando served as the book's organizational genius, showing amazing patience and detail-orientation from start to finish. It is my sincere hope to work with her again.

Kristen Ng provided her talent and time to transcribing the interviews and offered encouragement throughout the process. Her involvement always felt like that of a friend and I am grateful for her participation, talent, and collegiality.

David Oakley, featured in this book, was enormously supportive of the book and helped me reach out to many of the other advertising greats featured. I am incredibly thankful for his support and his belief in the project.

I am also thankful for my family, especially David, Daddy, Susan, and Chloe.

Introduction

In 1984, Bart Cummings published *The Benevolent Dictators: Interviews with Advertising Greats* (Crain Books). In that book, Cummings interviewed eighteen of the most influential people in the advertising industry. We see these icons of advertising—people like Bill Bernbach, David Ogilvy, and Emerson Foote—as heroes and luminaries. Indeed, they light our way to the future of advertising. Cummings called his book, *The Benevolent Dictators*. Why? He explained that for many of these leaders, their word was law. And as for the benevolent aspect? There is no shortage of talent in the advertising business. No shortage of brilliance. But some are not *just* brilliant. They are also good, kind, fair, understanding, empowering, and dedicated. Despite the diversity of the interviewees, Cummings described them as self-confident leaders who didn't seek out the role of leader and, importantly, as people who truly believed in advertising.

The eighteen people represented in *Advertisers at Work* are unique in their beginnings, roles, and views of the industry and, like Cummings' advertising greats, they *believe* in advertising. At some critical juncture, what Doug Fidoten referred to during his interview as an inflection point, they chose to make a difference in the field of advertising.

Did they know they'd end up in advertising? Overwhelmingly, the response is *no*. Fate took a role. Many were influenced by someone who ultimately served in the role of mentor. Jayanta Jenkins, David Oakley, and Doug Fidoten in particular share rich stories of the influential people who played a role in changing their lives. They and many others in the book then chose to mentor up-and-comers. For example, many of the interviewees offer career guidance. Luke Sullivan's entire interview can be viewed as career advice to young creatives. Kristen Cavallo and Ellen Steinberg speak to what it is like to be women leaders in the field. Jayanta Jenkins encourages young African Americans to consider the wealth of opportunities available in the industry.

Everyone featured in this book stepped up to find the career they dreamed of, to be challenged, to identify a place they'd long to go each day and contribute. They find advertising the perfect playground—a congenial yet serious place to create, influence, have fun, and make a difference. Time and time again those interviewed emphasized their love of the field, passion for the work, and enthusiasm for greeting each new project. Though each and every person represented in this book works incredibly long hours, they also can't imagine doing anything else. Kristen Cavallo shared her amazement at her good fortune, even though she initially took a pay cut to work in advertising. Others acknowledged the incredulous feeling that they could be paid and paid well to do work that was quite simply so much fun.

The advertising industry is a different beast than it was in the days leading up to *The Benevolent Dictators* and depicted by programs like *Mad Men* and even documentaries such as *Art & Copy*.

How is it different?

1) **Rigid organizational structures are dissolving.** *Mad Men* and *Art & Copy* expressed the days when the structure of agencies were fairly well represented by the departments of account management, creative, and media. At the core, perhaps these are still the primary tasks, but without doubt, the roles have expanded with the prevalence of digital media. The role of creative technologist is evidence of this shift. And importantly, particularly for creative work, these roles are not linear. For decades now, art directors and copywriters have worked together from ideation through to production. This shift highlights the change in the role of technology in advertising as well as the challenge in overcoming the silos. This is a theme that resonates throughout many interviews, including those of Kristen Cavallo, Susan Credle, and Edward Boches. Jim Russell gives us a deep view of the role of technology in agencies.

2) **Holding companies rule the industry.** Avid watchers of *Mad Men* know that the Sterling Cooper agency was bought by a holding company in the third season. Ownership limited the decisions the leadership could make. Ultimately, the limitations imposed by the holding company spurred the major players to launch out on their own. Once upon a time, agencies were truly run from the vision of their leadership. Today, four holding companies (the Interpublic Group of Companies, the Omnicom Group, the Publicis Groupe, and WPP) control much of the global industry. Holding companies set corporate strategy, direct

collaborative relationships among agencies within the corporation, and dictate operational and fiscal management of their agencies.

The advertisers featured in this book represent both agencies within holding company families and independents, as well as one holding company. Anne Bologna represented MDC Partners, a Toronto-based holding company that owns Crispin Porter + Bogusky (CP+B). Mullen (Edward Boches and Kristen Cavallo) and The Martin Agency (Mike Hughes) are brands within the Interpublic Group of Companies. Leo Burnett (Susan Credle) is a part of the Publicis Groupe. TBWA/Chiat/Day (Jayanta Jenkins) is part of Omnicom Group. Dentsu America (Doug Fidoten) is a part of the Dentsu Group. Others work in agencies that have retained or reclaimed their independence, including Wieden+Kennedy (Craig Allen), Cramer-Krasselt (Marshal Ross), and McKinney (Ellen Steinberg and Jim Russell). Independent, small creative shops are also represented in the book (Chris Raih of Zambezi, David Oakley of BooneOakley, Ryan O'Hara Theisen and Jonathan Rosen of Lucky Branded Entertainment, and Eric Kallman of Barton F. Graf 9000). Marshall Ross provides insight into the challenges facing agencies that compete as part of a holding company.

3) **Advertising is much more than print ads and TV commercials**. Advertising as a communication medium isn't as straightforward as it once was. It can go beyond a standard print ad or broadcast commercial. Advertising today can encompass both *experiences* and *messages*. Even among messages, it may be short-form or long-form film, text only, even an activity. What's more, the messages (or experiences) may be shared anywhere, anytime. Ultimately, advertising is *ideas* regardless of the media involved. This theme is explored in the interviews of Mike Hughes, John Zhao, Ryan O'Hara Theisen and Jonathan Rosen, Eric Kallman, and Craig Allen.

4) **Awards are still important**. There are many awards sought after in the industry, such as Cannes

Lions, One Show Pencils, Clios, Addys, and Effies. The interviewees and their agencies hold many of these awards. Mike Hughes discusses the role awards can play in driving the work of creatives, and Susan Credle explains in her interview how her team uses Leo Burnett's HumanKind scale to evaluate and judge the quality and potential of their ideas. Though awards aren't the only measure of an idea's success, they are critical to recognizing the value and influence of ideas. They are important to agencies as recruitment tools for both top talent and new clients.

5) **Consumers have power.** We can't simply interrupt them and expect them to care about our message. We have to offer them something of value. To some extent this is relevant to point 3, but even without the experience or the message or the medium, we must recognize that consumers are co-creators of our brand. Chris Raih embraces this theme in his discussion of passion brands.

Those working in the field of branded entertainment—communication whose main purpose is to entertain the audience rather than differentiate a brand, but which is overtly branded—John Zhao, Ryan O'Hara Theisen, and Jonathan Rosen, emphasize the need to offer valuable content if brands wish to earn time with consumers. John Zhao explains the challenge he faces today as he strives to be relevant to audiences in a world so crowded by content from a variety of sources. Ryan O'Hara Theisen and Jonathan Rosen expand on John's view with their contention that advertising must serve the consumer—and by that they literally mean serve the consumer of the advertising—and not just the product's consumer. Their views add credence to the view that advertising can no longer simply push products via an advert. Instead, it must add value to the consumer, and that value is likely in the form of entertainment, and specifically branded entertainment.

Branded entertainment is actually not a new concept in the industry. When television programming was in its early stages of development, brands like Proctor & Gamble sponsored programs of interest to its target audience. Today's soap operas are a byproduct of this kind of sponsorship. We are perhaps destined to return to this model as consumers seek high-quality, relevant programming, and brands seek to play a meaningful role in consumers' lives. Yet, the model will differ because audiences seek different forms of entertainment. For instance, entertainment may be sought online or offline and of varying lengths and genres. Branded entertainment as a niche of the advertising industry focuses on the provision of entertainment, sponsored, of course, by relevant brands. Ultimately, though, the success of branded entertainment, like award-winning advertising, is based on the story told.

Doug Fidoten shares the importance of storytelling, a theme that also arises in the interviews from Mike Hughes and Susan Credle. Many agencies developed in a time reverent to newspaper as the king of print and television as the king of broadcast. These days it's not uncommon to hear people anticipating the demise of traditional media and consequently the supporting advertising. Eric Kallman and Craig Allen take issue with such predictions, suggesting that there will always be a role for short-form films distributed via broadcast venues.

6) **The ad world *is* the world.** It's global. Audiences are exposed to messages from a variety of sources and origins. Brands pursue globally dispersed markets. Advertising is a cultural expression of meaning. When we seek to expand beyond our cultural boundaries, we must do so with an understanding of the culture we target. This is a challenge. Chris Raih, Craig Allen, and Jayanta Jenkins give vivid depictions of what it means to develop global advertising campaigns.

Everyone interviewed shares their personal stories, fears, challenges, successes, and insights for those of us who wish to learn from their experiences. Their openness and willingness to share made this project possible.

Chris Raih

Co-Founder and Managing Director
Zambezi

*Hailing from Minnesota, **Chris Raih** spent his early advertising days at Fallon Minneapolis, where he cut his teeth on accounts like United Airlines and BMW. He then joined Wieden+Kennedy in Portland, where he was a key account player for Nike and met creative partner Brian Ford. In 2006, at the age of 28, Raih co-founded Venice, California–based creative agency Zambezi (www.zambezi-la. com), with nothing more than a cell phone and a Gmail account. Since its beginning, Zambezi, a full-service agency focused on passion brands, has tripled in size, and opened an office in Shanghai, China. Its client roster includes Champs Sports, vitaminwater, and the LA Lakers, among others. In 2011, Advertising Age awarded Zambezi the title of "Small Agency of the Year-West Region."*

Tracy Tuten: Chris, how did you find your way into advertising? Did you grow up wanting to work in the field?

Chris Raih: Actually, I was always excited and intrigued by the notion of mass communication. Growing up, I dreamed of being a journalist. Specifically I daydreamed as a young boy of being a writer for *Sports Illustrated*. I was the kid who read every page of each issue of *Sports Illustrated*. I literally have read every issue from the age of seven to today—and I just turned thirty-four recently. Still to this day, I have *Sports Illustrated* on my nightstand. I love the idea of telling stories and communicating from a journalistic perspective and always felt an attraction toward the news media.

In college, I was a print journalism major, and I wrote for the school paper as a columnist. Then, the summer before my junior year or my senior year, I ended up with an internship at an ad agency, a dynamite ad agency called Fallon in Minneapolis, where I grew up. Truthfully, it came at the right time for me. When I saw the creativity and the spark that was happening at the agency, my excitement and enthusiasm for communications really went to the next level. Ultimately, that was the first big fork in the road for me. I moved more toward the creative side and away from the who, what, when, where, and why constraints of written journalism and news media. Once I had gotten a taste of advertising during that internship, I felt a strong pull to pursue it, which ultimately led to my first job out of school as a young account executive at Fallon.

Tuten: Did your past interest in sports journalism affect your development into advertising for passion brands?[1]

Raih: Yes, I was fortunate to tap into that passion, and I still do on a day-to-day basis. I played some small-time college basketball and I coached junior high teams even into my adult life. I definitely come from a sports family. At our agency, Zambezi, we definitely have a pedigree in sports marketing. We love working with sports and entertainment-related clients—it's our niche.

Tuten: How did your past experiences help or hurt your rise to your current position?

Raih: When I worked at Fallon as an account guy, I was fortunate enough to have the opportunity to work on some tough pieces of business. I worked on United Airlines during 9/11. Our client was a direct and immediate victim of the 9/11 attacks, and it created a really force majeure situation across the board. We, the agency, were keepers of the United Airlines brand. I will tell you that is a tough brief.[2]

Imagine—someone just took your product and used that product to kill thousands of people. How are you going to go market yourself and tell stories three weeks later? Really tough brief. I was really nothing more than a young whippersnapper on those teams, but I worked with highly intelligent

---

[1] A passion brand is one that incites a high level of involvement, commitment, and engagement from its target audience. Many passion brands are tied to interests consumers tend to feel passionate about, such as sports, music, and art. The overarching commonality among passion brands is that they relate to their respective target audiences through a shared vision rather than on the basis of a functional need.

[2] A *brief* is the planning document developed to guide any client project work at the agency.

and global-minded people who were able to help craft some awesome stories and help lift the brand out of the aftermath of 9/11.

The reason I tell this story is to say that I was toughened up at a young age in terms of what kinds of challenges you can face at an ad agency. I also [worked on] BMW while at Fallon, and then ultimately got a job at Wieden+Kennedy and moved to Portland.

I would definitely say that for a twenty-four-year-old guy, working at Wieden+Kennedy on the Nike business was a dream job. I worked there for three years, and I ended up becoming the lead account manager on the Nike basketball business. The basketball business is kind of the crown jewel of Nike. Obviously, Nike is a huge sports empire, and basketball is the highest-margin product. I was fortunate to work with incredible people all the way from the ad agency side to the brand side, and to the athletes themselves. That's also where I met my partner, Brian Ford.

Brian was a copywriter at Wieden back in the day and became the lead writer for the Nike basketball business. He and I made up the core of the agency team for Nike basketball. Brian and I had a great relationship right from the beginning. We complemented each other well.

In mid-2006, after several years of working together, we started to discuss the idea of opening a shop. We both shared the theory that it was possible to create impactful work without an apparatus of hundreds and hundreds of people. We asked ourselves, "Could we do it more efficiently? Could we work with brands in a more nimble way? Could we move as quickly as consumers were moving? Specifically, as quickly as young consumers? If we were quick and nimble, could we still tell really compelling branded stories with smaller groups of people?" This is something we were drawn to and I was always drawn to autonomy.

Some investors came out of the woodwork at the right time for us, and Brian and I were able to take the leap and move from Portland to Los Angeles. This was almost five years ago this month.

Tuten: What's it like opening your own agency?

Raih: It has been scary, frustrating, exciting, wonderful, and fulfilling and everything in between. This has been another huge leap for me personally, and in the development in my career. In terms of a learning curve, it is almost straight up and down as you go from the cozy confines of a best-of-breed agency like Wieden to starting your firm. I'm sitting there in Brian's apartment on day one with a Gmail account and a cell phone. We're saying, "All right, I guess we had better go find some clients."

We definitely learned resourcefulness and ingenuity. We learned to never victimize ourselves. At the beginning it was all about hustling. I had to learn the sales side of this business. I knew how to push ad campaigns out the door. I knew how to facilitate communication between all parties and keep clients happy. I could get things done, on time and on budget, and at a really high creative level. I had been trained how to do those things. But I had never been trained on business development or anything that would constitute the sales side of things. These were things I had to learn and learn quickly.

I am happy to say that through 2006, 2007, and 2008, we were building a really nice trajectory. During the global financial crisis in 2008 and 2009, a lot of things went south for many—not only in marketing and advertising, but across industries. We were working as a small agency with a number of mid-size clients who could and in some cases did pull their marketing in-house. Some clients put work on hold. The president of one of the brands that we work with called me in, like, November 2008, and said, "Hey Chris. Buddy, you know I love you guys, but we are pulling in our sails and we are getting ready for a storm in first and second quarter of 2009."

When we lost some business, we contracted a bit from a staffing perspective and definitely took some lumps, but I am happy to say we survived it. More than survived it. Fast-forward two years and we have been able to get back on the same growth trajectory. We are in a place I had hoped we would be. We have thirty-six employees in our Venice [California] office and another three in our new Shanghai office. We just opened the Shanghai office this week.

Just recently, Bridget [Bulters, communications manager] and I were in Denver, Colorado, for the *Advertising Age* Small Agency Awards. I am very proud to say that Zambezi was awarded 2011 Agency of the Year for the West region. We are definitely starting to get some recognition and we are starting to get some heat and momentum as a brand—as our *own* brand. As an agency, we are moving from a regional to a national and even an international profile.

Where we are now is where I had hoped we would be in late 2009. The global financial crisis set us back a bit, but probably in the long term served us well because it toughened us up. I see for myself that it toughened me up even more than any experience prior. It acutely helped me to develop a sense of resourcefulness, resilience, and ingenuity. It honed my basic instincts for business.

The agency is named after the Zambezi, or Bull Shark, one of the most infamous, resourceful, and adaptable creatures on earth, swimming between freshwater and saltwater in the Zambezi River, which flows through East Africa. It has become the muse for our logos and agency personality with our employees all coming to consider themselves "sharks." This actually seems pretty funny to us since we are all really nice people. A common refrain around the office is, "life is a river." It means you never know what is around the next bend. You never know what is going to happen. It isn't that we are ready for everything, but we are never shocked by anything. I would say that it has been rewarding and fulfilling and a great ride, and I look forward to what the future holds.

Tuten: Would you say are Zambezi's core values?

Raih: A couple of things are emerging as tenets of our agency and its brand. We have been able to prove ourselves to be able to work efficiently and collaboratively. Many agencies, specifically the big, established agencies, are often very hierarchical. It is very clear that unless you are a creative and, even more likely, a creative director, it is not your place to offer up ideas. We prefer to operate as more of a market. We are like a market of ideas being exchanged. An open bazaar of ideas. An idea exchange. We say the best idea wins even if that comes from the intern. If it's a great idea and stands up to internal rigor, then we will go present it to the client. If that idea sells, then the contributor will get the credit.

We are collaborative internally and we try to be collaborative with our brand partners as well. We love our clients! They are great partners. They are the reason we come to work every day. We actually presume high levels of intelligence, ability, and marketing proclivity on the part of our clients. We expect that they know their brand very, very well. We know they are a valuable resource. This has helped us to do great, provocative, relevant work for our brand clients. At Zambezi, we don't think you necessarily have to be bruised and bloodied on both sides in order to get a campaign out the door. In so many agencies, their reels[3] may be undeniably good. But at the same time, you know there may have been some infighting between the clients and the agency in the production of that work. We feel you can work together and pull in the same direction, and I think that has served us well. We are true partners for our clients.

---

[3] *Reel* is a term that refers to the compilation of finished broadcast ads an agency or individual has produced. Similar to the use of the term "book" in reference to a portfolio, it is a holdover term from the time when work was shown literally on audio or film reels. Today, work, whether that of a reel or a book, is presented via digital media.

Another core value concerns victimization. We don't want our people to ever victimize themselves. There are so many obstacles that arise on a day-to-day basis and to succumb to those daily obstacles would be detrimental to our people and our business. When our people face issues, we ask that they not simply complain but come up with a solution. If they don't like something, we tell them not to be a victim of circumstance. If there are conditions that are not conducive to doing great work, then suggest a way to work around it.

Our credentials deck actually includes a slide with some of these bullet points. Those are the big ones . . . collaborate internally, collaborate with our clients, do great work, come up with solutions and not problems. You can be nice and still do great work.

Tuten: Zambezi has been in the news a lot lately with the award for Agency of the Year and the press over the smartwater viral video. Can you tell us about the viral sensation?

Raih: There was an interview published yesterday about the project Zambezi did for smartwater. The project involved a video featuring Jennifer Aniston. We gave the video a cheeky title—"Jen Aniston Sex Tape." If you've seen the piece, you know that the video is *not* that. The title is used ironically. It is used as a poke at what it takes to create a viral phenomenon. The title was simply another layer to the joke. But, of course, in this interview, the title is quoted at least five times. "Chris said sex tape blah, blah, blah, sex tape, blah, blah." Yesterday, my mom reads the interview and calls me saying, "Your grandmother is reading this!" I'm like, "Mom, it is irony. Don't you know irony?"

Tuten: How do you approach new business development for Zambezi?

Raih: That is a good question, almost a two-parter. Part one is methodology for business development. Part two is what the criteria are of the kinds of clients we could really make hay with. What kind of clients are we after? That's pretty straightforward. We use the phrase "passion brands" for the kind of work we are after. Warren Buffett says, "Stick to what you know." Our staff is very youth driven. We are very diverse. We are multicultural and we are all ex-jocks. We are all into music and sports and entertainment. We do our best around brands that are consumer discretionary brands largely targeted to Millennials[4]—your sneakers, your favorite energy drink, your

---

[4] Millennials are people born in the 1980s and 1990s.

favorite headphones, your snowboard, your favorite NBA team, your out-door sports or action sports.

We are not chasing financial institutions. We stick to our lane. Typically, those are brands for which the purchase decisions come from the heart as much as the head. These are brands that produce things young consumers keep on their person on a day-to-day basis. As I said—sneakers, video games, energy drinks, and electronics. If you walked ten feet out of our front door onto Venice Beach boardwalk and grabbed any seventeen-year-old, these are the brands you'd find on that person. Any teen would have probably three of these products on his person at any point in time. Just stuff that he or she is passionate about and passionate about daily—those are the kinds of brands that we do the best with. The halo over these brands is passion.

Now about the first part of your question—about our methodology for creating needs and getting us into client offices. It takes a number of different forms. Back to the notion of being nice guys and being good partners with our brand clients. It has born a lot of fruit for us in so far as many of our clients currently have provided referrals. These days, marketing managers jump around from company to company quite a bit. I think I read that the average CMO[5] life span is under two years at any given company—just one anecdotal statistic. It is a transient business in a relatively small industry. It's a village in a way. We don't want to burn any bridges.

These days we find that somebody will shift to a new company and give us a shout. That's a new thing for us. It took a few years with a lot of phone calling, a lot of hustling, a lot of chasing down the third-party consultants to barge into pitches.[6]

We continue to be the small guy in a lot of our pitches. We are often the dark-horse candidate. We have gone up against some of the biggest and best agencies in the world and I am happy to say that every now and then we are able to knock them on their ass. These days we'd rather get a referral than hustle so much.

Methodology is always an evolving thing. At the end of the day, we just want to get in the room with companies that we consider to be passion brands.

---

[5] Chief Marketing Officer

[6] In advertising, if an account is "in review," the client will invite a few agencies to pitch for the business. Sometimes, determining which agencies should be considered depends on a recommendation by a third-party consultant.

Tuten: What's a typical day like for you?

Raih: On the personal side, I have a three-year-old daughter and a one-year-old son at home. They are up bright and early. My wife and I kind of have a negotiation at 5:45 each morning as to who is going to get up with them when they start squawking. Today it was me, which has brought on the need for strong coffee. Let's see. A typical day is that I am always checking e-mail immediately when I wake up. I check e-mail as I watch *Sesame Street* with the kids. This morning I knocked out about an hour of e-mail. We have clients in China, and typically there are a dozen or so e-mails from them when I wake up. We also have a number of East Coast clients and they are all up early. Each morning, I at least get the mission-critical e-mails answered before I even brush my teeth. Then I will make my way in. We don't have any kind of strict 9:00 to 6:00 schedule here at Zambezi, but usually I am at the office by 8:30. If the gods be good, I usually find about an hour or so to do house-keeping and organization, and then typically start a barrage of meetings or calls.

I think one challenge, personally speaking, is getting my head around our geographic expansion. It is simply no longer realistic for me to be aware of every moving piece of every campaign and every piece of business that we have. I am learning to be selective as a manager in terms to the kinds of situations that I need to insert myself and involve myself in. Those are typically more of a macro problem instead of a micro. If I am too focused on the creative rotation for this print ad, it is not necessarily the best thing for our company. Now if we have a particular brief that is a real sticky thing and we can't quite solve it or, God forbid, we have a dissatisfied client—those are things that it does behoove the company for me to get involved in. I am learning what those things are. All day long I am being selective.

Several times a day, I have to choose between this meeting or answering that e-mail, or taking this phone call, or reaching out to this person. It's like triage in terms of the things I take on. I do try to cross-train between the six or seven retained clients we do have and the five or six different departments we have. For instance, I make an appearance in a production meeting, go hang out with the studio designers, sit and work on deck with the strategic planners, go to lunch with creative directors, go get a beer with the senior account folks. It is a little bit like trying to clone myself.

Tuten: How involved are you in the creative work? Do you miss being more a part of the work given the time you spend on management and leadership?

Raih: Initially that was the spark between me and Brian. I think Brian has been taken aback—in a good way—as he sees my appetite and fluency with creative. Even as a mid-level account guy at Wieden+Kennedy, I had a strong opinion on the work. Truth be told, we would kind of try to work on the creative together.

It is not that I miss it because I stay involved. I pick my spots to be heard and to put my finger on some things. But yes, there are times I wish I could be involved with every single little piece that we are doing.

I'll tell you something my uncle taught me. I was home for Thanksgiving or something a couple of years ago. I asked him, "How do you decide what to take on or what to tackle?" I am going to butcher this relatively slick piece of advice he gave me, but I will do my best. He basically said, "Think about a bull's-eye. In the center of that bull's-eye is where you bill out at a high hourly level." Not to make it all about dollars and cents, but basically what he was saying is that as a founder, I am the center of this bull's-eye. I need to spend as much time in that bull's-eye to further the company's interests. The further I get out in those concentric circles, the less I am serving the best interest of the company. That is something that I took to heart. I try to stay in that bull's-eye as much as possible while not becoming detached from the front line.

Usually about once a day I catch myself weighing in on what kind of coffee mugs we need to buy for the kitchen, or what kinds of ficus trees we need for the lobby. I just catch myself and smile and think about my uncle. He is right. It is good advice.

Tuten: Do you have any rituals that are important to your ability to work effectively?

Raih: One is like a mental exercise and one is a physical exercise. On the physical side, something we do a lot of in our office is to just go outside. We are in Venice Beach, right on the boardwalk. We are literally fifty feet from the sand. Here in LA, I will walk out to the beach a lot with Brian or whomever or just by myself and take a deep breath and look at the waves for a second. When I try to not think about solutions so hard, sometimes the solutions come. Just by the physical movement of going out to the beach.

For the mental exercises, I'm usually stuck when a problem is a big, emotional problem. I'm an ex-athlete. I am a highly competitive person. I tend to get emotional and passionate about things. At those times, you are not necessarily thinking clearly. I am learning to take a deep breath and calm down in these situations. I try to wait before firing off an e-mail in anger and so on. I try to think dispassionately and try to deconstruct the complex problem and into simple, pragmatic next steps. That is typically how you start to get unstuck.

Tuten: Do you have a campaign that is a favorite? Something most meaningful to you?

Raih: Let me paraphrase something Dan Wieden said. I was able to spend some time once with Dan Wieden. He is such a Hall of Famer in our industry. He's an amazing business person who has accomplished more than anybody in advertising, maybe ever. In addition, he's the guy who wrote the line, "Just do it." He has accomplished everything that he has accomplished and he's still just a great guy. I remember sitting with him as a young account person at Wieden+Kennedy. We were with a bunch of folks working on the Nike business. I asked him this same question—what are you most proud of? What piece of work do you feel like, "Yes, we nailed it." The answer he gave me frustrated me at the time, but as I've aged and have grown more with experience, I understand what he meant. I said, "Dan, what is your favorite campaign or favorite spot this agency has produced?" He basically demurred, answering, "The next one, the next one we get, the next brief we get."

So my answer to this question is that the blank, white piece of paper is the one I am most excited about. The next one in the queue. I'd like to just plagiarize his answer right now versus going down memory lane or do a greatest hits kind of thing. I'll say what Dan said: "My favorite campaign is the next one."

Tuten: What is the next one?

Raih: We are developing work in China for our client, Li Nang. Li Nang is a sneaker giant. It's the third-biggest sneaker brand in the world. The reason I say I am excited about it is that the project is like ten-fold the hardest thing we have ever done in terms of taking our expertise about youth, sports, and entertainment, and amplifying that in a foreign country where business gets done in a completely different way than here. It has forced us to really stretch outside of our comfort zone. We have work airing in China. It is far and away the hardest thing we have done. We've worked on it both night and day. We're really proud of what our team and our clients have created.

Tuten: When you look around the industry, what's most surprising to you?

Raih: There is a sea change when you look around the industry seemingly daily. You know, even a month ago, we would talk about QR codes[7] and I would argue that QR codes are already passé. That is just one example of

---

[7] QR code is short for Quick Response code, a two-dimensional bar code used to house data that can be read with a reader using a smartphone or tablet.

how quickly tools and platforms and ways to tell stories are changing. We as an industry have been asked to be creative in the medium and now that is not enough. We need to be creative in the delivery of the message.

Tuten: With the nonstop news and industry developments, how do you stay up-to-date on what's happening?

Raih: At Zambezi, we try to keep the collective IQ high. We have instituted a multiplatform, internal entity called Bites. On a weekly basis, we curate and distribute an HTML recap newsletter of the eight or ten most pertinent stories in marketing, sports entertainment, and tech. We distribute it to not only to our people, but also to our clients, production partners, and media partners. We distribute that once a week and then we get together once a month for a Bites immersion session. These sessions are mandatory, all-company meetings. They are a chance to put the pencils down and get away from computer screens.

Sometimes we meet off site or bring speakers in. We may go see an art exhibit or a show. We may do a show-and-tell session. For example, our most recent session was Friday. We had a couple of different things going on. Some of our creatives presented side projects. These were cheeky videos which brought the freaking house down. Lastly we did a kind of deep dive on media. Our media staffers presented on key terms, industry developments, new metrics, and that kind of thing. It was very well received.

Last month we went to the Tim Burton exhibit at the LACMA, the Los Angeles Contemporary Museum of Art, and sometimes we will go to a Dodger game or what have you. We typically parlay a Bites emerging session with two goals: team building and keeping our collective IQ high. My perception, and maybe I am blind to it, is that our staffers really love what we do with Bites. It is so sharp and it's good enough that six months ago we started submitting it externally. Every client gets a copy of Bites from Zambezi, which underlines and speaks to being on the bleeding edge of what's new and relevant in marketing, pop culture, technology, and sports entertainment.

Bites is branded by Zambezi, and it serves as tangible evidence that Zambezi is curious and hungry to know more. Bites hits the inbox of all of our clients all the way up to CMOs and CEOs.

I almost feel like I am beyond being surprised about stuff now. It rarely happens that I am shocked or feel I completely didn't see something coming. Some of the things that jump out at me are especially related to marketing to young consumers. You can't sell to today's young consumers. You have to provoke them. We always try to be provocative in some way. The key word is relevance. We like to partner with brands that are relevant and our goal is to make those brands even more relevant in terms of how consumers view the brands.

It used to be when an agency rolled out a campaign, that we were kind of guaranteed certain things like reach and frequency. Everything kind of took care of itself—knee bone connected to the hip bone and here come the sales. Now there are so many tools, choices, and opportunities to avoid or ignore paid media. To overcome this, the trend is to provoke and to try to create the belief in relevance around the brands you are working with.

The key is to really try to distill the problem and solutions. We are always after a good idea. A good idea is a good idea. With it, we can figure out what screen to put it on. A QR code is not a good idea. It is one potential arrow in the quiver. It is not an idea. Start with the idea. Then we will find the right production partners to put it on the most pertinent screens.

Tuten: Give me an example of one of Zambezi's great ideas.

Raih: I would say one piece that was pretty funny is our work with vitamin-water. We worked with vitaminwater last fall on a fantasy football campaign. Fantasy football has become big business in the last five years or so. There are going to be like forty million people playing by this year and many of those are male consumers, eighteen to thirty-four, who are decently affluent. That's a pretty desirable audience. This audience is checking into fantasy football every single day from August through December, interfacing with their buddies. It's become a loud market place. Budweiser, Procter & Gamble, Chevy . . . they all spend big in fantasy football.

vitaminwater wanted to try to steal some of that spotlight, really hijack some of the attention that was going on with fantasy football, but with a fraction of the ad spend. We had a couple of things going for us. We have a highly relevant athlete, Adrian Peterson, who is a star running back with the Minnesota Vikings. A year ago, he was probably the number-one overall pick among the fantasy drafts. We had him do the pitch for vitaminwater. The concept was freaking zany—basically that this athlete retained an attack-dog lawyer to try to sue fantasy guys who had Adrian on their team. He is like, "I am on your team. I ran the ball thirty-five times against the Bears. I got two bruised ribs and a sprained ankle and you win all the money in your fantasy league with me. What is up with that? Where is my piece of the action?" This is obviously ridiculous because you and I know he makes millions of dollars a year to play football. This was very over-the-top, kind of cheeky.

We cast for the craziest actor we could find and trust me, we found him! We got Gary Busey to play the lawyer. The net result in terms of the content was a very funny, high-octane, two-and-a-half-minute digital film that was aimed directly at the twenty-five-year-old fantasy guy. The film talked about a specific flavor, vitaminwater energy. A kind of very high-octane energy that is pure in vitaminwater. The piece itself was minimum branding, but maximum storytelling. When I compute the facts, we did this using almost no paid media. Nothing even close to the spending of Budweiser and P&G. With the provocative content and really strong social media engagement using Facebook and Twitter, the video became very well trafficked. We were able to hijack the mindshare around fantasy football.

The day we released the video content, ESPN had its two-hour, kick-off fantasy special. ESPN aired the video in the special. I will never forget it. One of the best moments we could have dreamed of getting as ad folks and ESPN played the video in its entirety. All two-and-a-half minutes right there on ESPN at the beginning of the broadcast. They were like, "before we get started, this just came in from vitaminwater. These guys are crazy. Look at what content they put out. We have been watching it all day." Then they opened the broadcast full screen. I can't even imagine what a two-and-a-half-minute spot would cost in that slot. Again, zero paid-media spent, but we got there simply by being very relevant and provocative.

Tuten: What lessons have you learned during your career that you'd like to share with those aspiring to the field?

Raih: You should always be open to—not necessarily massive change in whatever your goals and dreams are—but be open to a circuitous route to get there. You never know what you may be able to see from the next vantage point.

I was in China a month or two ago. We were able to go out and hike the Great Wall. You think as you hike each section of the Wall—which is about half of a mile long—that the next section would be the end of it, yet it isn't. The Wall is all built on rolling hills, and you can't see the next one until you get to the guard tower. You can't tell until the next section is right in front of you. I think that would be a message to young people: be open to what you are going to find, be open to shifts, and be open to a line of development that isn't always a straight line.

Tuten: What's ahead for you and Zambezi?

Raih: As Brian and I discuss these kinds of things, we've realized some truths. First of all, we get out of bed every morning and we still have flat bellies and sharp spears. We still have the same hunger we had on day one. We still have a keen since of urgency, just as we did on that first day when we were sitting in Brian's corporate apartment trying to figure out who was going to be our first client. I would say in terms of goals, we are growing now but we want to protect the culture we've established here. We won't grow beyond the point at which we can't maintain the culture that we have tried so hard to establish. We round out at about fifty people and everybody still likes coming into work. If we are able to maintain that at five hundred people, that is fine too. We want to maintain the pride, the chemistry, and the culture that we have here.

Kristen Cavallo

Chief Strategy Officer
Mullen

*As chief strategy officer, **Kristen Cavallo** leads planning, analytics and business development for Mullen (www.mullen.com), an agency built to work with ambitious thought leaders like JetBlue, Google, NOOK by Barnes & Noble, Zappos, iRobot, and LivingSocial. In 2011, Mullen was named an Advertising Age A-List agency, as well as a Fast Company Most Innovative Company.*

A strategic storyteller, Cavallo spent 15 years planning strategy for Volkswagen, NASCAR, Coca-Cola, Hanes, Kohler, Charles Schwab, and Miller Brewing. For her work on VW's "Drivers Wanted" campaign, she was awarded the 4A's Jay Chiat Award for Strategic Excellence. She won a second Jay Chiat Award for the launch of Vanilla Coke, which also had the distinction of being named the Best New Product Launch of the Year. That same year, the Hanes Tagless T-shirt was ranked in the Top 10 Best Product Launches. While on Miller Brewing, Time magazine complimented the brand for "perhaps the best turnaround in American business history."

As growth officer for The Martin Agency, Cavallo focused on repositioning and differentiating the agency utilizing her planning background. During her six-year tenure, Martin experienced the best growth years in the agency's history. One of the fastest-growing agencies in the country, Martin was named to Advertising Age's A-List five consecutive years, and in 2010, Adweek named it Agency of the Year. Cavallo helped diversify their client portfolio with brands like Wal-Mart, Pizza Hut, Expedia, Microsoft, ESPN, Mentos, BFGoodrich, FreeCreditReport.com, The American Cancer Society, Kraft, and Johnson & Johnson.

Tracy Tuten: You recently moved from The Martin Agency to Mullen. What's the transition been like for you?

Kristen Cavallo: I was just joking that I have only been here a few months and it feels like it has been ten years. It feels good. It feels like it's been a lot longer—*a lot* longer. It was hard to leave The Martin Agency after fourteen years, but in some ways it was like coming home because Mullen was the first agency I worked for. Mullen's chief creative officer is Mark Wenneker. I actually worked with him at the Martin Agency too—on the Saab account. Back then, I was the planner and he was the art director. He went to Goodby [Goodby, Silverstein, & Partners] for nine years and I stayed at Martin and then we reunited here. There were only two folks I didn't know—the heads of media and account management. Everyone else I'd worked with at some point in my career.

Mullen is a more progressive agency today than when I was here years ago. The physical space is very different. Mullen used to have offices in Wenham and now we are downtown. The agency has been on such a growth spurt. About two hundred people [out of 375] have been hired in Boston in the last two years. The agency feels young and vibrant and has solid, digital skills. It feels forward leaning.

Tuten: You were with The Martin Agency for such a long time. How did this shift come about?

Cavallo: Initially, Joe Grimaldi [Mullen's chief executive officer] reached out to see if I had any recommendations for the role. We've stayed in touch over the years, so the call wasn't unexpected when the role of chief strategy officer came available. After a few discussions, I decided to throw my hat in the ring.

We toyed with the idea of my family moving to Boston and for various personal reasons that did not pan out. I withdrew from consideration for the job. I was really disappointed about it and I thought it just wasn't in the cards. Then in February, Alex Leikikh [Mullen's president] called back and said, "I am staring at *Fast Company*'s list of the top ten Most Innovative Marketing Companies in the country." Mullen had made the list. He said, "It occurred to me that we are not being very innovative about this, so let's start over. Let's rewrite the rules and figure out a way to make this work."

I thought, "How we can do this?" I have a fourteen-year-old son going into high school and a seven-year-old daughter going into second grade. I thought, "I don't want to not be there for them and their activities." The job requires that I manage twenty-five people in Boston. My husband and I discussed it and we came up with a proposal for me to spend three days and two nights a week in Boston and four days and five nights a week in Richmond. Mullen said yes! So I usually fly up Tuesdays and I fly home Thursdays.

It is amazing I am able to still live in Virginia and keep my family unit tight. My parents live in Virginia, my in-laws live in Virginia, and my extended family live in Virginia and that way everyone was able to stay in a great family unit. I am able to come to work and be a chief strategy officer and manage a team of rock stars and I feel enormously blessed. I feel happy that I work for people that didn't let the traditional rules stop them. I feel enormously fortunate that I have a husband and kids, parents, and extended family who all said "we are here to help." And I thank God every day for technology. Because if I didn't have technology, this would not work. Whether I am Skyping or Facetiming with my kids, or Skyping or Facetiming with my co-workers, technology enables this whole thing to happen.

Tuten: What led you to advertising as a profession? Did you grow up wanting to work in the field?

Cavallo: Heavens, no. I worked in sales and I got my undergraduate degree in business from James Madison University. I had been working for Clairol as a sales rep all through college. When I finished college, I really wanted to go into the marketing department in New York City. I asked my boss, "How do I get into the marketing department?" When I was in sales, I felt like I was on the front line with consumers. I would see people frustrated when they bought products that didn't work or super happy when they bought products that made them look great. So much of their self-esteem is built into the products. I heard the pros, the cons, and the whys of every product in the line. Sales was the front line of consumer research.

I had all this great input to contribute about consumers, but I felt like I wasn't being tapped to share that input. My boss said I could absolutely go to New York, but the requirement is an MBA. I struggled with it because I had just spent four years getting a degree in business and I didn't have a desire to go back and get another one. But I decided to go for it. I did an accelerated program at George Mason University. It was a one-year program. I decided to major in something different since I had the marketing slant from undergrad. I focused on statistics. With my masters, I felt like I was coming out with some form of added value, so to speak.

I moved to Boston after my MBA program and interviewed around with a bunch of great companies. In the process of networking, I was introduced to an ad agency by the name of Houston Effler that had the Converse brand. At the time, I thought to myself, I am so not interested in advertising. My impression of advertising was like that of *Melrose Place* with Heather

Locklear. You know, with a lot of really short skirts and frivolous airheads. Then I went and interviewed. The agency was young and vibrant and fast-paced.

I am an Army brat and I love change. Change feeds me. My fear is boredom. Boredom stifles me. I felt like this industry would feed my desires and squelch my fears. I almost took that job, but the next day I had another interview with an agency named Mullen. It was up in Wenham on the North Shore of Boston. It was located in this old monastery and it had kind of a *Dynasty* flair for those who remember that show. Very regal and strong in conviction and spirit. It was unlike anything I had ever seen. I thought, "This is where I want to work." I was hired to work on Timberland and BMW—two really strong brands. There was only one other planner, a guy by the name of Kevin Kolbe who came from Chiat/Day. He had great energy and experience, and really took me under his wing. I loved it.

My father refused to talk to me for about a month after that. He said I was the only person he knew who the higher my education went, the lower my salary went. I think my starting salary was $18,000 a year at Mullen with an MBA and I had left a job in sales making probably about $50,000. It was a pretty significant cut, but I was so happy, very alive, and thriving in the chaos that is advertising. So I really just lucked into it. It was never really part of the plan.

Tuten: Do you think your background in sales helped you as you developed in advertising?

Cavallo: Definitely. Persuading somebody to back my judgment with their money is the heart of both sales and advertising. At this level, most of the agencies that we compete with are as capable as we are, and we are as capable as they. We all have good case studies. We all have great people. We all have the ability to hit the ball out of the park. Sometimes what makes the difference between winning and losing is a game of inches—one team being slightly more persuasive than the other. My sales experience definitely helped me hone that skill.

Tuten: Here's the inevitable *Mad Men* question. *Mad Men* has reinforced some of the ad industry's early stereotypes. Are any of the types of people and situations represented in the show still prevalent in the industry today?

Cavallo: Oh sure. I think Don Draper and his very focused perspective on creative is very much still true. The stereotypes represented in the show in terms of the positions are still true. Like the account guys being very focused on the clients' point of view and the creative guys focused on the creative perspective and what will be award-winning—all that is still very true.

The biggest shift in my mind is the role of women. Seeing *Mad Men* reminds me how far we've come.

Tuten: What advice do you have for women as we seek to advance?

Cavallo: Take yourself seriously, read, travel, be well-spoken. When you go into the room, take a seat alongside key decision makers. Believe that you belong there. If you don't believe you belong there, or if you sit shyly on the sidelines, then you won't be invited back.

Tuten: What's it been like for you as a woman, working in the field and working in positions of leadership? And how do you balance that with family time?

Cavallo: It can be difficult to balance obligations. It is hard to be a working parent. There are times you leave vacation early for a pitch or times you leave work early for a game. For years, as a single mom, I tried to do it all myself to prove I was capable. But that was misguided. Doing something well matters more than doing it all. When I realized this truth, I asked my boss at Martin, Earl [Cox, Martin's chief strategy officer and partner], for help. I asked him for flextime to work from home one day a week. Earl made it clear that he didn't help me out of pity, but because he valued my contribution. I learned to accept actions like these not as symptoms of weakness, but as evidence of my worth.

When I was considering this job here at Mullen, I saw Sheryl Sandberg [chief operating officer at Facebook] speak at TED.[1] She spoke about the lack of women in C-suite jobs. I was surprised to hear her chide women for walking away from top jobs. She said that by doing so, we didn't allow companies the chance to be progressive and contemporary in their approach.[2] I took her advice to heart and that was a major reason I asked Mullen to consider my work schedule proposal. It's working for me and for Mullen and for my family. My kids and my husband and my family are my biggest cheerleaders.

There's one other thing that comes to mind. This is from another TED talk. It was a talk by Madeleine Albright [former US Secretary of State]. She said, "Guilt is every woman's middle name. Plenty of women asked me why I wasn't in the carpool lane or told me I wasn't prioritizing my kids. Is the

---

[1] TED is a non-profit organization that supports the spread of ideas through presentations by thought leaders. Learn more at www.ted.com.
[2] TED, "Sheryl Sandberg: Why we have too few women leaders," www.ted.com/talks/lang/en/sheryl_sandberg_why_we_have_too_few_women_leaders.html, December 2010.

carpool lane the only way to show I care? I believe there is a special place in hell for women who don't help other women."[3]

Tuten: What's a typical day for you like, if there is one?

Cavallo: My typical day . . . I have about twenty-five people in my strategy group, twenty-five who report to me. They are a mix of strategic planners and analysts and statisticians. The planners are traditional strategic planners, so to speak, and the analysts have master's degrees for the most part in analytics or in econometric modeling. It's a broad group of smart thinkers and there are a variety of specialties including mobile, digital, innovation, and storytelling. My favorite time is spent managing and growing the team. I spend a good chunk of my time developing specific client strategies for current clients like JetBlue, Google, NOOK, and Zappos. I probably spend twenty percent of my day on agency issues like diversity and inclusion, revenue generation, and such.

Tuten: Kristen, you have won several awards for your work on past campaigns. Now, in your management and leadership role, are you as involved in client work?

Cavallo: Well, this is not an industry of martyrs. No pitch has ever been won or lost and no case study has ever been based on just one person. Although a lot of people would have you sometimes believe that. Very often, one person might be a driving force. But it takes a lot of people to make what we make, lots of cooks in the kitchen. Collaboration and working with other people is key. I'm probably more involved in client work right now than I was in my past job as director of new business, but probably less so than when I was a planning director. When I was a planning director, everything was client work. As a business director, I didn't work for any one specific client. Instead, my client was the agency. Now it is split for the most part with maybe a little heavier focus on the clients.

Tuten: Are you enjoying having more client focus than you did in your role in business development? Has the work at Mullen been positive so far?

Cavallo: Oh yes. Absolutely. Mullen really has a sweet spot with thought-leader brands. By thought-leader brands I mean brands that tend to be outspent, brands that tend to not be the market share leader in that category.

---

[3]TED, "Madeleine Albright: On being a woman and a diplomat," www.ted.com/talks/madeleine_albright_on_being_a_woman_and_a_diplomat.html, February 2011.

Thought-leader brands must challenge the product category and do business differently. These are brands that have to think their way out of a problem because they don't have the luxury of throwing money at it. Market share leaders tend to have the lion's share of money and customers. It's a totally different situation in how to approach the market. With these brands, usually we move at a really fast pace and are constantly asking ourselves, "What's next?"

Our clients tend to feed their consumer-based social conversations with lots of initiatives, or topics in succession, much more frequently than maybe a market share leader would. That's because they are trying to turn the category conversation in their favor, always trying to pull people to their brand. And since they don't spend more than the market share leader, they have to say more provocative things to cause consumers to reappraise their choice.

Tuten: How would you describe the Mullen philosophy? Is it similar to your own approach to work and life?

Cavallo: I actually think that Mullen's philosophy and my personal philosophy go hand in hand, which is one reason why I am here. Mullen's philosophy has a name—it's called "unbound." It means that we don't work in silos and all the disciplines are smashed together. We are a bundled solution with everything under one roof—media, digital, creative strategy, social, performance analytics, everything. We don't, for instance, have a digital department. Instead there are digital people throughout the whole company. Everyone is focused on solving business problems and just moving the ball down the field—helping our clients win. Other agencies separate their media teams from their creative teams—often they even work in different buildings. I don't know how to solve problems that way.

Mullen is pretty entrepreneurial and doesn't labor over titles and such. People frequently move in the agency and try their hand at different things. It's encouraged even. I love that about the agency. As far as my own approach to work and life, I'm an Army brat. I moved a lot growing up and I was exposed to many cultures. I learned to play instruments and sports. I have a lot of interests and I thrive in an open environment. Mullen suits my personality. Plus I'm surrounded by other misfits like me.

Tuten: When you look around at the industry now—expanse of media, consumer control, interactive and social, challenges for print and traditional media—what's most surprising to you?

Cavallo: Many agencies are known for expertise within a channel. Like digital or media or direct or experiential. There are so many agencies set up like that. People in these agencies need to be able to play across channels, but they can't really because of the agency specialization. Like, "I only work in digital," or "I only work for the media company," or "I work for the direct company," or "I work for social media," or "I am at the experiential agency."

The industry did itself such a disservice when it started splintering things off as a way to not deal with competitive conflicts. The industry sold the idea to the client that they should hire agencies based on best in breed. I am not saying you can't. While I know there are great agencies within those silos, I don't believe they are structured to solve business problems because they have to execute solutions within their own boundaries.

When I was contemplating changing agencies, I had a handful of criteria that I was unwilling to compromise on. One was that I would not go to a siloed agency. The prevalence of siloed agencies surprised me. That alone dramatically narrowed my field of agencies. It was the biggest funnel shrinker of all my criteria.

Another one of my criteria was that the agency had to have a strong creative backbone. And lastly, the agency had to have a reputation for integrity —both in how they treat their employees and in their decision-making. If I was going to move, it had to be for an agency that had a reputation of integrity and a sense of honesty in an industry that I don't always think rewards that. Those were high bars. I wasn't willing to sacrifice those parameters for money or a title.

Sometimes I think the industry isn't its own best advocate. I think if it wants to be taken more seriously, then it needs to take itself more seriously and it needs to keep a high bar. The tactics that we use now will change. The tactics that we use are different than the tactics that we used six years ago. It will be different six years from now, but the values that we operate with should be sustained.

Tuten: Do you think the industry will rebundle and shift from the focus on silos?

Cavallo: I hope so. You are starting to see some agencies starting to rebundle now. They are bringing media back inside and digital inside, but it is not enough just to have the capabilities inside the agency. It really comes down to the people and the process. Agencies with bundled disciplines tend to hire different people than siloed agencies. In bundled agencies, you reward people based on how collaborative they are and for the accomplishments of the group instead of the accomplishments of a person.

That will take years for siloed agencies to build because we're talking about behavior and it is hard to change behavior. It is easy to just move somebody into a building, but it is hard to get them to act like a team. I hope that it happens. For those agencies that are trying it, they need to know that they can't do it in just a year or two. It will take longer. They have a longer road. An interesting thing is that there were a few dinosaurs that didn't unbundle when it became popular to do so. Those few dinosaurs are now pioneers in an industry of super-siloed agencies. They should be justly rewarded.

Tuten: How do you stay on top of it all?

Cavallo: Let's see. It's so hard. I read constantly. I travel extensively. I attend shows and go to museums and people-watch. I definitely realize I don't know everything I should, so I surround myself with really smart people. I believe Twitter to be both my chagrin and my pleasure. I pay attention to creative work. I read magazines and I shop. I talk to my kids. You just have to have an unending curiosity and willingness to learn, and when you get into a specific pitch or review or process, you have to be able to quickly immerse yourself in an industry and a brand. Being a quick learner and avid reader, being open-minded, and having a big, curious appetite are all necessities for this job.

Tuten: Do you still watch television?

Cavallo: Yes, but I watch it all online. I watched all four seasons of *Mad Men*, but not once did I watch it on TV. I downloaded them all on iTunes and watched them. I watch almost all of my television after the fact and online. My time to watch TV is at 11 p.m.—never when it is "on," so to speak. I do still have a TV and my kids watch it sometimes or they use it for Xbox.

In fact, my son and I were talking the other day about radio and how everyone thought MTV was going to kill radio. The first video ever played on MTV was "Video Killed the Radio Star" by the Buggles. We were talking about how in fact that did not happen and even more so now people are paying for radio. People may be listening to Sirius or using Pandora, but clearly radio has not died at all! Recently I turned on MTV and I couldn't find a video to save my life.

Now I go to YouTube for videos. When my daughter wants to find the latest Taylor Swift song, we go to YouTube. We don't go to MTV. I still think MTV is a cool brand, but it is based purely on yesterday's momentum and equity, not anything they have necessarily done lately. The last thing I think they did with any kind of momentum and buzz factor for me would be the reality show with Puck from *The Real World*.

Tuten: Do you have a favorite campaign, one with special meaning for you, that you worked on? What made it a favorite?

Cavallo: I love working on brands that feel they have something huge to overcome—brands with a strong sense of mission and purpose. I have found that in a number of client brands. Volkswagen was my first love because it was an outlier brand. It had a desire to become more beloved while staying true to its identity.

Kohler plumbing is one of my favorites. I have worked on that brand twice— once at Mullen and once at Martin. Now every time I redo a new house, I redo it in Kohler from head to toe. I just love the whole mythology of that brand. I love the fact that Kohler is the name of the brand and the town it originated in, and the head of the company is the mayor of the town. The work they do is beautiful. They have a soul. They have one of the largest artists-in-residence programs of any company. Ten feet away from someone spray-painting enamel on a toilet, there is someone painting a fresco of Milton's *Paradise Lost.* Mr. Kohler wants his employees to feel like artisans, not workers in a factory. That passion is reflected in the beauty of the Kohler products. I love that! I loved the whole spirit of the company.

Miller beer thoroughly embraced being a challenger brand. They were number three, Coors was number two, and Bud was number one.

We came up with this idea to make it a two-horse race—to laser-focus on Bud, the number one, and ignore Coors, the number two. To ignite the beer wars. We did a lot of mental chess. If Miller did this, what would Bud do? If Bud did this, what should Miller do? And so on. We came up with a campaign based on chapters of a book. Every quarter we would write a new chapter in the story of Miller and figure how it worked vis-à-vis Budweiser. Miller had a roster of agencies—us, Ogilvy, Y&R, Wieden+Kennedy—and we all got together for strategy sessions. I loved it. It was awesome to open up *Time* magazine and have *Time* say it was one of the most inspiring turnarounds in business history.

Now I feel like a kid in a candy store that I get to work with brands like JetBlue and Zappos, and Google and NOOK. NOOK is fascinating as Barnes & Noble goes from a paper company to a digital company. They have so much ambition. They stare down big companies like Amazon and Apple each day. Every meeting is a game-changing meeting. Every one of them. They don't have the luxury of an enormous budget, huge market share or ample shelf space. They fight for every piece of it. But they have smarts and vision and courage, and that is beyond fun.

Tuten: What's been your most exciting moment in your advertising career thus far? The best moment?

Cavallo: I've had lots of great moments. Seeing the VW "Milky Way" commercial [aka the Pink Moon spot] on TV alongside my parents was one.[4] That was a favorite not only because of my passion for Volkswagen, but also because it was the first time my parents thought what I did for a living was cool.

When we won the Wal-Mart account at Martin, certainly. It was the largest review of the year and we were the underdog.

When I had the recent pleasure of standing alongside a newly minted senior planner during her first new business presentation. We'd rehearsed over and over and she really knew her stuff. When the big day came, she wore a new scarf she'd bought online with a cool design that connected to our client's business. It was subtle but I loved that she wore her passion for their brand like a badge of honor. In the middle of her speech, the client interrupted to compliment her scarf. It was a good moment.

The opening of the first Microsoft store—let me tell you, it is surreal to walk into a structure that I actually had a hand in designing. And to see people walking out with our shopping bag in hand. Our team designed the Microsoft Store logo and it gave me chills to see the logo lit above the door to the store, on the bag, and on employee uniforms.

The BFGoodrich pitch was the first one I ran after I became director of new business. It felt like the Super Bowl to me. It was a test. I'd never managed a review before. Then on the last day, we were waiting to hear if we'd won or lost the account. I felt we'd done well, but this business is finicky and it's hard to predict a win. It was a rainy day and we were dressed casually. Even more so than usual. We'd pulled so many late nights on the work and we had given it all we had. The consultant called me and asked me to pull a last-minute meeting with the core team, saying that there were "issues with compensation." He insisted the client needed to have a conference call right away and that things were on edge. I was so angry! To have this wonderful work and thinking and chemistry come down to a disagreement over money was frustrating.

I got everyone in a room and we prepped for the call. About two minutes before the call was to start, I got a note from the receptionist that I had a visitor and they were insisting that I meet them in the lobby right then!

---

[4]The Volkswagen "Milky Way" spot aired in 1999 and was thought to be Volkswagen's best advertising until its 2011 spot, "The Force." Readers can see the ad and learn more about it at www.adweek.com/adfreak/battle-vw-ads-force-vs-milky-way-11593.

Awful timing, right? I sprinted to the lobby, trying to think of ways to ditch the visitor and get back to the call. When I got to the lobby, the receptionist pointed me outside. There, in the rain, was the entire BFGoodrich marketing team. They were holding a banner with our proposed tagline and they were chanting for us to come outside. I called the team down from the conference room. We all ran outside, popped champagne, and danced and hugged for like twenty minutes. In the pouring rain! They said they knew we were the right choice after the first meeting and each subsequent meeting had just confirmed their gut reaction. It was a great ending to a great pitch and a great beginning to the relationship.

I never tire of those moments. When you get to see your work come to life, when a client's business improves, when an employee believes in themselves, when a brand chooses your agency to represent them. These "votes of confidence" motivate me and keep me going.

Tuten: Do you ever think about running your own place? Having your own name on the door?

Cavallo: No, I have never felt the need to have my name on the door. I feel the need to travel, to go places, and do things. I need to meet people and work on lots of different kinds of business. I work with some clients that I have been fortunate to work with again. I have never felt the need to see my name on the door.

This is probably an irrational fear, but I also have it stuck in my head that to run a place means I have to settle down and stand still. Maybe it's because my role models—Joe Grimaldi, John Adams, and Mike Hughes—have all worked at their agencies for thirty-plus years. My desire for freedom is greater than my desire for power.

Tuten: Are they your mentors?

Cavallo: I am learning so much from Joe now. He is passing the baton so beautifully. If I'd built Mullen I know I would have a hard time letting others drive. But Joe is remarkable. He is curious about our approaches, our thinking, our reasoning. His default mode is supportive. He assumes we're right, which gives us so much confidence. I feel like a plant being watered every day. And it makes me more determined not to let him down. And yes, at Martin, Mike Hughes and John Adams both served as my mentors. Mike taught me that genuine compassion is in short supply. We work in an industry where shortcuts, breakups, and cynicism seem to dominate. In sharp contrast, Mike wins employee loyalty with praise, wins competitor respect with compliments, and wins client attention by listening . . . really listening. When Mike was inducted into the Creative Hall of Fame, John Adams pointed out that people can be intimidated by Mike, but not for the usual reasons. Mike intimidates people because he talks about the kind of advertising he wants them to do. He tells them he wants them to change the world. He insists that they think bigger than they're able to think. Then, as they sit there, he tells them what he finds remarkable about them and how knocked out he is by their talent. They leave proud, off to find a wall to walk through for him.

John is the CEO of Martin and another big influence on me. Initially I was afraid of John, but after working with him on one new business pitch, I placed myself directly in his path. He pushed me and the strategies I was creating to be more surprising. He would question my logic until it was smarter. He would rehearse me over and over until my presentations were powerful and concise. He invested in me and I am better for it.

Tuten: Think back to when you were just getting started in the business. What do you wish you had known then that you know now?

Cavallo: When looking for a job, one's inclination early on is either to pick the one agency that you admire or to pick the account that you want to work on. What I have found in my twenty years of being in the business is that neither is the best way to choose. Work for somebody who inspires you every day to try new things and think more deeply. Don't worry about the brand or agency name on your résumé. Follow amazing people. I always learned the most when I worked for someone I admired. When I worked for somebody who pushed me—regardless of what agency I was at or what account I was on.

The reputations of the agencies can get distracting. I know plenty of people who have gone to work for the "agency of the moment" with all its magic fairy dust, and it didn't turn out to be what they thought it would be. This is why you have got to find the great people. Be willing to search for those people. Sometimes it may take a while for you to find them. Once you do, you can build that "agency of the moment" with them.

Tuten: What's next for you? What next steps, dreams, aspirations still await?

Cavallo: Personally, I want to raise good, stable kids who are productive members of society. I hope my kids see their parents as people who find creative ways to solve problems and who love them. Work-wise, I have been given a rare gift to work for two companies back to back, which have high integrity, creativity, and regard for my personal growth. I plan on embracing that. Someday I'd love to work abroad. I grew up in Europe and I would really love to give my kids the experience of living in another country during their childhood.

I feel like my answer is all over the place. I don't make firm career plans because I worry it will give me tunnel vision. Have you seen Steve Jobs' speech to the Stanford graduating class? I'm sure it's online.[5] In it, he talks about how new opportunities will present themselves to you. They will be opportunities that you never thought of. These opportunities occur when you follow your passions. They don't happen because you followed a career ladder or some predictable schedule for career growth—just when you follow a passion and are committed to excellence in your work. You earn the opportunities with your passion, but you can't take advantage of them unless you are open and smart enough to recognize the opportunities when they come. The choices may not always seem rational. But when you look back, they will make sense to you. And what's even better, you'll have fun with your career. That's the best way to describe what's next for me. I'm open to the opportunities and I plan on enjoying every moment.

---

[5] Read the transcript and watch the video of Steve Jobs' Stanford commencement address at www.npr.org/blogs/thetwo-way/2011/10/06/141120359/read-and-watch-steve-jobs-stanford-commencement-address.

Luke Sullivan

Former Creative Director
GSD&M Idea City

*After 30 years and 21 One Show Pencils in the ad business, author **Luke Sullivan** is now chair of the advertising department at the Savannah College of Art and Design (SCAD). He's the author of the popular advertising book* Hey, Whipple, Squeeze This: A Guide to Creating Great Advertising *(Wiley, 2003); the blog* Hey Whipple *(www.heywhipple.com); and a memoir,* Thirty Rooms to Hide In: Insanity, Addiction, and Rock 'n' Roll in the Shadow of the Mayo Clinic *(CreateSpace, 2011). Sullivan now lives in Savannah with his family. He reports that he enjoys the indoors and likes to spend a lot of his time there.*

Tracy Tuten: What led you to advertising as a profession? Did you grow up wanting to work in the field?

Luke Sullivan: I grew up reading comic books—*Spider-Man, Daredevil.* Then I started making my own comic books, which if you look at a comic, is basically a storyboard. Telling stories with words and pictures. It took me a couple of years out of college to put those two together: telling stories with words and pictures equals advertising. Lordy, I remember the first book I put together to get into the business. What Tom McElligott and Ron Anderson [of Fallon] back in Minneapolis saw in me I will never know. It sucked, but somehow I got in. My blessings to them both.

Tuten: How did your background—school, earlier jobs—help or hurt your rise as a creative director?

Sullivan: The habit I picked up early that helped me most was definitely reading. In 1966, I discovered my first Doctor Doolittle book by Hugh Lofting. I remember sneaking pages of it in during my sixth grade class because I found it more interesting than the class. I have read voraciously ever since. I recommend students do the same. It doesn't have to be classics. It can be anything. Stephen King, romance novels, _People_ magazine, history, I don't care. Be curious. Stay curious.

In high school, I enjoyed putting together magazines and other "underground" publications. One publication I released—to the irritation of the vice-principal—was a twenty-page book called "Student's Guide to Better Skipping, Smoking, & General Misconduct." It was a detailed manual on how to forge hall passes, which were the best doors to sneak out of school, and the best places to hang out during school hours.

After college, I spent three years refinishing wood and working on a construction crew while I figured out what I wanted to do next. One day I stumbled upon a book of the best ads from the Minnesota ad community. Each year advertising groups publish an annual of the best work. That was really the first time I considered advertising as a career. While I wasn't ready to get into the middle of the business, I did land a job as a typesetter at Dayton's department store. I didn't write the ads, I didn't art direct them. I just set the type. But at least I was on the edge of the business and I wasn't refinishing woodwork in the third floor of a brownstone in the July heat.

Tuten: You've recently left the chief creative role at GSD&M Idea City to run the advertising department at SCAD. Can you share the decision-making thought process you went through as you made the choice? Goals for the future? Fears? What played in to the choice to mentor young talent in a school setting rather than in an agency?

Sullivan: I often think there are three main chapters to a creative person's career. Getting famous, getting money, and getting settled. When you first start, you're all on fire and you want to show the world you can do this. Your focus tends to be on awards because the recognition is evidence that you can do the work. Then after you've convinced yourself, "Dang, I really can do this," you think, "Hey, I should get paid more for this. I do it really well." That comprises much of the middle of one's career. And then there's that time when you want stability more than anything else. You have kids. You don't want to move around as much anymore. So you look for a long-term home, a place you can see yourself happy in for ten, fifteen years.

Maybe that doesn't describe your path, but it does mine. As I approached this third chapter of my career, I wanted some stability. But stability in the advertising world is a scarce commodity. Even if you're an established player, forces outside of your control can make your job go away overnight. Things like a change in management or the loss of an account can shift everything in an instant. So I started looking outside of advertising, as I think many people in my position do. Education was a natural, at least for me, because I have enjoyed mentoring kids all these years. I think I have it in my blood. My mom was a teacher, and so was my grandfather. He even has a school named after him in Daytona Beach, Florida—R.J. Longstreet Elementary School. Good ol' Poppa. I love carrying on the family business.

Tuten: *Hey, Whipple, Squeeze This* is among the most-read, most-loved advertising books and one I, like many other advertising professors, recommend to students. What's it like to *be* Luke Sullivan—the person who wrote such an influential book in the industry?

Sullivan: I wrote *Whipple* when I was at Fallon. I had been saving speeches and articles for a few years in a file. Gradually I started adding other people's advice, insights, and articles and the file eventually grew unruly and bad-tempered. It would no longer fit in my file case and I didn't want to buy a new one. Changing my storage system would've thrown off the design of my office. I'm serious.

Then one day I had to give a speech at the Portfolio Center in Atlanta and I raided that file for all it was worth. I handed out the notes of the speech and later learned the notes were turning up as screen savers in agencies here and there.

In addition to being flattered, I began thinking there was a market for a decent book on advertising. Most books—at least at the time—were pretty bad. All you had to do was look at the examples of "good advertising" these books contained and you could tell the authors weren't practitioners of the craft, at least the craft I practice.

So I just started writing. I didn't have a publisher nor any hope that such a book would be welcome on the shelves of bookstores. But that was beside the point. I *had* to write this book—mostly to get it out of my system. I wrote it out of an obsession. Once I had the idea in my head, I literally could *not* stop working on it.

After I had finished, I showed the first manuscript around to about forty people I admired. These were just folks in the business. I showed it to creatives, account folks, directors. Every one of them was kind enough to read the entire thing and give me criticism. I am still in debt to those people. After that, it was just a matter of getting it into the hands of the right publisher.

Not knowing the first thing about the process, I just wandered over to the Barnes & Noble in downtown Minneapolis and bought some books on how to write book proposals and other how-to manuals. I followed what they said and that was pretty much it. It's been fun. It's made money, but not John Grisham money. First-time authors rarely make money. It's more of a love and pride thing.

Hey Whipple has been a constant source of joy for me because so many young people write to me and say, "Hey, your book is what got me into the business." That does *not* get old, I assure you. It feels great knowing you've had a positive effect on someone's life. That is, if luring someone into the dark alley of advertising can be described as positive. It's in five languages now and the fourth edition is out in 2012. The new edition will include coverage on creating for social media.

Tuten: Your latest book is *Thirty Rooms to Hide In.* It's quite a departure from *Hey Whipple.* Tell us about the book and what inspired you to share stories of your childhood.

Sullivan: It's titled *Thirty Rooms to Hide In: Insanity, Addiction, and Rock 'n' Roll in the Shadow of the Mayo Clinic,*[1] and about the best way I can describe it is *The Shining* . . . but funnier.

It's the story of growing up with my five brothers in a big dark house in Minnesota back in the fifties and sixties. Winters raged outside and our father raged inside, and yet we managed to have a wildly fun, thoroughly dysfunctional time growing up, thanks mostly to our mother's protection. Dark humor was the coin of our realm, and The Beatles, they were true north on our compass of Cool. We made movies, started a rock and roll band, and wise-cracked our way though a pretty grim landscape of our father's insanity, Eisenhower's Cold War, fallout shelters, and JFK's assassination.

Although I had two agents repping the book, we were unsuccessful in selling it to a major publishing house. My agent described the problem when she said, "Luke, I love the book, but you are about ten years too late to a market that is now flooded with memoirs." Every crybaby with a typewriter out there—and I include myself among them—has written a memoir. Seems to me there are plenty of "my childhood sucked more than your childhood" books out there. It might have started even way back when with *Mommie Dearest's* "No more wire hangers"!

Tuten: Did the process of trying to get *Thirty Rooms to Hide In* published remind you of the approval process in advertising?

---

[1] Available on www.BN.com and www.amazon.com.

Sullivan: Absolutely. First, can we just agree that whenever art and commerce meet, there's going to be tension? Sometimes compromise, sometimes conflict, but *always* tension. The creative world bristles with examples.

Take Hollywood, where producers can dictate "notes" while screenplays suffer the "death of a thousand cuts." Or advertising, where clients can grind excellent work into vanilla-flavored poop. Christ, even The Beatles were pressured by the financial people, and to this day, their producer, George Martin, regrets being forced to release "Strawberry Fields Forever" and "Penny Lane" as singles when he knew they should've been part of the *Sgt. Pepper's* album.

On the other hand, artists aren't always right—even the great ones. I'm thinking of Michael Cimino. Here's a guy who creates one of the best movies ever—*The Deer Hunter*. It wins a bunch of Oscars and so Hollywood decides Cimino is a deity and gives him carte blanche. He then immediately turns into an orgy of creative excess. You may remember *Heaven's Gate* as an expensive, so-so movie? But actually what it *was* a creative indulgence, which actually closed the doors of the United Artists studio. Even more, what's ironic is that United Artists was originally formed by so-called "creatives." It was formed by actors like Chaplin, Fairbanks, and Pickford—to wrest control from the financial people.

Here's where I'm going with this: artistic control seems to be moving away from the financial people and into the hands of not just artists, but consumers. We've moved from being a downloading culture to one that uploads, and now everybody with a cell phone can have their own movies on YouTube and any crybaby—including me—with a computer can be a "published author."

There's no financial entity keeping us in line anymore. No conference calls about "studio notes" or "client concerns." Content is king and we artists can't blame our mediocre output on "The Man" anymore.

Tuten: What's a typical day like, if there is one? Do you have any rituals that are important to your ability to work creatively?

Sullivan: When I was a working copywriter, yes, I had many little rituals I observed in order to have a productive day. All creative people are different. I happen to like a clean environment that offers no distractions. I read recently that author Jonathan Franzen, who wrote *The Corrections*, wrote on a little MacBook while facing a white wall in a small, bare room. He further removed distractions by having no internet access on his little machine.

There is a marvelous book about the creative process called *The War of Art*.[2] The title is a nice little play on that old chestnut, *The Art of War*. In this book, the author posits that many of the roadblocks creative people encounter are of our own making. We have an unconscious resistance to writing that we have to be aware of in order to defeat.

I defeat it by working in a room without distractions. In a quiet, well-ordered, empty, and totally clean room. I cannot work well with music of any kind playing. Well, okay, I cannot work with music with lyrics. I cannot work well with distractions. Many people can. I am unable to. No e-mail on the computer. No phone about to ring. Nothing. Just the white page or screen. It focuses me. And as for time of day, I always liked my morning brain better. Ten a.m. was prime thinking-time for me.

And as for a typical day? There never was one. That's the thing about this business. There are so many things going on, even at a small agency, that things stay pretty lively. And even when you have something approaching a routine at the office, it goes out the window when you go on a shoot or any kind of production.

Tuten: Do you have a favorite campaign you worked on? What made it a favorite?

Sullivan: It's a radio campaign, for a teeny little client that we had at Fallon McElligott in 1995 and 1996. It was a technical school called Dunwoody. They trained kids in what was once called "the trades." You could get a degree in, say, heating and air conditioning, architectural drafting, computer repair … you know, *real* jobs. I had a great client who never changed a word of copy, trusted that I had their best interests in mind, and just let me at it. I've posted my fave spots from this campaign on my blog, heywhipple.com.[3]

It never won Best of Show anywhere, but I don't care. Well, okay, maybe I was a little bummed. I still think the work was great, but listeners can decide for themselves on heywhipple.com.

Tuten: Are there campaigns that have special meaning for you? Can you share one with us?

Sullivan: Way back in 1986, I won an advertising contest. *Reader's Digest* sponsored a competition to agencies worldwide. "Who can come up with

---

[2] Steven Pressfield, *The War of Art*, (Black Irish Entertainment LLC, 2012).

[3] Hey Whipple, "My Favorite Radio Campaign. I Mean, That I Personally Wrote," www.heywhipple.com/2010/10/05/my-favorite-radio-campaign-i-mean-that-i-personally-wrote/, October 5, 2010.

the best poster to keep high school students from drinking and driving?" The first year, two famous knuckleheads at Fallon won it—good ol' Bob Barrie and Mike Lescarbeau. I was at The Martin Agency at the time and when they ran the contest the second year, I sat down with the express purpose of winning. You could enter a few concepts, and so I sort of put my chips on different creative strategies and sent the work in. Each campaign I submitted was with a different Martin art director. There was one with Cabell Harris, one with Diane Cook, and another with Hal Tench.

The work with Diane won. The winning concept Diane and I did avoided the clichés of the category, which in this case were gravestones, morgues, and toe tags. Over an image of a high school boy with his date in the back seat of a car being driven by his mom, we had the headline: "If losing your life doesn't keep you from drinking and driving, imagine losing your license." We got lucky, and Diane and I won the grand prize, which was a *very* expensive trip to Europe. We flew to London with our spouses on the Concorde and spent one week there in a five-star hotel, The Savoy. Then we rode the *Orient Express* to Paris and spent another week in a five-star hotel there. After that, we spent a week in the south of France at a castle. Then to wrap it up, we took the *Queen Elizabeth 2* back to New York City. It was a total blast to have won a tough little nationwide contest *and* to score such a cool trip.

Tuten: You've worked on award-winning campaigns—and it's clear from your writing that you *love* the work. In your new role, how will you satisfy your passion for the work?

Sullivan: There was a time in my life where the greatest joys were either seeing my work air on TV or winning a Gold Pencil for it at the One Show. But as I've aged, my joys are more often felt on behalf of the successes of other people. In part, I think this has something to do with becoming a father. I have mentored juniors off and on throughout my working career and it always thrilled me when their work was sold and produced, or resulted in a winning pitch. Now as I enter the educational field, I imagine it may be somehow similar—coaching kids, helping them stretch to their limit, and then seeing the fun when they succeed.

Tuten: Think back to when you were just getting started in the business. What do you wish you had known then that you know now?

Sullivan: Many young creatives I see today remind me of myself. They are just full of fire and gasoline and insanity and must-must-must-get-ahead drive. But I think that is good. It's good to try hard. It's good to stretch to see what you're capable of. But unbridled, such aspirations can curdle and burn a young person out. This happened to me back in the eighties when I let it all mean too much to me. I tried too hard and when I struck out, oh, my . . . that was the end of the world. Bertrand Russell said, "One of the symptoms of an approaching nervous breakdown is the belief that one's work is terribly important." That sure described me. So now, I wish I could go back and tell myself, dude, it's just advertising.

I was also poisoned by this obsession many of us have with winning. I still see it today in many students. After school is over, they begin to tear their hair out and worry, "Oh my God, what if I don't land a job at one of the five or six elite agencies in America? I'll be a *loser*."

Having been around the ad schools over the years, I've overheard this same conversation in hallways and computer labs all over: "Dude! You know Bill? Yeah, he got into Goodby and I didn't even get an *e-mail* back from them. God, I suck."

Here's the thing: they probably don't suck. It's just that they've been raised in a culture that places a lot of emphasis on winning. We believe in sayings like, "winning isn't everything, it's the only thing," and, "winners never quit," and all the others.

The fact is, America has been obsessed with winning ever since we won first place in World War II. We copped a silver in the fifties space race—damn that *Sputnik*—but we came back and nailed the gold with *Apollo II*. Ever since then, we've been all, "Who even *remembers* the second man on the moon?"

It seems we've left the grading system and become a pass-fail society. In fact, more like winners/failures.

"What? You didn't get into Harvard? Just Notre Dame? Duuuude."

"What?? You didn't win the Super Bowl, just the AFC title? Ouch."

This is what I want to stay to students: "Students, repeat after me.

I did not get a job offer at Goodby. Or Crispin.

But I did get a job offer from, say, Shelby & Hammerstein in Chicago.

And they want to pay me for my ideas.

I am not stocking Bic pens on the shelves of Wal-Mart.

I have landed my first job in a creative industry.

From here, I can probably go anywhere.

Because I have a career now.

It has begun."

This is an important lesson. And, let us bless our friends who did land jobs at the high-profile agencies. Those jobs come with some extra stress. Not everyone really wants that.

Let us be kind to ourselves and become "recovering perfectionists." Let us leave winning to Charlie Sheen.

Tuten: This business changes so rapidly and there are always new things to learn whether its new consumer trends, new technology, or just keeping up with industry news. What's your approach for knowing everything you need to know?

Sullivan: The only way to do any of this stuff is to *do* this stuff. It sounds silly, I know. But that is my experience and it's what I am seeing the successful agencies doing. They just start, they dive in, they figure shit out as they go. You, too, will figure shit out as you go, but first you have to dive in. You will begin to realize what you bring to the party and what you don't after you start. If you enter it with a willingness to listen, to learn, and every once in a while to just shut the hell up . . . you will meet in the middle.

My best advice for people is to do a few critical activities. Stay focused on the work. Read the awards annuals. Read everything, go online and watch the reels, read library books, read the sports section, the business section. Read history, read comedy. Soak up the culture around you. I go to a movie a week. Never fail. Movies are storytelling. As is a TV commercial. Movies have all the new cinematic techniques, also germane to my craft. And they are a good escape from the business.

There's a tendency to stay cooped up with yourself when creating. Don't stay in your copywriting ivory tower. Get out there. Learn and learn some more. It's a process that'll never end. The ability to read massive amounts of material, the ability to integrate all that data, to be disciplined in your study process? That's what college is anyway. It's not about what you learn. It is about learning *to* learn. It is about the process.

Tuten: When you look around at the industry now—expanse of media, consumer control, interactive and social, challenges for print and traditional media—what's most surprising to you?

Sullivan: What I find most surprising about the digital shift is the speed at which it happened. Often revolutions take place over time. I remember watching this wave coming towards me back in the early nineties. I remember thinking, "Wow, this is gonna change things." I thought I'd have more time than it turned out we did. By 2000, the train had crashed through my living room and the whole advertising world is completely different. Today it's different than the industry I grew up in, it's different than the early nineties, the early 2000s. The curve of change is now almost vertical. It hurts my neck just to look up this curve and think about the changes to come.

Tuten: So many people struggle with balance between work and personal life. How do you achieve a balance?

Sullivan: When I was young, there was no boundary between work and life. Work was life. That may still be okay for those without spouses or children and for people who know how to keep sane in a business that does not promote sanity. But in my middle and later years, I drew a line in the sand and said this is work and this is home.

I always tried to be in the car at 5:50 or 6:00. I was fortunate enough to work at places that weren't driven by what I see as a destructive work ethic. We all hear about them. These are places where you work until midnight all year long. Personally, I think such an ethic is destructive, even for young people. It's not a sustainable model, not on a personal level anyway. It's probably sustainable for the shops—they just need to keep the new meat coming in the side door as the burnouts are being poured out the back. But it's not for me. Nothing is that important anymore. Only my family.

Tuten: You have a magic, fairy wand. If you wave it, you can change one thing about advertising that you hate. What do you change?

Sullivan: Clients would no longer ask agencies to do creative for new business pitches. The clients would simply pick a few shops based on the kind of work they've done previously. Then the clients would visit each agency, get a feel for the people, and make a choice. I can think of no other business where we give away our product for free. Where we work ourselves to the bone, where we lose weeks, weekends, holidays, slaving away with limited information in a crunched time schedule, as we try to quickly throw together solutions for complex marketing problems . . . *and doing it all for free.* I think it's just an absolute shame. But until the whole industry locks arms and just says "No," it's going to keep happening.

CHAPTER 4

Mike Hughes

President
The Martin Agency

Mike Hughes, *president of The Martin Agency (www.martinagency.com), a full-service advertising agency based in Richmond, Virginia, is a 40-year industry veteran. Hughes served as The Martin Agency's longtime chief creative officer, relinquishing this title to John Norman (former executive creative director for Wieden+Kennedy's Amsterdam office) in 2010. The succession of creative leadership to Norman was brought about in part by Hughes's illness; several years ago he was diagnosed with lung cancer and so he set about to identify someone who could guide Martin's creative group forward. A survivor still, Hughes isn't ready to retire. He's set out to direct The Martin Agency beyond the making of ads, to serve the greater good—and nurture people along the way.*

Hughes was inducted into The One Club's Creative Hall of Fame, the advertising industry equivalent to the Baseball Hall of Fame. Virginia Commonwealth University Brandcenter, one of the top graduate programs in advertising, named its building Mike Hughes Hall. He's also a member of the Virginia Communications Hall of Fame.[1]

Creativity *magazine named Hughes one of the 50 most influential creative thinkers in the United States. Adweek called Hughes one of the nine best creative directors in America, and Ad Age listed The Martin Agency as one of the three best creative agencies in the world.*

---

[1] A nice tribute to Mike Hughes can be seen at www.youtube.com/watch?v=KfPursqlLbE &feature=player_embedded.

A former director of the American Association of Advertising Agencies and chairman of its creative committee, Mike has also served as a director of The One Club for Art & Copy, a judge at the Cannes Advertising Festival, and a leader in the Advertising Council's post-9/11 Freedom and Homeland Security campaigns.

Tracy Tuten: It was David Oakley who helped me get in touch with you, and I really appreciate his help. He had given you quite a compliment at the end of his interview.

Mike Hughes: It's a shame that you can't believe a word David says [laughter]. But that's awfully nice, that's awfully nice. That makes me feel very good.

Tuten: He obviously thinks the world of you.

Hughes: Well, I think he's crazy as a loon, but there's a huge place in my heart for David. Huge.

Tuten: Let's get started. What led you to advertising as a profession?

Hughes: Fear. I was a newspaper reporter who thought I wanted to be a magazine editor. I considered moving to New York City from my hometown of Richmond, Virginia to try to get into the magazine business. But I was scared. I was nervous about moving. My father had sold typography to ad agencies in Richmond, and so he knew a lot of agency people. I thought I would at least try that for a year or two before I moved to New York to make my mark, and I've been doing this ever since. So it was fear of moving to New York I think, and then—getting into this business and finding some things I really loved about it.

Tuten: What are those things that you really love?

Hughes: When I was a newspaper reporter, a young newspaper reporter, I'd have to go out and ask hard questions of people. And then on deadline, you'd have to write a story about it. There were hard questions. I remember having to go to a bus crash where some young people were killed, and I had to talk to their families. I have nothing but admiration for the reporters who do that work, because it can be important, but it's hard, very hard. But in advertising, they bring you all the information and you can take some time to figure out the right way to present that.

Let me tell you about my first assignment, when I showed up at an ad agency and didn't know anything. They gave me a four-color brochure to write for Reynolds Metals. They gave it to me at nine in the morning, and at 9:45, I gave them the copy because that's how we did things at an afternoon newspaper. They said, "What is this? No, we expect you to spend a week on this." I said, "Doing what?" But there was time to work on the craft of writing in a way that surprised me at an advertising agency. I didn't know. Reporters—newspaper, magazine, and all kinds of reporters—they go out and cover what's interesting. In advertising, the content may or may not be inherently interesting. We have to *find ways* to interest people in what we're writing about. So it's a different kind of discipline.

Tuten: How did you practice that craft?

Hughes: You know, I don't think I'm a great "big idea" person, but I think I have some ability to help other people make their ideas work. I was lucky to come into advertising in a generation where it was assumed that you would sit across the desk from an art director all day and work on the ideas. My contribution was to be very patient while the art directors came up with the ideas, and then I would stay up all night and just write thousands and thousands of headlines to go with their ideas. And then I'd get them to edit that for me. It was a puzzle that was worth figuring out, especially figuring out why should anybody care about our message. They're not going to care just because I come up with a clever pun. I mean, why should people care about whatever the product is I'm trying to sell, and how can I be honest in trying to present that?

Tuten: Did you have a mentor who helped you as you were developing your skills?

Hughes: Over the years, I had a number of mentors. Actually, going back to when I was a reporter for the afternoon paper in Richmond, Virginia, the metropolitan editor, who was pretty interesting because he knew—like, you know, here I am at this very conservative newspaper, and I'm a bleeding-heart liberal who reads *The New York Times* every day, like all the reporters. And he suggested back then that I also look at the *Daily News*. He said there's a big segment of the population that's more comfortable with the writing that you see in the *Daily News*. That was an interesting thing to me—to this day I read *The New York Times*. But that editor taught me that I also have to learn to write for people who are different from me. I had to figure out how to write for people who had different views and interests. And to try to think about what those people did and what they were like. That was valuable.

And then in my first job at an advertising agency—even though everybody else had copy and art together—the agency still had a separate copy chief. After I'd been there a few months, my boss said I was pretty good at this. He said I should start looking for a better agency to work for after eighteen months at his agency. In fact, he said if I was still there in two years, he'd fire me. And so at eighteen months, I went to another agency.

I just kept discovering new things about the business. Like my first agency was not a good creative agency, but at least it was serious about the business of selling things or interesting people in the products. Then I got to a better creative agency, and I learned about things like award shows that I didn't even know existed. I certainly didn't know that an agency in Richmond, Virginia, could do the kind of work [that would win awards]. I was really taken with it, and so I spent long days and long nights to try to do the kind of work that would appear in those places.

Then I bounced around to a couple of other places in my twenties. I worked a series of jobs for eighteen months each. Then I had a place of my own for a while. When Harry Jacobs, who at that time was president of The Martin Agency and creative director, offered me a chance to go there, I figured, "Well, this will be a huge cut in pay, because my little company is doing really well, but I have a lot to learn from Harry." So I joined The Martin Agency thinking, "Well, I'll do that for eighteen months." That was in 1978, and I've been here ever since.

Tuten: What was so magic about eighteen months?

Hughes: It just seemed to be the way things had worked out for me. I had always gotten a really nice offer after eighteen months from all these different places. I was given a contract at one of the last places that said that I had to give them three months' notice. I was getting married at the time. I didn't know where I was going to go, but I figured I had some time to find something. So I told them that I was leaving in three months. There was this very talented, very beautiful writer in town, and the people who ran the office wanted to hire her right away, and so I ended up with three months' pay and I didn't have to go to work. That allowed me to set up my own business. I did that until Harry Jacobs gave me the opportunity to come here.

Tuten: What was it like being a part of Martin all those years ago? How is the agency different than it is now?

Hughes: We were a lot smaller then. We had a wonderful time over this period. But, there was probably never a time we didn't struggle, you know? In all the years we've been here, I bet once a month the entire time I've been here, someone comes into my office and closes the door and says, "This agency is at a crossroads." We're always at a crossroads. I think every company always feels it's at a crossroads, and advertising's an industry that can make you feel pretty paranoid because business can come and go. But the things that I think we worked on here were just basically about being good people. Like every young creative director, when I came here—and I guess I was associate creative director under Harry, or some title like that, when I was twenty-nine years old—and I came here and I would have said that the only thing that matters is the work, the work, the work, the work. As I've gotten older, I think I've come to understand that while nothing is that much more important than the work, what's really important are the people, the people, the people, the people.

If you can find a way to be a good place for good people to work and you give them some room to develop their own ideas, then you can have longer-lasting success, I think. You can't guarantee that any client will stay with you forever, but if you keep attracting good people, you'll also keep attracting, hopefully, good clients. And so this has been a place that really treats people well.

Tuten: You've talked to me about your philosophy on the importance of people and nurturing people, and you talked to me about how you had come to join The Martin Agency and work for Harry Jacobs. What's been the highlight of your work experiences?

Hughes: Well, the thing I'm happiest about is I have a fabulous family, and on the professional side, it's that I'm surrounded by such wonderful, inspiring, and talented people. At Martin, we try to be a magnetic place for the best people. You know that everybody wants to talk about their culture as if they're a family. Every agency will say that. But you also know that it's got to be tougher than that. It's more like a team because you never fire family members, but . . .

Tuten: [Laughter.] Sometimes you wish you could.

Hughes: Yeah, sometimes you wish you could. Putting together a team where people support each other and help each other, that feels awfully good. But now *making* them support each other and help each other, that isn't something I can dictate. It's something that people do, and so I feel very fortunate that I've got a great group of people to work with. I feel strongly that everybody should be able to go to work and do work they love with people they love. I think that's the gift the people here have given me.

Tuten: If you were going to give some advice to people who are getting started in the industry now and who want to achieve the kinds of things that you've achieved—which is pretty much every award in the industry, all kinds of honors, buildings named after you and so on—what kind of advice would you give them?

Hughes: Well, I don't think you set out for those things. You know, like everybody else, I was once a paranoid young copywriter who felt that I wasn't quite up to the job, and so I worked really hard and really long.

I wish—I *wish* I could say that you could do that in an eight-hour-a-day job five days a week. But everybody I know who has made a real difference in whatever industry has really put in a lot of time and a lot of hard work. I'd say to these young people, I don't think you should try to get ahead of yourself. I never in my life asked for a promotion. It was always a matter of just trying to do the work as well as I could and as conscientiously as I could, and surrounding myself with other people that thought that way.

I think the best advice I ever got was from my dad when I started working in the professional marketplace. He said, "Just don't ever lose your sense of humor," and I think that is still the best advice I ever got. Because, you know, in any world, whether it's journalism or advertising, there are so many ridiculous things that happen and so many things you can't control, but if you keep a sense of humor about it all, I think you can go through your life and do good things and make good things happen.

Tuten: Do you have a favorite campaign that you worked on?

Hughes: Well, it's kind of hokey [laughter]. I have a favorite spot—a TV spot I did with an art director named Jerry Torchia. It was for Wrangler jeans. It was probably nineteen years ago. I was actually the copywriter on the spot. It was about a father giving his son a driving lesson. I was giving my son driving lessons. My son had knocked over some trash cans during his lessons. So in the spot, we had a kid knocking over some mailboxes. The story was simply about fathers and sons, first-time driving lessons, and comfortable blue jeans. That spot always has a big place in my heart.

Tuten: Do you get to work on client work as much as you want to? I know you're doing different types of things now.

Hughes: I have to be careful that nobody feels that I'm trying to be the creative director. I was creative director for a long time here and people can shut down on their own work and opinions if they feel I have a strong opinion on the path a creative idea should be taking. I kind of underestimated how hard that would be. I think people have defined me in that role for so long that it's hard for me to be part of a discussion without someone thinking, "That's the creative director talking."

But I do have wonderful relationships with several of our clients, and I work much more in the strategy level than I do in the creative level, and I like that a lot. I really like that a lot.

Tuten: So for those clients, are you advising on marketing for their entire business or strictly for the advertising campaigns?

Hughes: It's mostly about marketing. Every company now is trying to be so innovative, and yet nobody has a budget for innovation. Nobody is actually staffed or resourced to do it. And so what we have to be able to do is to go in and talk about innovation and maybe different ways that they can approach their customers—not in terms of the advertising creative campaign, but just in terms of how they build their story.

One of the things that I've been working on a lot for the last year and a half is this notion of storybuilding. Once upon a time we were brand storytellers. Now we start a story and the *audience*—our customers and our observers and everybody else—joins in on the conversation. We don't tell the stories. We build them. That also means that storytelling is no longer media-specific. The story can be told through all the things a brand does. We're trying—I'm trying—to encourage companies to be a little bolder and not so thin-skinned about what people say and how people add to their stories. It's hard for a company to respond quickly to what happens online, for example. But, on the other hand, companies must be responsible with their responses to how others expand their brand stories.

Tuten: Do you feel like your clients are willing to take risks?

Hughes: Well, I think it's the rare businessperson who isn't at all concerned with risks, and I think agencies too often categorize their clients as too risk-averse. Too many agencies blame their clients for the work they do. To me, that's just not acceptable. We are responsible for the work that we do. Some clients make it harder than others, but I completely understand why they don't want to be too risky. I think one of the things that agencies make a mistake in doing is they go in and try to sell innovative advertising by telling the clients, "Well, this will really be risky." When agencies do this, they are daring the client to go with the concept, when the fact is bolder, smarter, more creative advertising works better than other kinds, so the risk is doing something that is not as interesting.

Tuten: What's your favorite thing that Martin's working on right now? The thing you're most excited about?

Hughes: A couple of our people are developing a new kind of media technology that I can't talk about yet, but it is incredibly exciting. I'm incredibly excited about some of the content things we're developing. I'm not as close to the day-to-day in the creative work these days, but it still excites me a lot when something big comes through. No agency is as consistent as it wants to be.

Also, I feel extremely good, although I'm not planning to retire—I'm planning to live forever and work forever—I'm very excited about the people in the next generation of management at our company. Both John Adams, my partner, and I are very, very excited about the next generation of leadership.

They probably want to push us out the door, but right now it's exciting to watch them work.

Tuten: How would you describe Martin's philosophy?

Hughes: I think we try to be both a big-hearted agency and a big-shoul-dered agency. It is surprising to a lot of people that this agency in Richmond, Virginia, can take on things as complicated as Walmart or Pizza Hut or some of the really involved campaigns we do—like the interesting process we're in with Johnson & Johnson on Tylenol. Those are not easy assignments. Nobody expected the car insurance category to get very good. And I think our GEICO work—Steve Bassett is the creative director on that—I think the work Steve's led over the years has helped raise the standard for that whole industry.

You know, I would love to have more technology business, automobile busi-ness, and sports business, but working in unexpected categories is rewarding in its own way.

Tuten: If you had a magic, fairy wand and with it you could change one thing about advertising, what would you change?

Hughes: If I had a magic wand, I would drastically reduce the cynicism in the industry. The industry attracts a lot of the smart, bright people. There's always a tendency for smart, bright people to get pretty cynical about things and underappreciate the opportunities they have. That cynicism takes a toll. You can actually see it sometimes in the advertising. Some advertising can be very sleek and impressive, but I think long term, no matter how hip you want to be, it's helpful if you can reduce that cynical edge.

Tuten: Any advice for how to do it?

Hughes: Yes, I think you shouldn't make advertising for your peers. You become a creative director and you start judging all the shows, and then it's hard not to want to impress your peers. Your peers, they are often young, highly energized, "type A" males. It's hard not to get a "fraternity" kind of voice.

One of the things I'm so proud of at our agency is this thing we've started called "The Mom Complex."[2] It was started by Katherine Wintsch [vice president and group planning director], an amazing young planner here who

---

[2]The Mom Complex is a think tank that seeks to inspire moms to teach the rest of the world about the challenges of motherhood. It was inspired by the idea that marketers owe mothers more meaningful and true marketing communications. Learn more about The Mom Complex at http://themomcomplex.com/site/about.

has also led the planning for the biggest marketer to moms, Walmart. She is doing what she calls "opinion parties" with mothers around the world. We must improve the quality of advertising to women. If you watch a football game this weekend, you're going to see better commercials than if you watched, I don't know, *The View.* That's just a fact. And so I think we must find ways to radically lift the level of quality of advertising to mothers on a more consistent basis. Certainly, Nike has done some wonderful things aimed at women over the years, but the whole category needs to be lifted up. And I think that would be a huge opportunity for us.

Tuten: Is that part of Martin's mission at the moment?

Hughes: It is. Absolutely.

Tuten: Which clients are you working on it with?

Hughes: We are working with Kraft, Walmart—both our normal, US client and Walmart International—E! and Hasbro.

Tuten: This is not something the brands have to compete about. They can all have better advertising directed to women.

Hughes: Yes. What Katherine has done is this: her research has uncovered some true-life things for moms and the struggles moms have no matter what age their kids are. And it's not that this will dictate a style of advertising, but it is more real in the way people talk to the most important consumer in the world.

Tuten: How do you think we ended up with the advertising that didn't do the moms justice to begin with?

Hughes: I think a lot of it is because creative departments everywhere except in the fashion industry are dominated by young men. And there's a lot of testosterone, and there's a lot of energy there. It's not all bad. Yet there is nobody more efficient in the office than the young, working mother. She gets things done. She has to get things done. The guys often are just off playing ping-pong or something. But the young mother is efficient and then she gets home to her kids. Those guys might hang around the office all night long. And they will create something competitive, competitive within the industry. They'll want to win the awards—more so than the young mom. But the mom will be more responsible. Of course, what I'm describing here are huge generalizations.

Tuten: Right.

Hughes: So don't get me in trouble here. But, the moms will tend to do something that might be better for the client and the audience, but the work may not win as many awards. And so the industry has put itself on that kind of hamster wheel, where we're chasing the kinds of things that win awards, and the kinds of things that win awards become a style for people, rather than looking at and listening to the real world.

Tuten: That's a debate we hear a lot about in the industry, whether we should be chasing awards or trying to meet client objectives.

Hughes: What you should do is both. It's not that it's about the awards. It's that if you're not at least interested in the awards, then you're probably not as interested in the craftsmanship that's so important. But, on the other hand, even the best award shows have a lot of stuff that reflects the cynicism or the fraternity atmosphere.

Tuten: Tell me what you're reading right now.

Hughes: I'm an old English major who reads very few books. I *constantly* read newspapers and magazines. I've got a friend who's a publisher, and he gives me some grief about this. I read the free samples I can get on my iPad from different books and rarely get the rest of the book, although I do occasionally. Every year I get a book called *The Best American Magazine Writing.* The magazine editors put it together. You can't even get it on a reader, and so I'm reading the real physical book and I'm just loving it. All these very interesting stories.

Tuten: I've never heard of that before. I'm going to have to get it.

Hughes: I highly recommend it. It's a paperback. It comes out every December, and it's the best magazine writing of the year. There's a lot of serendipity because you go into it and you don't even know what the topic is going to be for this next story. It's amazing how much you can get into all the different topics.

Tuten: Mike, I told you when we spoke before that David Oakley summed up his interview with me by saying that he wanted to be more like you, so if you think of this chapter as being an opportunity to say anything you want to say to people who are developing the industry, people who admire you, people who feel you mentored them, what would you want to say?

Hughes: One of the advantages we have had over the years is that we were far enough away from Madison Avenue and the big agencies and everybody else in the industry that advertising people could be our heroes. They could *really* be our heroes. When I was in my twenties, I would read every word that Ed McCabe[3] wrote or that David Abbott[4] wrote. They were heroes to

---

[3] Founder of Scali, McCabe, Sloves advertising agency in the 1960s, and later founder of McCabe & Company. McCabe was the youngest person ever elected to The One Club Hall of Fame and is known for developing several iconic advertising campaigns.
[4] Founder of Abbott Mead Vickers BBDO and a member of The One Club Hall of Fame.

me, and they still are. But now they're also friends. And now I also know that David Abbott is a very elegant, fabulous man, and Ed McCabe, who is also a good friend, sometimes pretends to be crazy as a loon. This knowledge was hugely helpful.

For the last twenty years, I haven't wanted The Martin Agency to be like any other agency. You know, it's hard not to want to strive to be like others. I love and admire and I'm the biggest fan in the world for Wieden and Goodby and Crispin and Chiat. I'm the biggest fan in the world, but I don't want The Martin Agency to be like those agencies. I want us to be the best agency we can be in our own way. But in the eighties, we made a lot of progress because we kind of did say, "Okay how can we produce at that level." At the beginning of the eighties, we said we were going to go be like those top agencies. And when I was a young writer, one of the things that I would sometimes do was in my head say, "Okay, how would Ed McCabe write this headline? Or how would David Abbott write it?" And it was an interesting exercise to go through. Have you ever seen this little red book that our agency puts out for employees? *Our Beautifully Imperfect Company?*

Tuten: No, I don't think I've seen it.

Hughes: I will get Helen[5] to send you a copy. A few years ago, I gave a talk. It was a graduation speech, and it was well received. It got some attention, and the guys at work surprised me by turning it into a little book that we now give every employee. It talks about how everybody thinks they want balance in their life, but what I believe is that you don't really want balance in your life. What you want in your life is joy. You want fun, and you want work that you find meaningful, and you want to work with people you care about. When people talk about the search for balance, that isn't really right.

For me, my life has always been about joy because I like my work and because I'm married to a wonderful woman and I get to go home at night to her. She doesn't expect me to clean up the house or do anything that doesn't bring me joy [laughter]. And joy for me means that I have to find ways to engage in every part of my life, not just the work part. And so I think what a person needs to do to find joy is throw yourself into things that excite you. I think you should always seek wisdom. One of my disappointments in myself as I am getting old is that I'm not wise. I thought I'd be wise at this point. But what I love is that I am a better student than I've ever been in my life. College would make more sense for me now than it did back

---

[5] Helen Vennard, Hughes's long-time executive assistant.

when I was eighteen. I go into every meeting to see what I can learn. Even if I'm the presenter at the meeting, I can learn from my audience.

I'm also getting involved in serious discussions at meetings. A couple of years ago, I was kind of frustrated because I'd go to meetings and I'd hear the same people speaking up in every meeting. I wanted everybody to speak up and I thought we needed to hear more diverse voices. I developed this thing I called "Beer and Popcorn." People came into the room at four o'clock, and I put some subjects up on the wall. I said, "Let's pick which one we are going to talk about today." These topics had nothing to do with advertising or the agency. One day we ended up with this conversation about religion. Of course, that's one of the things you're not supposed to be able to talk about, but I wanted to demonstrate to people that we could talk about anything. We had a *fabulous* discussion that continued in e-mail messages for weeks afterwards. Being part of the conversation, being part of the thinking that goes on in a company that is supposed to be both strategic and creative, that can be an exciting possibility.

Tuten: You talked about not achieving balance, not really even *seeking to* achieve balance. I think that's going to be something that people have to practice on a day-to-day basis because you're always working at it—at balance that is.

Hughes: Yes, you know, there's this—I don't care much what hours you come to work as long as you get the job done well. And, you know, we're subject to the same laws as any other business that sells its hours and so it's important that we record certain things. But one of the reasons that we don't have any set vacation times for the majority of our people is that you can work your own schedule out. And you can even make up your own job, which is what I used to do. As long as you can say, "Okay, the company needs to make money on what I did and it needs to line up within one of our definitions of what we do as a company." But from then on, you can just make up your job. What I want to do is take away excuses for not doing something fabulous.

Tuten: Although that could be intimidating, I imagine, for a lot of people who work with you.

Hughes: It is, it is. Some people want to do that and some people don't, and it's not that it's an instruction that you have to do it. For some people, they want and need a regular job that lets them go home at five. That's fine, too. But if you're going to throw yourself into doing really special things, it's hard. You will end up constantly frustrated if you have that typical 9-to-5 job.

We now have a lot of production facilities inside our own agency, but still, for an agency like this, we are in Richmond and so if you're a creative person, you will spend a lot of time on the road for different kinds of video production.

That can be a hard life, and it can be hard on families, and so we want to help people in any way we can to take some of that burden away.

For example, if you're going to be gone for a month in Los Angeles on a production, we'll fly your spouse over for a weekend in the middle of it or we'll fly you back home and do things like that and—even for more than a weekend—because we know that travel such as that is asking a lot of people.

These are things that are important for us—to take care of our people.

Tuten: Tell me what's ahead for you. You've already designed your perfect job. So what do you still dream of? What do you still aspire to?

Hughes: Well, I've got to make some of these things real. It's hard to come up with a good idea, but it's harder still to bring those ideas to life and to make them happen. I want to see if I can make some of these things happen. One of the things Helen tells me all the time is that I like starting projects and she likes finishing them. I've had all these different projects going at any one time, and I am very guilty of starting things and then not bringing them to fruition. So I want to see if I can get a little more disciplined for myself and make these projects happen.

Tuten: So what's the number-one project on the list—if you can tell us?

Hughes: No, I can't even tell you about the second project.

Tuten: You can tell me after the book comes out. You can share later, just because I'm curious.

Hughes: Okay. You know, one more thing about David Oakley. What I like about David is his craziness. I wish I had a little bit more craziness. One of my partners told me recently that I was so rare because I was a creative director who was also a grown-up. I thought that was an insult. I think maturity is a trap in this business, and so a big part of me wants to be more like David Oakley. So I guess we have this mutual admiration thing going on.

Tuten: I can definitely see that. When I talked to David, he definitely gets joy out of everything he's doing, every day. That was my impression of him.

Hughes: Yes, yes.

Tuten: It seemed like he was always going to do his best work, but he was never going to take anything so seriously that it would get him down.

Hughes: That's true.

I'm flattered that you asked me to be a part of this, so thank you.

CHAPTER 5

Susan Credle

Chief Creative Officer
Leo Burnett North America

Susan Credle joined Leo Burnett (www.leoburnett.us)—the agency responsible for such iconic characters as Tony the Tiger, Morris the Cat, the Jolly Green Giant, and the Marlboro Man—as the agency's chief creative officer in September 2009. Her career began, upon graduation from the University of North Carolina Chapel Hill, at BBDO New York. Over her 24 years at BBDO, she rose from a receptionist to ultimately become executive creative director and a member of the BBDO New York board of directors. Throughout her tenure at BBDO, she created award-winning work for big-name brands like M&M/Mars, AT&T, Pepsi, FedEx, and Visa.

Credle sits on the Creative Review Committee of the Ad Council. In 2004, she was inducted into the AAF Advertising Hall of Achievement. In 2008, she received the first New Generation of Leaders Award from the University of North Carolina Journalism School and currently sits on the school's Board of Visitors. Credle was chosen by Boards magazine as one of their Advertising Women of Excellence, which recognizes leaders who have made significant creative and business contributions in advertising.

Tracy Tuten: Susan, what led you to advertising as a profession? Did you grow up wanting to work in the field

Susan Credle: No, not really. I actually really loved the theater and started performing on stage in about the seventh grade, and I danced a lot. And I really didn't associate the theater and dance as a way of having a livelihood. It was more the fun part of my life. When I began to start thinking about what I was going to do for work in South Carolina, I thought my choices were teacher, doctor, lawyer, businesswoman, banker, and things like that.

I was actually clerking for a law firm one summer and had to serve a subpoena on an advertising agency. I walked in—I think I was sixteen years old—and I was like, "What is this place?" It felt like the theater. People walking around, you know, kind of a little bit more gregarious, a little less business-like. And somebody said, "Oh, we're an advertising agency." I never thought that the ads, the work that I saw out in the world, had to be *made*. And it felt like an artful business, and I think that's the first time I started thinking about it as a possibility.

Tuten: So did you go into college thinking about majoring in advertising?

Credle: No, as a freshman I went in thinking I would do drama. I just started there, but I got nervous about it. Maybe drama was a major that I couldn't turn as quickly into a different source of careers. I was worried I was pigeonholing myself too much. I started looking for a major that could be more useful for careers. I actually ended up in the journalism school, not necessarily thinking about advertising, but the journalism school's curriculum was much more broad because they needed you to know a lot about a lot of things. I liked the broadness of the curriculum. It also had a great reputation at the University of North Carolina. So I thought, "Well, the school's got a great reputation and the curriculum is somewhat broad. That could help me—that could be good for any career I would want to go into." Because, I mean, when you're nineteen years old and you're making these decisions, you just don't know what's best. I didn't know.

Tuten: I don't know that anyone does, even at middle age.

Credle: Right. So I was looking for the best education that would give me the broadest sort of sensibilities about anything I might want to do when I got out of college. Something that would have the broadest appeal across different careers. Then when I ended up in journalism school, I did discover the advertising sequence and a professor that I really liked named John Sweeney.[1] That was the first time that I really started thinking, "Wow, maybe this might work."

---

[1] Sweeney is the head of the advertising sequence at UNC Chapel Hill's School of Journalism and Mass Communication.

Tuten: Did you know David Oakley[2] at the time?

Credle: Yes. I didn't know him that well, but yeah. He was always a talent.

Tuten: So Mr. Sweeney has quite a history of producing advertising brains.

Credle: Yes, that's true. Another one is Stacy Wall, who actually started off in advertising and then went on to be a director and now owns a production company [The Imperial Woodpecker].

Tuten: That's amazing. One of those "small world" kinds of things.

Credle: Yeah, yeah [laughter].

Tuten: So how did you get started then, moving from college into your career? I think I read that your first job was bathroom-break girl?

Credle: Yeah, I went to New York. I actually didn't choose New York because of advertising. I chose New York because of my age. I was like, "I'm twenty years old. I've lived in the South. I need to see the world, but I don't have much money, so if I'm going to see the world without a lot of travel, I think New York City might be the place to bet on." So I actually went there to be exposed to as different a world as I [could] imagine as quickly as possible, and I thought I would be up there for three months. As it turned out, I never left until I took the job [with Leo Burnett] in Chicago.

When I got to New York, I thought, "Well, advertising is still of interest to me, so I'll start with it." That was in 1985. I went to BBDO because it was the agency of the year and I thought, "Well, if they're that good, I'll start there." The only job I could get was giving the receptionists their bathroom breaks. So I did. I said, "Sure. I'd like to be around the best." So I started doing that and really got to know the company. I started introducing myself and asking the heads of department what they did, how they did it, and what kind of skills it took. I was really open to anything. I found all the different departments very interesting.

At BBDO at the time, the creative department really seemed to be the department that everybody else served. And, coming from a background in theater and making things—the creative side of things appealed to me a lot. So I started focusing in on the creative department as a place I would want to work.

---

[2] Oakley is co-founder and chief creative officer of BooneOakley. He is also featured in this volume.

Tuten: So you started as a creative and you've stayed true to that thus far?

Credle: Yeah. And, you know, it's funny. I think that I probably have a little more of a planner[3] in me, but we didn't have planners when I started. Instead, we kind of started with thoughtful planner behavior creatively and then got to the craft of the message. So the planning part comes at the front end. Some people are better at the front, and then some are better at the back end. I enjoy that whole process.

Tuten: Did you have a mentor?

Credle: It's interesting. This is an interesting question because I'm sure some people that greatly shaped my career would say that they were mentors, but I'm not sure that they were mentors as much as people that I admired, that I observed. I think we define a mentor as someone who sort of guides you and maintains a dialogue with you. Quite frankly, the atmosphere that I grew up in, people were too busy to do that. But what I did get in terms of great mentorship was simply watching some of the best in the business at the time do their job and seeing how they got it done, where they paid attention to work, how they crafted things. The mentors in my life were the result of just the incredible gift of being around very talented people.

Tuten: Anyone you'd like to name?

Credle: Phil Dusenberry and Charlie Miesmer were two. Later on, a guy named David Lubars,[4] watching how he worked. And then I was fortunate that a lot of my mentors or a lot of people that helped me be better were actually people that I got to work with who were often times much younger—like Gerry Graff. Any talent that you're around and you get to observe how they work, it becomes impressive. And it helps you—even if it's not a formal mentorship.

Tuten: Just soaking it up.

Credle: Yeah.

Tuten: Were there any special lessons that you learned from any of those people?

---

[3] Planners are the voice of the consumer in the agency; planners research target audiences and work to plan strategy for the brand.

[4] Phil Dusenberry was an industry legend and former vice chairman of BBDO. Charlie Miesmer is also a former vice chairman of BBDO. David Lubars is BBDO's current chairman and chief creative director.

Credle: Phil Dusenberry—his love of craft was just amazing. And he always explored options. I remember Charlie Miesmer saying something to me at one time, this is when we worked mostly in film, but he said, "Susan, you should walk around when you're on set and just frame up—frame up film." He meant frame up what you're seeing and find things that you believe are done the right way. And never be limited by what you thought you were going to go in and get. Always be expansive and always push the work and look for ways to make it better. It's never static until we shift. So we're always looking for, "Is this the best way we could say this? Is this the best angle? Is this the best piece of music?" And just that push to always better something. That was a big lesson.

Then some of the lessons I learned were what to take, what deserves a lot of attention, and what you should let just go. That's a hard one because you can, in a subjective business like creative, worry every little thing. What happens is that you have clients that grow to the point that they get irritated because it becomes so difficult. So, you have to know how to hold onto the things that really do make a difference and to push those, but not be so myopic that everybody who works with you gets exhausted.

Tuten: That sounds like something you'd have to work on every single day.

Credle: I do.

Tuten: Do you have rules like, "I'm always going to pay attention to *X*? *X, Y,* and *Z* are always important?" Or do you just evaluate every situation?

Credle: Every situation. You know, I think it's like children. There are children that you have high expectations from and you demand more from, and there are children that you just pray that they get their teeth brushed in the morning. I think ideas and brands are like that. There are some brands that you feel you can push, and I think that starts with a good relationship with the client. Then it's understanding their stomach for adventure and wanting to try things. Those are the ones that I pay attention to and then push harder and harder. And then there are some clients that I know we need to take baby steps with and slowly get them used to the idea of doing certain things—and those I don't push as hard.

It's hard because you want them all to be great, but I think understanding that appetite for creativity is important. I had a client once say he didn't like me. He didn't *not* like me. It was that he didn't like my goals at work because I said I wanted to hit home runs, and he said, "I just want to hit singles and get around the bases." It was an interesting, honest conversation. At the time, I was younger and really needed to prove that I had a decent portfolio. Single bases didn't seem like a very good career move for me.

But for that brand, single bases were probably what he felt he needed at the time. Whereas now, when you're in a more senior position, I think you've earned the right to understand just how far you can push. I think that's why younger creatives are so aggressive with their work, and I don't blame them. That's what makes or breaks their future.

Tuten: Can you give me an example of a brand that you pushed? I know you might not be able to given client confidentiality and things like that, but if you've got a story you can share, please do.

Credle: Well, you know, there's a brand that we all pushed together. It was M&Ms. In 1995, my partner Steve Rutter and I were told that we were going to run the M&Ms account. We were kind of bummed because it didn't seem like a very creative account. We went out to talk to the client. At the time, the client was Paul Michaels, who's now the CEO. In one conversation, we realized he was on our side. He was ready to go. He wanted to push this brand to a place that the company, quite frankly, probably wasn't ready [to be in]. Or if they were ready to go, they hadn't thought to go there. Together we recreated the M&Ms characters and went on to give them unique personalities.

Today, those personalities that we pushed and created are represented in a store in Times Square. The M&Ms have very distinct personalities and are very character-driven. That was an incredible experience, where we took a brand to a completely different place—but [Paul Michaels] gave us permission because he said he wanted it so badly.

Tuten: Is that the same time that you helped to create Blue?[5]

Credle: Yeah. We actually did all the characters' personalities straightaway, because we wanted them to play as an ensemble. The first ones we introduced in the new character form were Red, Yellow, and Blue. Blue was sort of the observant part of the ensemble. If you think about an ensemble cast like *Seinfeld*, Jerry Seinfeld sort of plays the role of commentator. You know, the character observes and the comedy comes out of his observations.

[Think of Blue] versus Red and Yellow. Red would be much more like George, the blustery comedian, and Yellow would be much more like Kramer. Then we went on and added some other characters, but we purposely made them play like an ensemble, a comedic troupe.

Tuten: And did the characterizations start off with *Seinfeld* in mind?

---

[5] Blue is an M&M candy color brought on in 1995 after an extensive voting campaign by consumers, who chose the new color.

Credle: No, we started off with archetypes. We went back and studied any comedy troupe from Shakespeare on and looked at which quintessential characters worked together well. They're easy. You can dissect any comedic troupe into some basic types. There's usually the blustery character—the blustery one thinks he's smarter than any other character. There's usually the idiot savant, the "clueless but is always okay" character. There's usually an observant commenting on the characters' character. There's usually a nebbish—a nervous or a paranoid, overly intelligent character. And then there's a female [laughter], a female or two that are usually like the Lucille Ball, comedic, almost physical character, and then usually there's somebody who's the sexy and "in control of my femininity" character. You could do that. You could break that down with almost any comedic troupe, and you'll see similar shades of these iconic characters.

Tuten: So your drama training is coming into play heavily in your creative work?

Credle: [Laughter.] Yeah, probably. Yeah. I always said that brands were like roles. If you were an actor, you'd look at a brand and say, "Okay, how would this character behave? What would they wear? How would they talk? You know, how would they react?" And if you think about it, brands are a lot like a character. What role do they play in people's lives? How should they talk, how should they act, how should they be? The more you can understand the role of a brand or what that brand's character is, I think the stronger the work holds together.

Tuten: And that's how Green came about?

Credle: Well, Green came about because we had basically worked a lot with Red and Yellow and Blue the first couple of years. We thought, "I bet we can refresh the brand just by using new characters that are in our ensemble and giving them a stage." So we said, "Let's do Green." You know, Blue had had a little campaign. Red and Yellow had been carrying the brunt of the work. We knew Green was going to be a female and [we] kind of knew her personality. There was a great myth in my high school about green M&Ms. I forget— either the green M&Ms made you horny or you got pregnant. There was always some kind of sexual myth around the green M&Ms. We came up with a campaign called, "What is it about the green ones?" That kind of defined her role as this kind of provocative, sexy, confident girl character.

Tuten: How did you end up being her voice?

Credle: Well, I haven't done much of her voice. [Another] woman, Cree Summer, does her voice most of the time. I think she's Canadian, but she has a little bit of a twang, and every once in a while when we were doing demos, we would get used to something that was on the recording that I had done, and we would say, "Oh, let's just leave that little piece." But it's not much.

Tuten: You look happy right now, so that must be a fond memory, being the voice of Green.

Credle: Yeah, yeah. Just the whole character-driven campaign and the fact that it's still going strong even though I'm not there anymore. It's a pretty amazing thing to have happened.

Tuten: Do you have any favorite campaigns that you're working on now?

Credle: Well, I really think the Allstate "Mayhem" campaign work is a favorite. You know, we started that—it broke last summer, so it's about a year-and-a-half old.

Tuten: That's one of my personal favorites.

Credle: I'm so glad to have gotten something like that out, coming into Chicago. Allstate's been a phenomenal client, a great partnership. The way that came about is we were sitting down with them, and they were very clear that they were ready to go. They wanted to push it. We had some nice dialogue about how far [to push]. We tried to make sure that we didn't just do comedy for comedy's sake, but that the campaign actually had a point, which is that the brand is about protection. Even though "Mayhem" is funny and amusing, it really has a very strong protection message to it.

Tuten: Yeah, definitely. Last year, right around this time, my husband and I had gone to get a Christmas tree.

Credle: [Laughter.] Oh no.

Tuten: And my husband didn't do the best job tying it to the top of the car.

Credle: Yeah.

Tuten: It flew off, on the highway.

Credle: Mm-hmm.

Tuten: At sixty-five miles per hour. Hit the car behind us.

Credle: There's *nothing* that works better than truth.

Tuten: The very next day, my mom calls and says, "Oh my God! You've got to see this Allstate commercial."

Credle: That's great. Oh, that's wonderful. When you can relate to the ads— that's it. I think the one spot or two spots that people have really enjoyed are the GPS spot, the "recalculating GPS spot," and "the blind spot," when he says, "You're good." Like your experience with the Christmas tree, the more you've almost had something happen because of something we're showing you, you're like, "Oh my Lord. I have met Mayhem."

Tuten: Exactly, exactly. So it definitely hits home and made it all the more hilarious to our entire family.

Credle: That's great.

Tuten: Your current role is chief creative officer. What's a typical day like?

Credle: Oh my goodness. Typical day: I usually start at nine. I walk—I try to walk to work. It's a little cold right now, but I have about a thirty-minute walk to work and get in about nine. My day is pretty packed because we have over fifty brands that we work with. If you just do the math, the amount of people that want to come in and talk about what they're up to, what their ideas are—it's back to back. I've learned to put blank holes in my calendar so that I have a little bit of time every now and again. But it's meetings all day, and then around six o'clock, the meetings stop. And I would say from about six to eight, I try to catch up on all the e-mails that I probably missed—and correspondence. Then, I try, on an average day, to get out [of the office] between seven and eight. When we're busy, you know, you just do it. You stay until the work's done or you're done. I used to—ten years ago, I think—work all night. I have to get a little sleep now. You do get to a point where you're like, "I can't. I've got to go to sleep." [Laughter.]

Tuten: How do you prepare mentally for each day?

Credle: Well, three days a week a trainer comes to my house. We do a lot of breathing exercises and stretching and just kind of finding a place where you find some strength. And I think it's important, too, because in this position, what you find is that when you start work, at every second of the day, you are *giving out*, whether it's advice or like how we're talking and I'm giving you this story—but it's always helping other people.

Tuten: Right.

Credle: And I find that starting the day with someone helping me is a good gift. I try to start every day thinking about—and this is going to sound so corny—"How can I be a positive influence today?"

Tuten: No. I don't think that sounds corny. I think that sounds amazing.

Credle: [Laughter.] I think as a leader or as someone in this position— sometimes I just want to go kill everybody. But as a leader you want everything to be right, you want everybody to come through for you. I think if you're not careful, your first instinct is to really be frustrated with people, and while that's the feeling, I don't think it gets you anywhere. So I'm trying to reframe everyday frustration into something else. If I'm frustrated, it means that people need me to help them do something that they're not doing right now. To me, I'm blaming myself as much as the people that I need to do something. It's like, "I must be doing something wrong because they're not getting where we need to get." So, that's a hard one.

I did have a boss years ago who said something beautiful. I asked him, "How do you lead? How do you get people to do stuff?" And he said, "You know, interestingly, it's not one leadership style. For every individual, I have to think about what would motivate them—because we're not all motivated by the same things." And that was really interesting. He said to really think about people. "What can I tell them? What can I do for them that will motivate them to be better?" There's no one answer.

Tuten: In the group that you lead, everyone is a creative?

Credle: Well, it's interesting. When I came here, I said, "I didn't come here to run a creative department. I came here to run a creative agency." And I think if you have the creative mindset, you'd bleed over to all departments, because they're all part of getting us to the best work. So I work with lots of different people, but my line of sight should be the creatives.

Tuten: If you're in a different area of the agency, I think we have the stereotype that creatives are all alike. You know, they're different from us [my background is in research], and they're the same within—but when you think about how to motivate them, is everybody different?

Credle: Incredibly different. I have creatives who, if you're hard on them, burst into tears and become dysfunctional. I have creatives who, if you're not hard on them, think you're a weak leader and aren't getting anything from you. I have creatives who, if they're in a vulnerable situation, start acting like jerks, so I have to work to make sure that really strong people surround them so that they don't get scared. I have creatives who believe they're better than they are. I have creatives who believe they're not as good as they are. I have creatives who, if you give them too much, shut down. I have creatives who, if you give them too little, they shut down.

Tuten: Did you know that you were going to become a psychologist when you took this role?

Credle: [Laughter.] I do know. I told somebody, "The higher up you go in this job, man—you're just a therapist!"

There's a lot to be said for playing the role of therapist at work. Forget the creative department or an agency. I think once you get to a *leadership* role—

and by that, I don't necessarily mean a job of "leader" because I recognize that there are leaders at all levels of an organization—or even a management role, you have to consider the needs of the people and how to work based on their needs.

Tuten: Right. When I was studying your background, I read about the scale you use at Leo Burnet to judge the creative work, the "HumanKind scale."[6]

Credle: Yeah.

Tuten: That's what you use to judge work or that your whole team uses to judge work. How did that scale come about? How was it created and how do you use it creatively?

Credle: Well, my boss, who hired me, Mark Tutssel,[7] was largely responsible. It [the HumanKind scale] was created before I got here. I think just before I got here, so that was over two years ago. I think it's like any good idea: when it seems to be brilliant, there are a lot of people that claim it's theirs. When it's a piece of crap, everybody runs from it and says, "I didn't do it." This one, thank goodness, a lot of people want to be its parent, but I credit my boss, Mark Tutssel. If he didn't come up with the whole thing, he pushed to have it.

It's interesting because I, without naming it, have been kind of practicing HumanKind in my career without knowing it—that is, I always believed brands could have meaning in people's lives beyond "it makes my hair clean" or "it makes my teeth not fall out." That, if [brands] have a voice, they can do so much more than just sell a product, and that by doing more than selling a product, you build brand loyalty. It's all in service to capitalism. But when I saw the HumanKind scale—well, that's one of the reasons why I took the job at Leo Burnett. Because the scale showed me Leo Burnett is a company that's dedicated to the same things that I'm dedicated to, which is not just quarterly sales but making a difference in the world—or attempting to. Making a difference in people's lives gives this business a lot more value. Personal value for me.

Tuten: Can you tell us how it's used?

Credle: The first way we use it is to really ask, "Where on the scale do we think the work we're looking at lives?" And if the idea is, "Okay, you told me

---

[6] The HumanKind scale is a scale from 1 to 10 that Leo Burnett uses to judge the value of ideas and creative work. The higher the score, the more valuable the idea or the work. Leo Burnett strives to never produce anything below a 5.

[7] Leo Burnett Worldwide's global chief creative officer.

why I should buy this brand—that's a five." If it's a beautiful way of telling me—that's a six. If it's really well crafted—seven. Eight is if it starts to really change the way I think and feel. Nine changes the way I live. That's a really hard one to do. And then ten changes the world. But it gives us something to aspire to.

Tuten: When your teams come in and share concepts with you, do they introduce it that way? Do they come in and say, "We think we've hit a seven here?"

Credle: It's starting to happen. It's young in our culture, so I think they're intuitively starting to think that way. We meet quarterly as a global company. Some of the top creators from around the world get together, and we actually look at the work and we grade it. So creatives will know what the *company believes* their work is living up to. We put numbers to it so we can kind of put some math to how we're doing and what we're doing.

Tuten: It's such a subjective business, and so to have some objective measures can help.

Credle: Yeah, it does. We are working with the research team to show how the work that is getting scored high in our global meetings tracks from a business standpoint. And we're seeing significant parallels: that the work that this company believes is living in the six, seven, eight numbers is actually producing work that's helping clients.

Tuten: Have you had any nine or ten ideas?

Credle: I think there was one nine—no tens. The one nine was for Earth Hour. It started in Sydney. Earth Hour is on Earth Day. Everybody in the world turns off their lights for one hour. It's been a bigger concept in Europe. The important thing is—it changes the way people live. Just to have over a billion people turn out their lights on one day is a big gesture.

Tuten: Yeah, that's amazing. Do you have people who've set a goal like that, to say, "This year I want to come up with a nine or a ten?"

Credle: Yeah, I hope they all are saying that, but it's really hard even to get an eight. We don't give out many of those in our company. We feel like a brand is healthy if it's getting solid fives. That's good, strong work, but still a five is just a nice solid, good job. Sixes—sixes start to be interesting. And sevens are really where we hope brands start to live.

Tuten: I love the idea of the scale.

Credle: The bottom of the scale is really great, too. When I see an idea is destructive, then I can say, "We as an agency won't put this out." It might be funny, it might break through, it might make noise—but we don't do that at this company. And then two is no idea. Rarely do you see twos. Three is a hard one because it means the brand or the idea is invisible. And that's what I think we, as an entire industry, are largely guilty of: putting out work that says and does the right thing, but nobody sees it.

Tuten: It just blends into the background.

Credle: Yeah.

Tuten: What's your favorite campaign that never was, the one you wish has been produced but wasn't?

Credle: [Laughter.] Oh, let me see. I'm sure there are lots of them. There was a campaign that we wrote years ago for Gillette that I loved. It was called "For the man, not the masochist." I wanted to do it so badly because I thought to put the word "masochist" into the world would be great. It was a good vocabulary word. The point was to get people to go from disposable razors to a real Gillette razor. The whole campaign was about people who loved pain. The tag was something like, "The only reason you should be using a disposable razor is if you really love pain."

Tuten: And why didn't it fly?

Credle: Because everyone thought nobody in America would know what the word "masochist" meant [laughter].

Tuten: Oh, that's sad.

Credle: [Laughter.] I know, but I'm still on a mission. That's my point: when we put words like that out there, I think we make a contribution to the world because we're actually teaching vocabulary.

Tuten: Absolutely. I can remember when I was in high school some kid studying for SATs or something had come across the word "instigator." That became this little trend for a few weeks in the high school—everyone was trying to fit the word "instigator" into regular conversations.

Credle: Well, it's interesting. There are tons [of other examples] if I sat down and thought about it. Every day there's something that doesn't fly and you're like, "Ahh. That would have been good."

Tuten: Do you have a special file you stick them in in case they can come back to life later?

Credle: No. I probably should. But it's funny. I've always believed that the work that I really love usually works so well for the one brand that it shouldn't be too easy to push into something else.

Tuten: Leo Burnett is known for its eraserless pencils. Can you tell us about those pencils and what they mean in terms of the organization's philosophy?

Credle: Well, I think the first thing you'll see if you come to the company is a lot of illustrations that show that the work that we make comes out of the pencil. You know, when Leo Burnett [began], print was really the craft or the medium, so there was a lot of writing. Print was a very copy-driven medium at the time. When Leo Burnett started [the company], his point was that you have to write and write and write and write—down to the nub to get where you need to go. And to think about how our work comes through this very simple machine, the pencil, powered by a human brain. What is nice about the eraserless pencil for me is that it says there are no bad ideas and you should never erase—because the bad ideas get you to the better ideas. So, it's okay to write down everything. And don't think that the thing that you wrote doesn't have value.

Tuten: I love that idea. It relates a lot to Malcolm Gladwell's ten thousand hours. You can't get to ten thousand if you didn't start with one.[8]

Credle: Yep. It was funny. My dad was asking me for some help. He's with UNC Memorial Hospital and he needed to name a residents' program that he was working on. We were hanging out, and so I said, "Okay, I'll think about it." About fifteen minutes later, I sent him an e-mail across the room with an idea that I thought would work. He e-mailed me back saying, "How much do I owe you?" And I e-mailed him: "$30,000." And he said, "That only took you fifteen minutes." And I replied, "No, it took me forty-eight years. You just saw the last fifteen minutes."

Tuten: [Laughter.] With the history that honors the pencil, what is it like for Leo Burnett to work in the digital age?

Credle: [Laughter.] I think it was Clay Shirky[9] that said "when a medium is taken for granted, then it becomes important." In a weird way, creating for new mediums, as long as they've reached a point of being important en masse, it shouldn't be an issue. As a creative person, you think about how you communicate in your life and you use those tools to do that. So from a creative standpoint, I think it kind of almost happens naturally.

---

[8] In his book, *Outliers* (Little, Brown & Company, 2008), Gladwell surmised that the most successful people in any field have at least 10,000 hours of practice before they become a top performer.

[9] Clay Shirky, a scholar of the effects of the internet on society.

I remember when I first signed up for Facebook when it first started, and there was nobody on it. It was hilarious. People were like, "Well, what do we do here? ... I don't know." And then, as it became more and more mass, you start understanding how you're using it, what you do on it, how people use it. And then as a creative, you go, "Okay, if people are using it like that, why don't we do this?" So you start using the mediums when they become a place where people are taking them for granted. That's okay.

I think where we're having to play catch-up is on the actual delivery—in *making it*, because these back ends are incredibly complex. [Doing it all ourselves] would be like saying as a creative department we have to build the elevators for a company's building. It's like, "Whoa. When did that get in our line of sight?" And what I'm wrestling with right now is how much of this company should be in the production digital delivery business versus the ideation and strategic business of using new media. And then we go to the best-in-class, back-end delivery places to make it.

It really follows the film production model. Very few agencies keep a great film production [capability] in-house. There are a couple of reasons why: because the talent's always changing, so you would date yourself very quickly by building that. The other is the amount of the work—when you're in production, the intensity and the amount of hours that it takes. It really works better in a freelance basis, where people come in, work hard on a job, and when it's done, they take a respite.

I think this is going to be the future—outsourcing to the best-in-class back end. The problem is that in the past in film production, the film companies rarely, if ever, competed with the agencies for creation of the content. They stayed on the other side of making the content. Whereas in new media, there's such a blurred line of creating and making, and there are agencies that want to do both. Right now the competition is there.

Tuten: So when you hire, you still hire art directors and copywriters. You're not hiring creative technologists?

Credle: Yeah, we are hiring those people. It's just a question of how many of them. I really want the kind of creative technologist that knows where to go to make film work and how to supervise it, in the same way that film producers knew the best directors, the best editors, the best music houses. They knew even before the set, they could look at the scope of a project and say, "We're going to need two cameras or we're going to need three days or we're gonna ..." They became very well-equipped to understand bidding and what was needed to create ... to turn an idea on a piece of paper into the real thing. And I think that with creative technologists, we need people that can look at a social concept—you know, whether it's a social media idea or a game, whatever we're doing—and be able to look at it and say, "What kind of team? How long? How much money? Who would we go to? How would we put this bench together that will get us to the best-in-class delivery?" This is all theory right now, but I've believed it for ten years, and it's not over—it seems to be going faster and faster towards that than away from that.

Tuten: We'll see what happens.

Credle: I know. I'm putting it out there.

Tuten: Susan, what's been the best moment in your career thus far?

Credle: Hmm—wow. There's so many. One will always be the M&M characters. To have created something that doesn't go away is pretty special. We'll see. Maybe one day they'll stop doing the characters or they'll change them, but right now, we're seventeen years strong, and what we created in 1995 is alive and well and surpassed all of the possibilities I thought they had. So that's what I'll talk about I think long after I'm finished with this career. The other thing is just the incredible talent, throughout my twenty-five years, that I've been able to work with and chat with and talk with—from directors to actors to musicians to editors. It's just incredible the kind of people I've been allowed to engage with.

Tuten: I see a bottle of champagne on the desk behind you. Is that from something special?

Credle: No, that's actually from Stacy Wall's new company, Imperial Woodpecker. This is how Imperial Woodpecker announced the latest director: a bottle of champagne with Peter Martin's name on it. So we're actually celebrating the new director, Peter Martin [laughter].

Tuten: That's a fun way to introduce someone.

Credle: Yeah, that boy's creative.

Tuten: What inspires you?

Credle: What inspires me? I think what inspires me are talented people. They give me energy. Smart people, dreamers, people that go, people that have characteristics that I don't have.

Tuten: What are those?

Credle: [Laughter.] Humor, comedy.

Tuten: You don't think you have that?

Credle: Everybody says that I'm funny, but I don't know. I've never thought so. I guess that's why a guy like Gerry Graff I just enjoy being around so much—because of his wit. And I think it's just a guy kind of locker room humor that I just find hilarious. I don't understand at all. Some guy told me, "All you have to do is get a bunch of sugar and then just don't edit yourself and you can get that sophomoric comedy coming out of you."

Life inspires me, just observing. I was thinking today, "Man, I've been in the office so long. You know, I just want to go see stuff." Like I was in the Museum of Contemporary Art this past weekend, and I saw this cool thing. And it was great. It was just so simple. An artist had done an exhibit where he had taken old TV sets and plugged them into the wall—so you just get the static. And he had painted scenes on the screens, and the static became water. It was just beautiful. That was just great.

Tuten: What an amazing idea.

Credle: Yeah. And, just watching people, break the conventional, see things in a different way. That's always amazing to me. I love it.

Tuten: Imagine you have a magic, fairy wand and with it you can change one thing about advertising. What do you change?

Credle: Impatience. Well, maybe not impatience. Maybe that's not the right word. The one thing I would change is I would love to make people believe that experimentation and doing is not going to hurt them. The idea of having to test something or quantify it or get enough people to agree is not going to get us to the best place fastest. It's actually swinging, you know? Taking some chances is not a dangerous thing. We overworry everything, whereas if we would simply just act and do, we would get so much further faster.

We did a thing for Secret this past year. This is a great example. There was no [creative] brief, but a woman on the team really felt—she really wanted to do something for anti-bullying. She designed all these cool t-shirts, or had Leo Burnett design them. I just thought it would be a nice thing for Secret to give to girls, but we couldn't figure out how or where. Then we were talking, and I said, "I think the problem is that you have this thing that you want to do, but it doesn't relate back to the brand at all." We went to Secret and we said, "We have a movement that we think we should start. It's called 'Mean Stinks'. And it will be our anti-bullying campaign."

And so there was no brief, there was nothing, and the client said, "We have two print insertions in *People* and *Cosmo*. Let's see what we can do. And we can do a Facebook thing." And we said, "All right." So we had very little money, very little media, but some good scalable media. And we did a couple of print ads and a little bit of a Facebook thing. The print ads said, "Say something nice behind someone's back at Facebook Secret: Mean Stinks." And within two weeks, we had over 200,000 girls talking on the Facebook page and apologizing and saying they wished they had not been bullies. It continues to grow and Procter & Gamble gave "Mean Stinks" their Global Purpose Award this year.

It all happened just because they did it. It didn't go through testing. They just put a little money behind it, just a little bit. Like no harm, no foul. It wasn't like they bet the bank on it. They said, "Just run a couple of print ads and let's see what happens." And now they're like, "Holy cow. This might be our campaign." We could have hemmed and hawed and said, "Well, that's not really what we're doing . . . ." But they took a chance. They did something that wasn't quite in their line of sight. And we are all benefiting now.

Tuten: That sounds like a nine to me.

Credle: Yeah, but we don't do enough of that. We don't do enough "Let's try stuff." If we have an idea for a client and it's an easy thing for them to do, they should just do it. Yet we'll spend seven hours talking about, "Should we? Should we not? You know, we probably shouldn't." And in the time we analyzed it, we could have done it and seen if it was something that would have resonated. That's the one thing that I think [that's different], than the old school way of using focus groups. I think this new media and this way of getting people's opinion in a more organic way—I think we'll see some significant changes in that in the next five to ten years.

Tuten: Just doing it and seeing what happens?

Credle: People forget that the reason we did such rigor, especially to television commercials, is because it's not that the commercial was expensive to do—I mean, it costs money—but it's that you're going to put $30, $40, $50 million dollars behind it in media. And, if there's a way to get a good feeling of which communications you want to put a lot of your mass media money behind, we should be doing it.

Tuten: And you can do it in social for very little and see what happens.

Credle: Yeah, exactly.

Tuten: One last question for you. What's ahead for you? What next steps, dreams, aspirations?

Credle: Well, it's interesting. Okay, I think the short-term answer is I really would like to see Leo Burnett and its HumanKind philosophy strongly come to life. So more things like "Mean Stinks." I would like to be able to talk to you about that and you—in the same way that you know what "Mayhem" is—be able to say, "Oh, I love it. It's doing such great things for the world."

I'd really like to see this company have a lot of famous work that lives the HumanKind scale, or lives at the top of it. I'd like to see the business of advertising regain its focus a little bit. I think we're, as an industry, all over the place. And the question is: have the basic principles of marketing and communication really changed that radically? Or do we need to get back and kind of relearn some of them?

I really like building brands versus doing advertising. And I'd like to turn around in a couple of years and say that the M&Ms' story that I have—there are a few more to go with it. As for the dream, I was thinking when in your life do you kind of get off of the career path and get into the "give back" path? What I realized is that while I think I would get a lot out of working with children and volunteering and all of that—I think I would love it—but I can have more impact staying in this career and working on the HumanKind scale and as a sort of "giving back" path. I could give back by tutoring a child on Monday night, which I have done, but I can give more through my career.

Tuten: The level of reach is completely different.

Credle: I think that the personal reward is better on the micro scale, but the effect is more on the macro scale. And it also seems like that's a great way to pay off a quarter of a century investment.

Tuten: In yourself?

Credle: In the career. It's like, what was the point of getting here? I'm not very motivated by money. I mean, it's not bad [laughter]. But it's not a huge motivator for me, things and stuff. But influencing and trying to make a difference—those are pretty big things for me.

One of the things I do is encourage agencies and brands to realize that besides doing entertaining work that breaks through and sells stuff, we have a social responsibility to put something out there that hopefully does something in this world for people. And it doesn't mean that it has to be altruistic. I mean, M&Ms—we believe that we should tell really good jokes. We should write really well. The characters should be very, very well developed and crafted. But I loved working on the brand because we just were telling people, "Don't forget to have fun." You know, smile every once in a while. I truly believe that's good for the world.

Marshall Ross

Chief Creative Officer
Cramer-Krasselt

Marshall Ross is chief creative officer of Cramer-Krasselt (C-K; www.c-k.com) where he's been a part of the leadership team behind the agency's rise to the second-largest independent agency in the United States, with $1 billion in annual billings. C-K has grown by nearly 50 percent since 2005 with clients such as Corona Extra, Edward Jones, Hilton Hotels Worldwide and Porsche.

As chief creative officer, Ross has crafted award-winning campaigns for numerous clients, garnering everything from Effies to Webbys to Cannes Lions. Ross's creative passions are never ending. His ability to nurture cross-platform creativity—paired with the agency's integrated structure and culture—has helped the agency consistently deliver on its mission to "Make friends, not ads" long before it became trendy to do so: from CareerBuilder's Monk-e-Mail viral sensation; to helping Corona fans "Find Your Beach" online, offline, or wherever they find themselves; to enlisting passionate Porsche-philes to help create relevance for the expanding lineup of Porsche cars.

Before joining C-K, Ross was a copywriter and creative supervisor at Foote, Cone & Belding. At the age of 27, he started a creative boutique, Mitchiner, Ross & Kahn, which after a successful run was acquired in 1992 by Campbell Mithun Esty, where Ross assumed the post of executive creative director.

Tracy Tuten: What led you to advertising as a profession? Did you grow up wanting to work in the field

Marshall Ross: Well, I don't know that I understood what the field was. I knew that there were two things that had a gravitational pull for me. One was that my father was a lifelong salesman. That's what he did. And he worked for *Encyclopedia Britannica*—actually, *World Book Encyclopedia*. He sold it door to door. And then by the time I was around in his life, he was a furrier and worked for a large furrier in Chicago and managed the store and always had this amazing rapport with customers and was able to help them see their way to saying yes.

I think some of that has to be hereditary because when I was thirteen, I remember working in my uncle's store and being a pretty good salesperson. I mean, I was a little kid, and I was selling clothes to adults. When I was in high school, my father got me a job at a big clothing store. And I was sixteen, seventeen years old, and I was selling suits to grown men and their wives.

I always sort of had this sales thing in me, and at the same time, I was a designer. I was an illustrator. I was always drawing. I was very fascinated by the worlds of art and design. I had no idea what I was going to do with either of those things. I don't even think I was thinking about what I would be doing. I had a high school teacher whose husband worked at Leo Burnett,[1] and she said, "You should be an art director in an advertising agency. You're very facile at this." I didn't even know what the word "facile" meant. And I said, "Okay. That sounds like a good idea."

I learned a little bit about it. Somebody had gotten me some unwarranted interviews around town. I met some people from Leo Burnett and met some people from Ogilvy & Mather, and I decided, "Yeah. That's what I want to do." I started applying to art schools and universities, and that sort of became my identity fix all the way through my education—my sort of upper-education career. And that's kind of what I did.

The weird thing was I thought I was going to be an art director, and I was. My first job was as an art director for Foote, Cone & Belding.[2] I was actually hired as an art director, but it became obvious to me early on that—at the time—art directors really got sort of bogged down in the execution piece of things and were out of sync with their writers. I was an English minor, and I'd always liked to write. I thought I was pretty good at it. I taught myself to write better, and I switched from art direction to copywriting. About a year into it, I became a copywriter. So, anyway, that's how that happened.

Tuten: How long had you been art directing when you realized that copy was more of your passion?

---

[1] Leo Burnett is a leading advertising agency, founded in Chicago in 1935.
[2] Another advertising agency also based in Chicago.

Ross: Maybe two years.

Tuten: And did that feel right once you did it?

Ross: Yeah, absolutely. The speed was right for me. I think I am a decent art director, but I am a much better writer. I was much more adventuresome with language for some reason than I was with design. And I don't know why that is. I think it's because it was faster and it helped me play more easily. Playfulness is a big part of this job. You have to be willing to put yourself in a place where you are having fun and it was easier for me to do that with language.

Tuten: How does that translate into your work now?

Ross: Well, the writing piece or just the beginning piece?

Tuten: That beginning shift from art and design to language.

Ross: I think that what it does, or what it did, was instill in me a tremendous amount of empathy for all kinds of craft in the space in which we operate. I completely empathize with the struggles of photographers and illustrators and designers and art directors, and at the same time, I think I understand what marketing directors have to do to synthesize their points of view and how to help them synthesize their points of view. I think that I understand or empathize with the idea of the creative process from a lot of different angles.

Tuten: What about the sales piece, that growing up and having the sales experience? Do you find yourself selling now?

Ross: I think that all successful marketing people are successful because they understand how to link desire with solution, and so I think I do that. Probably seventy percent of my work is figuring out what that linkage is or articulating what that linkage is in a way that becomes really compelling. Sometimes that's helping writers and art directors or user experience people or developers turn that linkage into experiences. And sometimes it's about helping an audience of marketing people recognize why the path we're heading down is the right one.

Tuten: Kristen Cavallo at Mullen says sales is a major part of her job because you have to persuade someone to let you "run your idea with their money."

Ross: I think that's a very nice, succinct way of saying that the art of persuasion is to make sure that your idea is actually their need. That's why I call it "linkage." I think sales is about connecting. The art of persuasion is making that connection feel obvious, innate, and inarguable. If you've done a good job of making their issue and your solution become indelibly connected, their response is, "Well, what else would I do?"

Tuten: Perfect. Would you describe that as the C-K philosophy?

Ross: No, I think C-K's philosophy comes from a couple of other different things, but it does involve connection in a way. It's just a deeper one. C-K's philosophy is really simple, and it's about the idea of value. We think that a relationship between a person and a brand, or a group and a brand, is far more valuable, far more worthy of investment than buzz, than click, than even transactions. And so our philosophy is about how do we get past those first sort of shallow engagements, which could even mean a sale? How do we get past those shallow engagements into something that's long lasting, into something that's repetitive, into something that kind of brings joy to both groups?

And we have a little line that everyone here has to learn and learn what it means. It's simply, "Make friends, not ads." That's what we try to get the organization to do: think not about this thing you're about to create, but think, how do you help a brand and its publics become friends. We've been actually doing that long before Mark Zuckerberg took the word "friends" and did something with it—before he could probably shave. Anyway, that's our philosophy, and we actually have an interesting organizational structure. We have no profit centers between any of our disciplines. We don't have any sort of wholly owned subsidiaries. We have T-shaped subject matter people[3] who can flow all around the organization and work on anything they want as long as what they're providing is relevant, without worrying about where the budget is going. So that's our philosophy.

Tuten: Can you give me an example of how "make friends, not ads" has come into play for one of your clients?

Ross: Sure, I'll just give one of our really recent examples, because it's easier for me to think a few weeks ago than a few years ago. But if you look at the "Everyday Magic" campaign for the Porsche 911, it was about helping people who see a weekends-only sports car to see the 911 as a car they could drive every day. But what made it, I think, "friendship building" was that it was a campaign designed to help connect prospects with existing owners. The campaign let the owners tell their stories—how they used the Porsche 911, what they think it does for them—directly to prospects. The campaign

---

[3]T-shaped people are those who are adept at a broad range of subjects while still having a depth of expertise in a specific area.

created an intimacy that the brand was never able to achieve before with people who weren't directly a part of the owner group. So that was a really cool thing. You can see the stories from owners at www.porscheeveryday.com.

Tuten: Okay. Great. I'll take a look at that. Now, the second question, a follow-up to the philosophy question: you talked about how people can flow, and as long as they're adding value and what they're doing is relevant, they don't have to worry about where the budget is coming from. Is that something that's made possible by Cramer-Krasselt being an independent agency?[4]

Ross: Yeah, absolutely. We are not required to write a check every year to London or New York or Paris. We're New York. So we get to decide what our profit goals are, what our efficiencies are. Obviously, we're not in a vacuum. We benchmark on what's smart and what's appropriate. But, because we're independent, we simply get to operate in ways of our own choosing. It's unusual for a company of our scale to still be independent, and then even more so to run things without profit centers.

Tuten: Are there challenges that go along with that?

Ross: Well, it's very messy. It's definitely very messy. That's the biggest challenge, creating the right kind of connectivity all the time is messy. But the upside, more important than the challenges, the upside is that there's zero internal competition. We used to have a saying in this business, and it was kind of BS: "ideas can come from anywhere." That was sort of a code for "Well, everybody kind of has to be creative, and our creative departments are not egotistical, so ideas can come from anywhere." But the truth is now ideas *must* come from everywhere, and that's because the marketing landscape, the communications landscape, the media landscape—all of those "scapes" are so remarkably different, require so much coordination, that if you don't have tennis players on all sides of the court, and the courts are now six-sided, if you don't have somebody that can hit the ball back in every corner, you're just not going to make it. Your thinking is just not going to work. So it's a real imperative that this kind of play happens.

We found that if people don't need purchase orders to work with each other, if people don't need job numbers even to work with each other, collaboration becomes a lot easier.

---

[4] The vast majority of advertising agencies are now held as subsidiaries of a holding company. The four major holding companies worldwide are WPP, Omnicom, Interpublic, and Publicis. Few agencies have retained their independence, operating as private entities. Some notable examples include Cramer-Krasselt, Wieden+Kennedy, and McKinney.

Tuten: Is time tracking different at C-K than it is at other agencies?

Ross: I think probably not. I think what's different is that we don't have gates between disciplines, that things can be more informal, and you don't need department heads approving everything. People can seek each other out. People can agree independently. People can make the call independently. They can say, "Yeah, I think I can add value to that. It makes sense that myself or a number of people in my group be a part of this project."

I remember when I was at a large holding-company agency [Foote, Cone, & Belding, part of the Interpublic Group] and recognized one of the motivations for starting my own agency. I literally just started to keep track on a piece of paper where my time was spent. I figured out I was spending something like seventy percent of my time negotiating internally for what I could show to a client versus working with clients and working on the craft of making things great. That statistic just sort of blew my mind. I said, "This is insane. We're tougher. You know, we're a bigger hurdle than the world is." So that didn't make any sense to me. I think if you did an interview of folks around C-K, they probably would not list as a complaint, "It's too hard to get ideas in front of a client." If they had complaints, they wouldn't list that among their complaints. They might have others, but they wouldn't list that.

Tuten: Now, you mentioned your own agency, the shop that you created with your partners. How did that come about?

Ross: It was a combination of a couple of things. All of us had some sort of sense of missed opportunity at the places we were at. We all felt like, you know, "If we were doing this in our own way, it would be a lot of fun." I wish I could say it was headier than that, but it really wasn't. At the same time, we had compelling reasons to make Chicago our home. At the time, there really weren't a lot of interesting agencies to go to in the city of Chicago that would have been dramatically different from where we were.

In my case, I had a family. My wife was doing well, very well, in her [career], and her work was Chicago-based, and I didn't think it was fair to ask her to come to New York or some other place for me to seek something out. We have family here. And, you know, Chicago's a great city. So my partners and I thought, "Let's just try it." We had been kind of doing it anyway. We had this little company called After Hours Advertising. We never spent any of the money we made. We just kind of chucked it in the bank. We said, "Well, one day we'll either go for a trip around the world with our wives, or we'll just start an ad agency." So we did the stupid thing, and we started an ad agency.

Tuten: What was that like compared to what it's like to be with a big shop, like C-K?

Ross: At the start of the agency, we didn't know *anything* about anything, which was kind of amazing. The only thing we knew how to do was what was very specific to our jobs, and we quickly learned in the first two weeks that there were a lot of other jobs that got done that we didn't even know about. I mean, we literally didn't understand the manufacturing process at the time, which was pre-Macintosh. So we didn't know how to get an idea into the newspaper. "What? Like, how do you do that?" So, you know, we had to use our network of people at other places, made lots of horrible mistakes— some hilarious now, you know, [that made us] absolutely panic-stricken at the time, but hilarious now.

And so I think the biggest thing was just the heft of the work. We literally had two shifts, but it was the same people pulling both shifts. One of my partners and I lived downtown near each other, and we would just walk home at midnight, literally six days a week. So that was really different. I think that's still the big difference between now being with C-K and Mitchiner, Ross & Kahn: one, the scale, and, two, the pitchability of C-K. You know, that was the biggest problem at Mitchiner, Ross & Kahn. We did quite well, and we grew pretty quickly and lasted past the danger zone. We lasted for more than seven years. But you still ran into walls where a client of a certain scale would say, "You know what? You guys just can't handle what we need." I think today it's a very different environment.

Organizations of all sizes are able to have their at-bat with clients of all sizes, but at that time, which was the mid-nineties, it was different. And so I really welcomed the scale of C-K, the pitchability of C-K. The one thing I miss about our tiny place was that it was really flexible. C-K's pretty flexible, but Mitchiner, Ross & Kahn was *really* flexible. C-K is one hundred and ten years old. There's sort of a big historical obligation that's on the current watch. You don't want to be the management team that screws this up. We didn't have that at Mitchiner, Ross & Kahn. We were like, "whatever."

Tuten: So that agency was bought out. Is that right?

Ross: Yes, by Campbell Mithun Esty, which now I think is called Campbell Mithun.

Tuten: Did you stay put or did you leave when the merger occurred?

Ross: We were bought and absorbed into Campbell Mithun. Several of us moved right over to Campbell Mithun and took leadership jobs there. I stayed for a number of years until that agency was sold. I didn't really like the idea of what was going to become of that. Peter Krivkovitch [Cramer-Krasselt's CEO and president] and I had spoken over the years many times about me joining Cramer-Krasselt. I gave him a call, and I said, "Well, I think finally I can say, 'This makes a lot of sense.'" And that was that.

Tuten: And you've been there ever since?

Ross: Yeah, like sixteen years, which is a long time in advertising.

Tuten: It is a long time. Do you think that that's it for now? You're going to stay put?

Ross: I think I have a really important goal still left, you know, a big aspiration still left ahead of me here. My singular goal is to get C-K to what I call a "sustaining benchmark status." I think, for me and a lot of people here, it's important we sort of hit a place where we are a constant benchmark. There are a few agencies that I think have achieved that, and I admire them a lot. That's the goal—to get us to that point.

Tuten: Can you share which agencies you believe have hit that level of having a sustainable industry benchmark status?

Ross: For me, the agency that most models "the dream" is Goodby, Silverstein & Partners.[5] Probably Wieden+Kennedy, too. Those two, for the last twenty-five years, really have always been a place to look to and learn from. It's really the consistency of the reference point that I think is so amazing. It's one thing to do it for a couple of years. It's one thing to knock it out of the park in a way that makes everyone's head turn once or twice, but to just consistently do it, to build a culture and value system that makes that happen over and over and over again. To me, that's the goal: how do you build a self-repeating culture?

Tuten: What kinds of things are you doing to achieve that at C-K?

Ross: We're doing all kinds of things to try and do that. We're trying to hire people who are believers, who are willing to stay. I think that's a big part of it. We're trying to stretch the definition of talent. We're trying to leverage our independence in ways that make the culture feel unique and make the culture feel precious and something that people want to defend, something that people want to go to bat for. We're looking for ways to give people freedoms and challenges that they haven't had. We bring outside influences in a lot more than we used to.

---

[5] *Ad Week* announced GSP, an agency based in San Francisco and held by the Omnicom Group, the Agency of the Decade in 2009. Its founders, Jeff Goodby and Rich Silverstein, were named Agency Executives of the Decade.

We now have a huge program called "Right Brain," which brings speakers, musicians, artists, programmers, mad scientists into the company culture on a monthly basis. We ask people within the company to research things and bring them to the rest of us and have their own forum to do it without somebody approving what they do. So, those kinds of things.

Tuten: Do you think those types of actions are part of what's led *Ad Age* to name C-K one of the "agencies to watch for" the last three years in a row?

Ross: Well, I hope so. It's hard to say. I think that like all sort of culture-based businesses, it is so much about who's winning and who's not winning. So I think a large part of the *Ad Age* measurement is about business success. I think a second, big part is, how good is the work? I think that our work has managed to be pretty good. To me, it's really not at that place yet that I think gets us to benchmark. So, I love that *Ad Age* has done that and I'm grateful for it, but it's not really satisfying for me until the product is really able to be a reference point over and over again.

Tuten: Is your goal one that is shared by the rest of the leadership team?

Ross: Yes. I think it is. I think we probably have different ways of expressing it, but I think the idea of success—success with continuity, success on a large public level—is very much shared. And I know we all believe that they key to that is how interesting the work product is, whether that work product be media innovation, planning innovation, or creative innovation—that's what drives this business and is the first step to helping brands create friends.

Tuten: What's a typical day like for you?

Ross: Breathless. And it's kind of nutty. It's booked solid, and it has a lot of travel—a lot of travel.

Tuten: What kinds of travel? To meet with clients? Prospecting? Presentations like at ad:tech?[6] Everything?

Ross: All three of those things. Last week I started in Chicago, I went to Nashville, I went to Atlanta, I went to Frankfurt, I went to Stuttgart, and back again by Saturday. And then I leave again tomorrow for Los Angeles. And that's kind of typical.

Tuten: Now, if you're traveling that much and you're doing the important work as part of the leadership team, how much time do you get to spend really with the creative, with the work?

---

[6] ad:tech is an industry trade show and forum. Ross presented in my session at ad:tech New York 2010.

Ross: Not enough. And that's kind of—I guess that's what's expected. This goes back to that goal that I spoke about earlier. I would personally like to spend more time with the creative work, but I'm not sure that helps [us reach] the goal. I think the challenge for me, and for everybody on the leadership team, is to figure out how can the values that I might represent be present in rooms where I am not.

Tuten: Right.

Ross: My challenge is to figure out who the people are who can lead those moments and lead them well enough that I can do these other things. As much as I miss those moments, there are other things that have to be done. From my point of view, the job of chief creative officer has to be about goal setting and values driving, not ad tweaking. If I'm ad tweaking on a big scale or across the network, that's kind of a worrisome thing. And it's also impossible, really, to do that well. It's impossible because it's impractical.

We have offices across the country and clients across the country, and there's a lot of work. To bottleneck the work through me would be kind of egomaniacal, and I don't think it could work very well. And I think it'd be demoralizing. So I believe that if you have creative leaders in New York, in our other offices, even within groups in the Chicago office, they have to be able to take the ball to a certain point. The executive creative directors of the individual offices have to be able to take the ball all the way. They shouldn't need me. Ideally, they'd want me for certain things, but they shouldn't be requiring it.

Tuten: Do you ever have a brief come in where you say, "I just have to work on this project."

Ross: Sometimes. And, again, because of how I delegate it, I don't see all the briefs, but there are a couple of businesses I do stay tied with. A lot of new business is when I get a chance to do work either by, again, sort of setting the approach we might take and then creating an example of what that might look, sound, or feel like. New business is where I get to do that the most. And sometimes with Porsche, which is a personal passion.

Tuten: Can you give me an example of something you've worked on recently?

Ross: Well, I'm really happy to say that for Porsche's model year 2013, I wrote a lot of that work. Actually, I'm a little unhappy because I say that and yet I can't tell you what the work is because you're not even supposed to know what our cars are for the model year '13. But that's very recent. That's why I was in Germany last week, sharing that with our counterparts there.

Tuten: You enjoyed it?

Ross: Yeah, it was great. I mean, it was challenging to be in the role of copy-writer again, from a logistics viewpoint. I had to go in on the weekends, but it was really fun to just write and think about ideas.

Tuten: And is that one where other people came to you and said, "We need you on this one?" Or is that one that you said, "I have to work on this."

Ross: No, I think logistics created a hole. There were some people that were out on production and some deadlines that sort of overlapped. It was the luck—in this case the good luck, the confluence—where, really the only thing I could say without ruining other people's lives was, "Okay, I'll do it."

Tuten: And what did it feel like?

Ross: It was great. It was scary for the first couple of hours, but then it was great. It was a lot of fun. More fun than my usual days.

Tuten: Scary in the "I don't know if I can do this anymore" kind of way?

Ross: It's like anything else. If you don't play tennis for a while, the first time you find yourself on the court, you kind of suck, right?

Tuten: Right.

Ross: So it was that. I wrote a bunch of stuff, and I was like, "God! I'm going to fire this person." And then, then finally, I remembered that that's normal. And then it got fun. And then when it gets fun, it gets good.

Tuten: And then who served as your creative director?

Ross: It's funny because I asked a larger team to review the work. And I think they were pretty honest, and so I kind of reverse creative-directed. I said, "Okay, guys, now you're the creative directors. What sucks and what's really great?" And it worked. I think it did. We're really happy with the work.

Tuten: That's fantastic. What a great story. Say you have a magic wand and you can change with this magic wand one thing about advertising. What do you change?

Ross: Ooh, that's a good question. What's the one thing I'd change about advertising? I think I'd wish that the really horrible work wouldn't be successful. There's a lot of really bad stuff that you're exposed to that I consider to be visual and noise pollution. And a lot of it arcs [i.e., causes sales to increase in response to the advertising]. It makes me crazy. A lot of it sells a lot of stuff, and I just wish it wouldn't. And that would be how I would use that magic wand. I would say, "Okay, from now on, if it's really offensive and crass, it doesn't get to be successful. You can't even buy your way to success if that's the way you're going to market." That's what I would change.

Tuten: It's funny to me that you mention that, because that's one of the things that we always end up discussing in my advertising classes when it comes to creative. Is the objective to meet the marketing goals of the client, or is the objective to create really good work? Sometimes the answer is not the same for those two things.

Ross: Well, right. I think the challenge with how open-minded the marketplace is in terms of accepting, responding to work that's just horrific and work that's really great, is that it allows marketing directors to be rightfully conflicted about what's the right path for them. From their perspective, their jobs are on the line with the success or failure of their products and services. Unless they work for companies like Apple that are driven by the aesthetic and driven by a design point of view, they're up against it. If somebody brings them a formula with a box full of rocks and that formula works, it's going to be hard to get them off it with work that's more insightful, with work that's more human, with work that's more endearing, with work that's more memorable. Because the junk actually succeeds. It's very challenging.

Tuten: Are you in that situation with clients?

Ross: I think everybody in my job is in that situation with clients. I think it's a fair situation to be in. Our clients have, appropriately, a different lens with which they view the world. And like I said, the first topic we spoke about, if you can't link what you're trying to do with what they must do, you're not going to get to yes.

Tuten: When you look around the industry now, what's most surprising to you?

Ross: I think the biggest surprise—well, maybe it wasn't a surprise. We saw it coming, but everybody just sort of said, "Holy cow. That looks like what's going to happen," and then it happened. It's happened in all kinds of different industries. The surprise is how people who had nothing to do with advertising came to control the world of advertising. Did you know that Google is the world's largest ad agency? But Google doesn't care about advertising. These guys were out to invent a way to share information. Their mission is to bring information to people in a really usable way. It just so happens that their way of sustaining that mission is through ad sales. They've become probably the most powerful force in advertising. I think that's mind-boggling. On the one hand, it's kind of amazing and cool. On the other hand, it's like, "How did we let that happen?"

A lot of the issues that we seem to have with the industry come from the outsiders—complete outsiders. Look at the music industry. Steve Jobs came in and completely transformed the music industry [with the introduction of the iPod and iTunes]. All these music industry people, many of whom got into the business because they love music and they worship the artists that create it, suddenly found themselves not in command of the industry they created. That's what has happened to the advertising industry.

Tuten: So what do you think will be happening next in the advertising industry?

Ross: I think that change, among others, will probably spark a whole domino effect of new models for what the ad business is. I think that in five years from now, there will be a few pillars of constancy, but a lot of the land-scape is going to look incredibly different. It's going to be way more entre-preneurial. It's going to be absolutely more technologically fueled. It will be analytics-fueled, and somehow creativity will still end up being a huge differentiator. But the definition of creative is going to be real different.

Tuten: In what way?

Ross: Well, I think the palettes—the canvas and paints—are just going to be different. It wasn't that long ago when agencies were measured by the brilliance of their film. And now, already, it's become—in, I think, a positive way—the brilliance of their engagement props, or how well they're able to elicit participation and activate that participation into real results for cli-ents. That's changing the kinds of ideas that people create. And people that started in this business, interested in design and interested in words or interested in marketing are still interested in and motivated by these things. But they're deploying them in ways there's no way they would have imagined three or four years ago. That's really cool.

Tuten: When we teach advertising, we're still teaching people who want to go into the creative side to be art directors and copywriters.

Ross: As long as it's writing and art directing through the lens of how things work today, that still makes sense. I think there's a place—there has to be a place for the artist. I mean, you look at gaming, and you say, "Gaming? That's a technology field, a software field." It is, but it's movies. It's just movies that wait for you to determine their outcomes. There is still great writing, and there is still amazing art direction. So I think that those mindsets and those skill sets are still going to be in huge demand.

What's going to be different is, again, how they're deployed. We're going to have to understand that the paint comes out of the tube in a different way now. That's a huge challenge for people who are currently in the business, who've been in the business for a while, and even for the next generation, because they're still inspired by the past. That's what got them interested. The truth is, the past is not all that relevant anymore.

Tuten: What should we be doing in the classroom differently, do you think?

Ross: Well, I think that we still talk about the business and teach about the business in a two-dimensional way. We talk about ideas as marriages between images and language. There's a whole new dimension that I like to call "activation." The big idea is the cliché in the business—the goal is to develop a big, breakthrough advertising idea. I think that's over. We need to be looking for big, breakthrough *activation* ideas. It's about mobilization. I don't mean literally a mobile phone, although that's certainly part of it. It's mobilization of people behind actions. And that's very different than thinking about the world of perceptions and imaging. Now you have to do all of that at the same time. You have to create aesthetics in a world that galvanizes, mobilizes, and motivate people to actually do things earlier, more often, and in more ways than ever before. And so the role of art and the role of language have totally new jobs before them. And creative people, whether they wear a suit or wear jeans or whether they use a calculator or Adobe Creative Suite, have to look at what they're creating in a very different way.

Tuten: You've talked to me a lot in the last several minutes about changes in the ad industry and changes that have happened and what's coming. *Mad Men* is an incredibly popular drama now, and that reinforces a lot of stereotypes about the ad industry. Are any of those still true?

Ross: Well, obviously, *Mad Men* is fiction on a lot of fronts. I think that's what makes advertising a constant stage throughout the generations of television—you know, it started with the movies, right, with *North by Northwest*. And then TV picked up on it with *Bewitched*. Darren Stevens [of *Bewitched*] was in the ad business. And when I was in college, there was *Thirtysomething*. There's always been that stage for the industry because the one constant, the one truth, is the way ego shapes this business. That's still true. I think that, like Hollywood, advertising is a magnet for people with grand visions, egos bigger than they should be, who sometimes through amazing skill and brilliance, and sometimes [through] sheer luck, get the chance to exercise their egotistical point of view. And so that part's true.

Edward Boches

Chief Innovation Officer
Mullen

Edward Boches is chief innovation officer at Mullen (www.mullen.com), an independent full-service agency within the Interpublic Group of Companies (IPG). Mullen integrates disciplines from creative to digital marketing, public relations and social influence, media planning and buying, mobile marketing, direct response, and performance analytics. Mullen specializes in what it calls an "unbound" approach to marketing, a term that Boches pays homage to with the name of his blog, Creativity Unbound. Boches has been with Mullen since its early days, working in the creative department, ultimately as chief creative officer. Mullen clearly provided Boches room to soar as it ranks among Advertising Age's Agency A-List and Fast Company's Most Innovative Companies.

Boches created the role of chief social media officer and later, chief innovation officer, as he sought to inspire change and encourage people in the agency and industry to embrace new technologies, platforms, and consumer behaviors necessary to create cool and relevant ideas for clients. He proudly says, "Somehow I've survived for 30 years in a business that typically eats its young." In this interview, he shares a rare glimpse into the story of Mullen in its early days and a look at where, having learned many lessons from the advertising industry, his life is headed.

Tracy Tuten: What led you to advertising as a profession? Did you grow up wanting to work in this field?

Edward Boches: I grew up wanting to be in the media in one way or another. Even at an incredibly young age, like seventh grade maybe. I loved the printed page, newspapers, magazines, and everything about it. I was a bit of a news junkie, even back then. I also was interested in film, starting probably about early high school. By high school, I decided, well, I want to be either Walter Cronkite or Orson Welles or somebody who is making something out of the media to perform, persuade, influence, and entertain other people.

I liked the idea of being a creator of popular culture and ideas that mattered. I started college as a journalism major. I went back and forth between film and journalism. I actually thought I wasn't a good enough writer to be a great journalist, which may have been a premature conclusion, and then I also thought the idea of becoming a famous Hollywood director seemed slightly elusive, and I ended up majoring in a hybrid: public communication.

My first job was as a newspaper reporter for a weekly newspaper. I then went into PR, later became a corporate speechwriter, and then I ended up in advertising. It was sort of circuitous route, but it still seemed to be con-nected and related to my first love, which was [working] with the printed page and creating ideas and content where nothing existed before.

Tuten: I think you must have been an unusual high school student to already know—as others have reported—who Bill Bernbach[1] was.

Boches: Well, I knew the work, anyway, from all those great ads appearing in *LIFE* and *LOOK* magazines. I probably had seen pictures of him at the ad agency. I was certainly familiar with VW and Avis and Alka-Seltzer ads. I just seemed acutely aware of all of that stuff.

And what's also interesting is the first serious film I ever saw. I saw *Citizen Kane* when I was maybe . . . fifteen years old.

The whole concept of the auteur in cinema really intrigued me as well. At that time, I was making Super 8 movies. When I was in high school, I had a Super 8 camera, and I had the Moviola,[2] and I had editing slicing systems. In those days, you had to do everything with glue and cement and wait for the film to come back. I made political films that were either protesting against companies that polluted, or oppressive school systems, or whatever.

I guess I was a little radical, too, although I didn't think that at the time. I founded a newspaper in high school, a student-run newspaper called *The Mad Hatter.* It got me thrown out of school. I think I was only a junior in

---

[1] Bill Bernbach was a creative director and one of the founding members of Doyle Dane Bernbach (DDB). He is credited with being the first to team copywriters and art direc-tors into two-person teams.

[2] A device that allowed an editor to view film while editing.

high school—I know I didn't have my driver's license yet—and I got featured on some Boston news station for being one of the more active high school radicals at the time. So all of that sort of went together: being political, subversive, creating content, writing, expressing yourself. Advertising in some ways was the easy way out because it was fun. It was filled with instant gratification. You could be clever and irreverent even though you were selling stuff [to] people. It was a more attainable career than, say, being a filmmaker.

Tuten: All of those characteristics that you just named seem like they are still very relevant for you today.

Boches: In some ways, yes. I once said to somebody that social media was invented just for me because it sort of combined all of my interests. I actually got really bored with traditional advertising if you will—with things like print or outdoor or television. I got bored with just delivering other people's messages to other people's audiences with other people's money. It sort of lost some of its appeal over time. I've been doing this a long time. Now I don't quite have that passion for making "an ad" that I may have had when I was younger. I still have the passion for media and connecting people and generating ideas and finding new ways to influence. But the original thing that got me really excited was, "Oh, I can come up with an idea and put it on that blank piece of paper, that two-dimensional plan, and have it be something magical." After doing that for a number of years, it wasn't quite as exciting anymore.

Tuten: Is that what led you to the role of chief innovation officer?

Boches: Yes. I guess basically what happened was two things. It became apparent to me that all the changes that were going on were going to dramatically affect our business. We frankly had failed a couple of times to really evolve as quickly as we needed to in the digital social space. Part of that reason was because we always brought somebody in from the outside. We did that because he supposedly was or allegedly was an expert in digital or interactive. Those people never could quite fit into our culture or make change from the inside.

One day I just said, "Maybe I'll do that job. Maybe I'll be the person who tries." I don't know a whole lot about digital. I didn't know anything about social at the time. This was maybe three years ago. But I said, "I know an awful lot about our company, our clients, and our standards, and maybe I'll go and learn that other kind of stuff and try to become an evangelist for it." What happened was I actually got into it! I got into every aspect of it—Twitter, and blogging, and fast-generated content, and the power of conducting research via the Web, and so on.

I'm more interested in that and I started to find ways in which I could get clients excited about it. As that happened, I said, "Shoot. Maybe we should get somebody else to pay attention to 'the advertising part of things.'" I ended up hiring my replacement, who is probably a better creative director than I was.

At that point, I started really pursuing all of the new platforms and digital technologies. I've defined my job as I've gone along from being someone who actually made advertising to somebody who tries to inspire people to try to embrace new ways of thinking to the creation of more modern forms of advertising. The simple way to look at it was this: for a long time, we made ideas out of words, pictures, and stories. And now ideas are also made out of technology and applications and utility. Trying to get a company to think in those terms has been interesting and fun. It's fun to try to make that transformation happen.

Tuten: How much of your effort is spent on work that is Mullen's development in a specific area versus how much is spent on specific client work?

Boches: I don't do that much direct client work anymore. I run an internal innovation lab that tries to experiment and be a catalyst for new ideas. I write and speak about trends as a public face for the agency and its innovative thinking. I generate an awful lot of content that we use in new business that helps show clients and prospects new ways of looking at things.

And I spend time trying to generate things for Mullen. They range from a crowdsourced Gen Y blog that I incubated, called "The Next Great Generation." It really runs completely and totally autonomously and has recently become the Gen Y content provider to *The Boston Globe*. I work on smaller things like playing with new platforms, social digital participation, and that sort of thing. We just launched something with boston.com called "The Pulse." It combines content from *The Globe,* content from blogs, social media, data, and analytics, Twitter participation, geo-based access to content, etc. It sort of takes the user, the reader, the professional content, data, and a branded advertising platform and puts them together in a new kind of media content.

I think it's important to be playing around with those kinds of things for a couple of reasons. One is they could become new sources of revenue over time. They could set examples or be experimental laboratories for the creation of new things for clients that make a statement about the agency being progressive in its thinking. These activities help raise awareness, which helps with the recruitment of both clients and employees. So it's a new sort of unchartered territory that a number of agencies are paying attention to— like Wieden+Kennedy[3] with its incubator, or BBH Labs.[4] It's about agencies inventing their own brands and products. I don't know if anybody knows where this is going to go, but I think there's a sense that it could be important and we should be playing in those spaces.

Tuten: How big is your team there, the innovation team working with you at Mullen?

Boches: There are really only a couple of us. It's me and percentages of other people. I tap into existing developers, technology people, project managers, mobile people, media people, and a few Gen Y content generators. Almost all of them have other roles and responsibilities. One of the reasons for doing it that way is to make the lab somewhat virtual. You're more likely to spread the thinking and the practices and the technologies into other areas of the company rather than keep it off to the side as a completely contained department.

Tuten: You're not a silo. You're integrated.

Boches: Some silo and some integrated. If you're doing things for the agency and not the clients, those things by definition are siloed. If you're doing things with people who work on client business, they're bringing that information, that thinking, that inspiration back into the rest of the agency, and it will inevitably affect the client one way or another.

Tuten: What's a typical day like—if there is one?

Boches: A typical day is a combination of staying connected with people outside the agency via social platforms. I think another important part is bringing ideas and content in from the outside. I generate a ton of content. That's the second part of my day. Blogging, speaking, writing, appearances, and generating content for those things takes up a fair amount of time. Let's say it's a fifth of the time that I might be actually working on projects for the agency. Some of the things that I refer to that we might be trying to create or invent. The rest of the time might just be ad hoc. I'm dragged into meetings, or I'm asked to consult or counsel on something, or to meet with a client, or make a contribution to a pitch. And then, I work on a couple of clients who are aligned with the kind of modern things we're trying to work on.

---

[3] Wieden+Kennedy is an award-winning agency based in Portland, Oregon, best known for its work for Nike. Wieden+Kennedy is a contributor to the Portland Incubator Experiment (PIE), a joint project between Portland's technology industry and the agency. Learn more at www.wk.com/incubator.

[4] The global innovation unit sponsored by advertising agency, Bartle Bogle Hegarty (www.bbh-labs.com).

Tuten: You are one of the founding partners of Mullen. What was that experience like?

Boches: Mullen was founded by one guy, Jim Mullen, but three additional people became partners in the very early days. It was actually awesome. Joe Grimaldi, who's CEO, came here before me. I joined a few months later. At that time, the agency was already eight or nine years old and had about twelve or thirteen employees. Joe and I became partners along with Paul Silverman, my predecessor as chief creative officer.

We basically built this agency from nothing. We were in a house on the North Shore in the middle of nowhere. We were thirty miles from Boston and a million miles from Madison Avenue. We were smart and we balanced each other's strengths and weaknesses. We sort of knew what we were doing, but not really. But it was a lot of fun because we had the challenge of building something. We were doing it for ourselves. We were experimenting as we went along. We could decide what we wanted to be and then how to be it. Anyone who's ever worked in a start-up company when it was small and you were struggling and you were trying to turn it into something would say that was the most fun. The journey to get big was more fun than being big.

We successfully created a culture that was inherently entrepreneurial, that embraced change on an ongoing basis, and that was rooted first and foremost in creativity. Those qualities served us well as the world changed around us.

Tuten: Do you miss that now?

Boches: We try to create that to a degree whenever we can in pockets of the company, or on certain projects, or on certain pieces of business. But I do miss it. I do. There are benefits to being large, having more resources, being surrounded by professional, talented people who are good at specific things. In those days we had to figure out everything for ourselves from the most basic stuff like traveling and faxing, to how you did new business pitches to how you prospected for new clients to how you produced a TV commercial. Anything we were doing for the very first time. But at the same time, it was closer to rock and roll, like being in a band that nobody ever heard of and taking the show on the road, hoping to find an audience.

Tuten: Like you have a dream and you just work every day a bit towards the dream.

Boches: It was also at a time when there was nothing—there was no technology. We didn't have computers. We didn't have web, e-mail, internet. We had IBM Selectric typewriters and landlines. I can't even imagine that now. It seems like it would be so much easier today because you don't even need office space. You need a cell phone and an internet connection and people can work from wherever they are. You can set up a company. Back then you needed an office because you had to congregate someplace. You needed Xerox machines, you needed a little bit more capital expense than you need today. It should be a hell of a lot easier to do it today than it was then.

Tuten: That sounds like it was an amazing experience.

Boches: It was. It was great. I hadn't really thought about it for a long time, but as you ask these questions, I'm starting to get flashbacks.

Tuten: Anything specific? A special story you want to tell us?

Boches: Oh, there are some great stories. Oh God, I could tell you a story that was amazing. We had the biggest pitch of our lives. There were fourteen of us in the company. This must have been twenty-nine years ago, so this would have been 1982, '83. We were going up against the biggest agency in Boston, which at the time was HBM [Humphrey Browning MacDougall], and against J. Walter Thompson in New York. It was for Apollo Computer, which was a very, very hot workstation company that was on its way to being a *Fortune* 1000, if not a *Fortune* 500, company.

Joe and I were basically doing the whole pitch. He was running the deck and the presentation, and I was doing all the creative with my partner. We had a pretty cool campaign. We were writing every single word of copy to try to be as perfect as we could be. We knew that we had a great way to position these network workstations visually and verbally and with a level of confidence that rivaled BMW advertising. We were the dark horse, for sure. The local ad trade publications at that time, like *Ad Week New England,* said it was a joke that we were even in this pitch with these big agencies.

The night before the pitch, Joe gets a call that his mother had died. She was in Florida and she'd passed away. It wasn't expected. I think she had a heart attack or stroke and died. This is maybe six or seven o'clock at night a day and a half before the pitch. All I remember is Joe stayed up and worked through the night. We worked from seven p.m. straight through the next morning till dawn. We finished the presentation. We finished the deck. I finished the copy, and then he had to leave to fly to Florida. And he was the senior guy. We had to go and do the presentation without him. It was just one of these crazy, intense, dramatic things. We did the pitch, and we blew them away, and we won! It was a big local and national advertising story. "Who the hell are these guys in Beverly Farms in the middle of nowhere that no one had ever heard of?" We had just beat the biggest agency in Boston, and a giant New York agency. It was empowering.

Here's another. It was '87 maybe. We were in this magnificent building. We had renovated William Randolph Hearst's private estate into an impressive office space in Pride's Crossing atop a hill with a view of Boston and the tip of Cape Cod out over the ocean. I was in New York getting ready to do a new business pitch. I get a call that morning from Joe telling me that the agency had burned to the ground, just totally burned to the ground. Nothing was left. First I thought—it was April 2 and I had my dates confused—I thought it was April 1, and I thought the entire thing was a joke. It turns out it wasn't a joke. There had been a small fire that had started inside the building. There was a volunteer fire department in that town. A couple of mishaps happened, and the next thing there are some explosions inside that building and the building burned to the ground. So we lost everything—every file, every computer, every desk, every piece of furniture, every document, every deck, every piece of paper, everything—there was literally nothing left. Not a pencil, not an eraser, not a paper clip—nothing. But, you know what? We were up and running as an agency the next day because people didn't ask any permission from anybody—ever. They just did what they needed to do.

The three of us in New York finished our pitch and flew home. Somebody else went out and bought new equipment. Somebody else did this or did that. We returned to the little building that we had been in prior to renovating the estate, now with three times as many people. We put four people into an office. We were crammed on top of each other. We still went to work the next day. At the end of that year, we had lost no business, we lost no clients, we missed no deadlines.

In fact, I think we grew twenty-five percent. At the time, we probably had, say, maybe forty employees—my numbers could be off a little bit. What was interesting is we had a culture of "collective entrepreneurialism." It was a term that I coined years ago—collective entrepreneurialism, which was the idea of "we're in this together, but we're behaving as a unit of entrepreneurs." That kind of stuff was challenging and trying, but man, it was joyful at the same time. That aspect of our culture still permeates the place today despite that there's probably only—out of six hundred people—there's probably only four or five of us who were here when that happened.

Tuten: Do you tell these stories to your current employees so they can have that sense of culture?

Boches: Not really. It's kind of the classic story of mom and dad telling you they used to walk uphill both ways to and from school. I think it's in the lore, but the fire is actually one story that I don't think we make a big deal of.

Tuten: How do you keep the collective entrepreneurship alive?

Boches: That is a combination of things, I think. First of all, we're big believers in rights and responsibilities, so we actually give people more rights and decision-making authority than they might get at the same age or with the same title in a lot of companies, as long as they're willing to embrace the responsibility that goes with it. That's one thing.

I think a second piece of it is it's almost just inherently in the DNA of the company. It's one of those things where you couldn't get rid of it even if you tried.

The third thing is, as a result, it attracts a certain kind of people. We never, ever attract people who want to be tenders or who want to maintain the status quo. We tend to do a really good job attracting people who want to take over, who want to build things, who want to make stuff, who want to assume that level of responsibility. That kind of person perpetuates the culture. I think we would make an argument that one of the most valuable assets that any company has is that [type of] culture.

I was looking at growth charts with my partner a week or so ago. It's significant. We've gone from a $2 million agency [income] to a $110 million agency, whatever the numbers are. If you look at any time we've had a down year, we may have lost clients. One year we lost BMW and Timberland in the same year. Another year we lost Nextel, which was our biggest client by two or three times, so that year was obviously a dip in our income than our previous year. But if you look at the company, we have never, ever had two bad years in a row. In the three or four times in the history of the company we've had a down year, the next year was an up year that brought us back to close to where we had been previously. That's a cultural thing that permeates how we work and what we believe we can do. We call on that without even realizing it.

Tuten: How do you see Mullen changing in the future?

Boches: It's interesting because there's a big debate going on. It's been going on for a year or two now. Are we in the middle of an incredible transformation when it comes to advertising, which includes branding, yes or no? More people seem to think yes than no.

There's a question as to whether traditional media will become less important in the future than it's been in the past. Most people will say yes, but when you look at the actual numbers in terms of where dollars are spent, there's a tremendous amount still spent on traditional media and no real sign of it diminishing.

Then the third question that comes up in this debate is where is the industry going. Will clients of the future be more inclined to want integrated agencies that do everything well? Or will they want best of breed, specialist agencies that do social or digital or something else?

We may be at odds with the majority of people who think the specialists are still the way to go. But we believe that you can't be best of breed if you're not completely, totally integrated and you don't have convergence because everything is interdependent. How do you have traditional advertising that doesn't have social media, that doesn't have digital, that doesn't have platforms, that doesn't have apps, that doesn't have mobile, that doesn't have all of those things naturally working together?

So, when you ask where Mullen will be in the next four or five years, we'll still be in advertising. We'll still be an advertising agency. We will still be rooted in creative ideas. We will apply those ideas to more new places and platforms, to mobile and social and community kinds of things. The way in which we [create] will be more informed by creative technologists and developers and programmers, not just writers and art directors.

I personally am a big believer, even though some people don't agree with me, that the future creative person is going to come as much from other areas as they do from the traditional writer, art director, and the crafts. In fact, if you look at the biggest cultural influencers of the last three or four years, who are they? They're the Mark Zuckerbergs of the world, right? Programmers and nerds—not necessarily who we consider traditional communicators.

Tuten: Right.

Boches: They're Ev Williams, they're Steve Chen, they're the guys who are inventing things like YouTube and Facebook and Twitter. They aren't writers and art directors. They're programmers. They just happen to be creative.

Tuten: But we're still going to have to have content created, too.

Boches: Oh yeah, absolutely. But what is content going to be? Is content going to be a platform or an application? As I said earlier, I think future stories are going to be made out of technology and code and APIs [application programming interfaces] as much as they are out of words and pictures.

Tuten: So for my students now, or for your students next semester at BU,[5] what would you tell them about how to best prepare for being a creative technologist?[6]

Boches: Well, I don't know if they need to be creative technologists. I think what they [each] need to do is have a specific skill and have it really well developed. They could be a writer. They could be an art director. They could be a designer. They could be a developer. They could be a UX [user experience design] person. They could be a videographer. All of those skills are still completely and totally necessary. The difference in the future is that you need to have a much broader perspective than just your specific skills.

So you've probably heard of the expression, "T-shaped person," which is almost becoming a cliché.[7] Look at any project these days—whether it's Nike Plus or Garmin Connect or a Facebook app, or a mobile game, or a social experience, whatever kind of project that you look at—the team that makes that stuff now is much broader than it used to be. The people that you have to have in the room are well beyond what used to serve as a core creative team. There are now four, five, six, seven, eight roles maybe. Somebody who really knows social, someone who knows mobile, someone who can actually do front-end development, and so on.

The real challenge now is, how do you get all of those people to work really, really well together? In fact, how do you stay open-minded enough to believe that the idea that everybody is working toward may not be an "advertising idea," or a concept that emanates from a television script, but may be something that transcends any one medium or execution. The skill that everybody in that room has to have, even if they all have a specific skill—the second skill that they all have to have is to be a T-shaped person. In other words, they must be able to see and understand, appreciate, and leverage the value of every other person on that team. They must understand their relationship to the holistic thing that they're trying to do. That is way easier said than done.

I actually remember the days when art directors would refuse to put URL addresses in a print ad because it would ruin the layout. You would have one

---

[5] Boches will be teaching a creative design class for Boston University in 2012.

[6] Creative technologists are a relatively new breed of creative that visually create using the latest in technology trends.

[7] The T-shaped person is a metaphor among human resource professionals that describes the ideal employee. The T-shaped person has a depth of skill and expertise (the vertical aspect of the T), but is also capable of collaborating across many disciplines (the horizontal aspect of the T).

person who was building the web site saying, "Well, if you don't put the URL in the print ad, no one's going to know the web site and people aren't going to go there." The art director's attitude was, "Yeah, but you're really fucking up the layout." At the time, I actually engaged in those conversations. It was, "No, we don't want to put the URL in the layout. It's really going to look stupid." You look back at that and go, "Oh my God. That was the most ridiculous thing." You had two people who had no appreciation for what each other's contribution was to the project. The web people thought that all that mattered was the web, and the print people thought that no one was going to go to the web. Consumers were only going to read the print ads. Yet both the web person and the print person could make a remarkable contribution to the overall project. I guarantee you there's plenty of people in the business who remember those idiotic arguments.

Tuten: Now they're saying that about the little Facebook icon.

Boches: Exactly. Now we're forwarding to a thing where you have a user experience person telling somebody else, "I don't really think the way you have that hierarchy in the navigation is really working at all." Someone may say, "But it looks beautiful," but the UX person may say, "Yeah, but we need usability here." Even beyond that, the question may be, "what is it we should actually be making and creating? Should it be a platform? Should we actually be inventing something worth being advertised rather than simply advertising?" What I would tell students is, "Okay, develop a skill and master it to the degree possible, but then learn how to apply that skill within the context to where all these other rules are as fundamental as yours."

Tuten: Given what you just described, what does a creative brief look like these days?

Boches: That's a really, really good question because the creative brief probably looks as stupid as it did twenty years ago. The brief says, "Okay. Who are we talking to? What's the problem we're solving? What's the message we should deliver? What are the executional guides?" Here we probably have multiple briefs and the briefs depend on whether or not we're creating advertising, whether or not we're starting from scratch and trying to solve a problem with something that may be beyond creative execution.

I think the brief ought to start with the problem that we're trying to solve. The problem, by the way, may not be an advertising problem. It's what kind of problem are we trying to solve that would make our brand of more value to this consumer?

I think the second thing it has to address is the use of media, technology, content, and community by the users, customers, or target audience or community members. Thinking about how somebody interacts with stuff beyond just the brand and the category is really important. I would actually go so far as to have every brief basically say, "You can't solve this problem with an ad. You have to solve this problem with an idea that isn't an ad." Then you get to invent this idea or creative that might be worth advertising, right? I think another way to look at it is to really figure out the problem behind the problem. The problem can't be, "Oh, we want know about this product." The problem might be, "Well, what problem do these people actually have that we could solve?" And maybe solving it and actually doing something of value in the world of social media, etc., might be the reason that gets them to pay attention to us and might turn them on to the product we want them to know about. That's almost coming at it from an extreme perspective in order to fight the inclination to solve problems with a TV commercial.

Does that make any sense?

Tuten: Yes, it really does. But it also sounds like it's a really hard process to go through.

Boches: I think it really depends on the people involved. We do this exercise sometimes where I'll ask creative people, "Don't you think you should learn a little bit more about technology? Don't you think you should learn a little bit more about APIs or different platforms or whatever?" And often I'll get an answer that's something like, "No, I don't need to do that."

I'll ask, "Well, why not?"

They'll say, "Because I know that no matter what I think up, someone will be able to make it or produce it." Which is true. There's hardly anything you can think up that someone will not be able to do. Here's the downside of that. If you're not aware of the capabilities of technology and APIs and certain platforms, you may never think up the idea to begin with.

I think it was the day that Google did the Arcade Fire HTML 5 video[8] that I had this exact same conversation with somebody. I dragged him in my office and I showed him the video. I said, "Would you be able to think that up?" His jaw dropped open. It was the first time he'd seen it. He was blown away. I said, "Would you be able to think that up? I'm sure someone could make it. Obviously, here it is. But would you be able to think it up?" The answer was, "Uhh, gee, uhh, yeah, actually, I, I, I couldn't."

I said, "Well, why not?"

---

[8] http://thewildernessdowntown.com/

"Because I would—I had no idea that something like that was even possible. I wouldn't even know where to start." These days, creative people need to be incredibly curious and interested in everything new that comes along.

We're doing a project right now for Olympus where all of the content is being generated by users, and none of it by the brand itself, for a new camera. The campaign really just took a chapter out of Gary Vaynerchuk's *The Thank You Economy.*[9] We just gave out a thousand cameras to certain people who would be willing and promised to generate a certain amount of content. We then put in place an entire infrastructure using almost all open-source platforms—Tumbler and Google+ and Twitter and Facebook and YouTube—to generate, aggregate, collect, and spread that content all over the place. With a fraction of the cost of a media buy—of course, we still do some paid media—the social components make that paid media more effective. It takes a certain kind of person who will think that way and be open to thinking that way.

Tuten: You are encouraging your creatives to be aware of what's possible and what's new. But, what do you suggest that they do? What's your approach for keeping up with all these new things?

Boches: Well, my approach to keeping up with things is to build a community of people who can help me keep up because I don't think you can do it by yourself. I mean, we can all, with good intent, build up our RSS reader, fill our Pulse app[10] with all the stuff we hope to or plan to read every day, or even organize our Tweet deck according to different topics and subjects, but that's really hard to do on a daily basis. We can get good at using certain kinds of tools whether it's Springpad[11] or all of the stuff we might use to save things or bookmark stuff. But I think what you have to do is figure out how to manage.

I've got a certain group of people that I've developed relationships with offline and online around whatever topics I know matter to me—mobile, social, digital, education, brands, etc. So number one, I have people I can go to directly anytime I need stuff. Two, they know enough about what I do and what I care about and what I'm interested in that I'm pretty sure they're going to send me stuff that matters to me. They're going to filter content that's for me. I can use my Google+ circles more efficiently that way. It still

---

[9] HarperCollins, 2001.

[10] A news-reading app for smartphones and tablets.

[11] An app that makes it easy to take notes. Boches is a company board member.

takes a little bit of an effort because you can't simply just say, "Oh, okay, I'm just going to click on all these people and these names and just hope that they play that role for me." You actually have to make the effort to give back and to develop a relationship with them and a dialogue and then hopefully that leads to that kind of quid pro quo with this community of people helping each other stay up on what matters.

Tuten: Content-management through relationships.

Boches: Yeah. I mean, you can also read your ass off, but that takes a lot of time.

Tuten: Not nearly as efficient. Now, you mentioned Springpad, and that was something that you helped to create.

Boches: Well, no, no. I'm on the board of directors. I didn't help to create it.

Tuten: But it's something that you believe in strongly.

Boches: Well, I think that they have a lot of potential. They're still a start-up and they're pivoting from what they started-up being to what they're doing now. They've added millions of users, but they're a long way from being Facebook or Twitter. For me, being involved with companies like that, learning a little bit about how software companies think, is actually valuable for the advertising business. You can learn from hanging out with software start-ups the ideas of prototyping, AB testing, of being agile and putting stuff out on the marketplace when it isn't completely ready, when it's still in beta. Letting users define how to make products better.

Many of these things are in some ways like the antithesis to how advertising works, where we make our stuff so precious and we want it to be perfect and magnificently designed, and then we've got to produce it and then we put it out into the marketplace. That long, linear process might lead to something that's gorgeous and finished, but it's not always the best. In a world where things change daily and things are disposable more quickly, it's not always the best way to do things. I think we're going to see more convergence among and between marketing, advertising, and software and gaming-type companies over the next five years.

Tuten: Are you involved in any of that gaming work?

Boches: I'm not doing anything myself in that space really at the moment. The agency's doing some stuff, but I'm not. I'm not really there, personally. I support it, but I'm not working on it.

Tuten: You're really active outside of Mullen. Things like the Springpad board and the content that you produce, and teaching with institutions, and giving industry talks. Which aspects of your work do you enjoy the most and why?

Boches: I think the one thing that ties all of those things together is sort of sharing what I know. If I'm helping a start-up company with ideas about how to think about marketing, or I'm teaching a course, or I'm lecturing, or I'm running workshops, or I'm blogging, what ties all of that stuff together is the idea of sharing. And I think that's really interesting—there's a real interesting benefit to doing that.

Number one is appealing to an awful lot of different people in communities, many of whom will gladly reciprocate. The second thing is it really helps you interact with people that you might not naturally interact with. Doing so exposes you to a lot more new thinking and ideas and platforms and conversations—all of which are fodder for your own learning and progress. All of which is stuff that you can bring back to the agency and package as examples, or information from clients, or content that helps with doing business.

The third thing that it helps is that by sharing knowledge, say if you have to give a speech someplace, you've got to really clarify your thoughts, and you've got to organize them, and you've got to write them down. You've got to develop a point of view. All of that makes you sharper as a content creator and a salesperson. These are incredibly vital skills when you're trying to pitch and win business, or pitch and attract believers in an idea that you think would be good for the agency. I think everybody knows that really good creative people are combinations of idea generators and salespeople. I may not be making ads per se, but I'm applying certain aspects of creativity into some of these other areas.

Tuten: Do you have any rituals that are important to your ability to work creatively?

Boches: The only ritual I would have—and I didn't even understand this until recently, but it's become more clear—I would call it seeking collisions. I just read, and it might have even been a Steve Jobs's quote, that when you ask creative people how they do what they do, many times they can't actually explain or give a reason how and why they came up with ideas. His argument was what creative people inherently do is they combine things in different ways that create small explosions or that yield something that is an unexpected result of two things.

Also, if you read Steven Johnson's *Where Good Ideas Come From*,[12] you get that same thing. Johnson would argue, and others have argued, that cities are more creative than suburbs. [And he explains] why New York is more

---

[12] Riverhead Books, 2010.

creative than Paris. It's because Paris pushes the congestion of the new city out to the ring and they try to preserve the history of the old city, and as a result they have fewer collisions and, therefore, there's nothing really wonderful and creative that's emerging out of Paris compared to, say, Shanghai and New York, etc.

You see the same thing in a way in companies like Pixar and IDEO and other creative companies that now work in these little congested environments. My ritual is trying to mash things up that don't belong together, that come from different places, whether it's literature and advertising, or physical space and theater, or sources of content from different disciplines, or even just the people that you try to interact with and engage. I think good ideas come from collisions. I'll give you just a simple example, which we're excited about. Am I talking too much or do you want to hear this?

Tuten: No, I want to hear it.

Boches: Okay, so I was at Google Zeitgeist,[13] privileged to be invited. It was in Phoenix. I sat next to Sandra Day O'Connor.[14] I talked to Robert Reich[15] and Arianna Huffington.[16] I saw the guys who did the High Line[17] in New York and Pencils of Promise,[18] the inventor of Angry Birds, and all this really, really amazing stuff.

Here's the collision that happened to me. So Robert Reich talks about how the problem in America is that there's an "us and them" going on, and I've used that expression before in some of my presentations—that our communities of concern are getting narrower. Congress doesn't care really about unemployment because unemployment among college grads is only five percent and they're closer to college grads than they are to high school dropouts, where unemployment is thirty-five percent. To groups with whom we have empathy and interdependency, we care about, and those with whom we don't have empathy and interdependency, it's easier for us to dismiss.

---

[13] Google's Zeitgeist is an annual, two-day, invitation-only event that brings together about 400 of the world's most interesting people to discuss issues affecting the world. Presentations from past events are housed at www.zeitgeistminds.com.

[14] Formerly a US Supreme Court Justice.

[15] The chancellor's professor of public policy at the University of California, Berkeley.

[16] President and editor-in-chief of the Huffington Post Media Group.

[17] A public park in Manhattan, built on a historic, freight rail line.

[18] A non-profit whose mission is to build schools in developing countries.

Europe can basically now say, well, Greece isn't really a part of them, so do they really have to worry about Greece? This thought about community really struck me as being an interesting problem that we have.

The second thing is someone asked a question of Sandra Day O'Connor that was completely irrelevant to any of this. It was a conversation about juries and jury selection, and this thought of juries sort of popped into my head and I thought, "Oh, that's really interesting." Juries are people who are from different backgrounds, different socioeconomic backgrounds, and juries work really well. People take responsibility, they're incredibly diligent, they come to good decisions. Then I started to also think about what little I know about the military service, which is similar. Then I started to think about what I know about social media because all these things that we're talking about vis-à-vis Robert Reich are ironic in an age when social media enables us to all connect to each other. But what do we do on social media? We connect to like-minded people.

One of the things that college students do before they go off to college is to search on Facebook to find someone to be their roommate. They search for someone who will stay in their comfort zone as opposed to seeking some-body who's completely and totally different from another background.

Now all of a sudden, these three, four things crashed into my brain and I came up with an idea. The basic idea is "can mandatory social media service save America?" My thought is instead of having mandatory military service and mandatory community service, what if we had mandatory social media service? What if the basic idea was you get recruited and you get put into a circle, a Google circle if you will, with eleven other people from different regions, different ethnic backgrounds, different socioeconomic backgrounds, etc., and you get handed a problem? The problem could be obesity, or pov-erty, or unemployment, or the fact that young men get all their sex educa-tion from watching online porn. You get handed the problem and you have to solve the problem as a group, not unlike a jury. You have benchmark goal setting and procedure. There's a proctor who pays attention to this thing and the result comes out and gets posted on a common web site, where legis-latures and the press and academia and business can get ideas and begin to implement them.

Maybe we will solve problems and maybe we won't, but the idea is that we'd have a pretty good likelihood of increasing empathy, interdependency, and an understanding of other people's perspectives by having mandatory social media service. The service would not be that demanding since basically every eighteen-year-old in America is on social media already. And yes, there are three or four things we have to figure out, such as the multilingual thing, access to technology for everybody, and how to actually implement this thing. But it's the best idea that I've had all year. Do you think it's any good?

Tuten: I think it's really interesting. I'm wondering how you would assess the effectiveness of it.

Boches: Well, there are probably short-term and long-term ways of assessing the effectiveness of it. That's a very, very good question. I don't have all the answers to that, but I could ramble off a couple from the top of my head. First of all, it could be the reaction of the participants and whether or not they, in a post-participation survey, had a different perspective of people whose opinions are different from theirs. You could measure the effectiveness by the number of ideas that got posted on this web site that resulted in new policies or proposed legislation across all of these issues. You could also look at the quality of the content that came out of it. You could subsequently look at whether or not any of those were ever implemented or were effective. And you could also look at whether or not there was an increased overall empathy among people who just seem to go at each other among their differences. I think you could set up ways to look at it short term and long term, short term from as early as six months, long term—five or ten years out.

Tuten: And even maybe a longitudinal study of the success of the people who participate?

Boches: Exactly. Now, the real point is that while there may or may not be merit in this idea, it certainly makes for an interesting conversation. But it's an example of collision. Using collisions to generate ideas. So thank you for enduring that little spiel.

I'm thinking this idea will have to be seeded initially via schools or states, because I don't think Congress is going to pass the thing and make it mandatory. There's two points to that crazy little story. Point number one is collisions of ideas and thinking. If you seek them out or just make them part of your daily routine, you end up having interesting ideas. The second aspect is what kind of responsibility do brands have to fixing and addressing some of the social problems that are out there? At least in my own personal case, as I live in a new space, being influenced by so many new things and technologies, I become increasingly interested in things that are different, in things that are potentially more, meaningful than, say, advertising. There's still a relationship to advertising, because I think that in a world where we're connected to each other and we have things like social media to connect us, brands have a responsibility to addressing social problems. I also think it would be good for them businesswise.

Tuten: In terms of what it means to consumers or in terms of the growth it allows for the brand?

Boches: Both. I think that we will see brands that practice real social responsibility will actually do better profit-wise. They will do better, a) because they endeared themselves to certain constituencies and customers, and b) because they contribute to improving the world around them a little bit, which may actually generate better economic situations that yield more business. And then I think that they may actually learn what it is they should be doing. It might be less altruistic and less selfish and greedy. It has worked for certain brands. It's worked for Apple and Google and Nike. You do see it in some cases.

Tuten: It just needs to become more prevalent.

Boches: Yes. Pepsi made a really great effort with Pepsi Refresh.[19] I think at the end of the day, they're not sure it actually contributed to business as much as traditional advertising. People who want to preserve the status quo will make that argument vociferously. I think that in the longer term, especially if you look at a younger generation, for whom this stuff may matter more, I think it's already a good place to invest.

Tuten: What's next for you? What hopes and dreams and aspirations? Is it going to be in the area of creating collisions and social responsibility, or something more?

Boches: There are three things actually that I'm interested in. I would love to do a start-up or work more with start-ups. I don't know if any of the ideas about mandatory social media service will materialize or turn into anything, but if they do, maybe that will be my start-up. If I get a presidential candidate to believe in mandatory social media service and he or she gets elected and wants me to come and help run that program, maybe I'll do that. I'm still interested in changing this industry or helping it stay caught up and relevant. And then I also have become really excited about teaching, which has been a result of doing an executive-in-residence and running some workshops and lecturing in a bunch of classes. So I'll learn more about the potential for teaching from my experience next semester at Boston University. Teaching is something I am really drawn to.

---

[19]A project that directed millions of dollars to community grants.

CHAPTER 8

Doug Fidoten

President
Dentsu America

Doug Fidoten is president of Dentsu America, Inc. (www.dentsuamerica.com), a full-service agency that is part of the Dentsu Network. He is a graduate of Oberlin College, an experience he was able to customize to address his interests in business and photography. Fidoten's regard for photography has served him well as he moved from the creative side of the advertising industry to roles in account management and eventually to the leadership team at Dentsu America. Doug Fidoten led the Canon team at Dentsu America and remains active in that account despite the demands of his role. In 2006, he was named the first American president for Dentsu. Still an avid photographer, Fidoten lives in Manhattan with his wife and three children.

Tracy Tuten: What in your background brought you to this industry in the first place

Doug Fidoten: I didn't grow up in an advertising family. I really didn't know anything about it. It wasn't something that I was familiar with either from a relative or from somewhere in the family. My mother was actually an artist and an art teacher, and my father was really more in the analytical world. By the time I was conscious of what my father did, he had moved into the computer space and was working on computer automation for manufacturing processes and things that were really kind of at the cutting edge of what was happening in the earlier ages of computers. My father was focused on computers as they related to office automation and manufacturing automation.

You can see our household was filled with a lot of duality. On the one hand, I was exposed to a lot of art. We went to a lot of museums. We heard a lot of music. We did a lot of activities that were of high interest to my parents and, of course, they wanted their kids to be exposed to these experiences whether we, the kids, wanted it or not. When you're young, you don't really appreciate these things. Later on you realize, "Gee, I'm really glad I did this when I did." So that was one side of what it was like growing up. The other side of my development was based on influences from my father. He was involved in information systems, and he'd get invited to conferences, and he would take the family. He'd be at the conference for a couple of days and then we'd travel on vacation. My favorite thing as a kid was to visit the show floors at the conferences and see all the vendors displaying their innovations and wares. Not a lot has changed. That's still going on.

As a young kid, I loved walking around and collecting all the trinkets they were giving out, you know, the notepads and all the other little things. As we would walk through, my father would show me things and make sure I was exposed to the new developments in the world of technology. One of the best examples was Xerox's featuring the earliest example of a graphical user interface. And the mouse was at one of these shows for the first time. They were developed by Xerox, through their PARC [Palo Alto] research facility. I remember my father remarking about how amazing it was and what a breakthrough it was [compared to] what he was experienced with. Years later, obviously, that became the roots for the Mac and what inspired Steve Jobs and everything that came after, even though Xerox never figured out what to do with it.

My young way of bringing these two spheres together originally fell into the world of photography. I literally had my first camera in second grade and moved up the levels of sophistication as I got older. I think by the time I was in eighth or ninth grade, I had an SLR [single lens reflex camera], and I learned darkroom work. My father had given me access to work in the photo labs on the weekends at the company where he worked. Because of my mother, and remember she was both a teacher and an artist, was doing coursework at Carnegie Mellon, I would get access to work with etchings and lithography stones. So I had this passion that just grew over time. This passion really was both the science side of photography, which was chemistry and, if you want to understand it, the physics of light, and then the artistic side of it.

Tuten: Did you study advertising in college?

Fidoten: I went to Oberlin College. At that time, I was still continuing to figure out how to bring these halves—science and art—together. Oberlin's a great school, very intellectual, very willing to let students kind of chart their own path, and rather than adopt a traditional major, I actually had the ability to do my own major. I designed and named my own major, which, if I still remember correctly, was "Physiology, Perception, and the Visual Arts." My thinking behind it was a combination of how the physiology of our nervous system and our brain affects the way we perceive the world and the way we perceive art. The psychology behind it, which is not necessarily part of the wiring, and then ultimately, how that expresses itself in the development of art over time. Like the single-point perspective in the Renaissance, and things like that. That major gave me the opportunity to continue to use photography as my artistic expression.

Eventually that led me to an opportunity away from school in which I apprenticed as a photographer. I literally apprenticed in New York City with a professional photographer, a very famous guy by the name of George Tice.[1] He was not a commercial photographer in the sense that he was shooting for advertising. He made his money selling his work through galleries, selling books, and he'd won either a Guggenheim or a MacArthur. I really forget which, but something that allowed him to spend most of his time taking photographs and not so much making money. I went to work for him for that period and really learned the craft of photography and developed a passion for it in a way I'd never had a chance to do before. I'd never had that level of skill or mentorship.

Tuten: So this is how you ended up in New York?

Fidoten: This is another inflection point that would lead to a number of things. First, when I finished my apprenticeship, I went back to school, finished my major, and continued to do the photography I was doing and the coursework I had to do to graduate. After a very brief moment at home trying to decide what was next, I decided to go back to New York City. I had a pocket full of names from people I'd met during my apprenticeship, and I felt like that's where I belonged. I had been to New York when I was much younger because my family had lived on Long Island, but I've often said it was as if I had just been away on an extended trip.

There's no time for this romantic story, but I'll tell it anyway. I had been in school at Oberlin, and I hadn't been in New York in many, many, many years.

---

[1] George Tice is most famous for his large, black-and-white photographs of New Jersey. His work is included in many major museum collections throughout the world and is depicted in several books including *Hometowns: An American Pilgrimage* (New York Graphic Society, 1988).

I hitchhiked with a friend to New York. We ended up on Staten Island with our last ride, walked to the ferry, took a ferry ride to downtown Manhattan as the sun was setting and glinting off the World Trade Center, and for the first time, you know, as if I were an immigrant, I felt at home. It was that experience that really led to my coming back. After I graduated from school, I came to New York with a portfolio of pictures and a pocketful of names, wonderfully naïve, and just started knocking on doors until somebody would have me. I ended up assisting, [working] as a photographer's assistant. Terrible pay, worse than advertising, but tremendously exciting, and that's really where I met advertising people. I was in a commercial studio. We were doing ads for American Express and others, and for the first time I was learning about the field of advertising.

I met account people—I really didn't know what they did except they seemed to take the clients to lunch [laughter]—and art directors. That was my first inkling that there was a world outside of what I knew. In an odd way, advertising began for me as an effort to fund my career, which I thought was going to be photography. Sure enough, I first ended up in a little agency. Then I got the bug. I could see there was this connection between art and science—or art and thinking, art and strategy—that took hold of me. I started my next push and said to myself, "Okay, now I want to be on Madison Avenue."

That led first to AC&R and then BatesAlliance, an agency that I ran for Bates and, ultimately, Dentsu. As I said, [there were] all of these career inflection points: when I first met Kaz Kudo—my mentor, when I first found myself working on some Japanese accounts, and then years and years and years later, not only working this time for an agency that is headquartered in Japan and started in Asia, but working on projects for the greatest photographic company on the planet, Canon. How all those things happen, I couldn't tell you. Maybe that's part of fate or that's part of . . .

Tuten: Your destiny?

Fidoten: Some trail out there that we walk on and we don't even realize we're on it, but I couldn't be more grateful that all of that somehow fell together as it did.

Tuten: Tell me more about how you transitioned from those early days into really knowing where you fit in the industry.

Fidoten: This question reminds me about a campaign that I had done an awfully long time ago. It was my first actually. It wasn't my first job in advertising. It was my second job in advertising. But it was the first time where the work was really under my control and my direction, and I was still quite young. We were pitching business, and it was also my first pitch. Eventually I did two pitches with the same client, but the first one was the most significant.

Tuten: Yes.

Fidoten: The pitch was for Hertz car sales. This pitch was really kind of my bridge—a bridge that got me out of a little retail agency [and allowed me] to cross over to Madison Avenue. It was also the pitch that brought me to a person who served as my mentor—Kaz Kudo.

[He was my boss] at what I would call my first legitimate Madison Avenue agency. He's an interesting story in and of himself because he is Japanese, but he was not working in a Japanese agency. At the time, nobody had even thought about a Japanese agency. This was very much a traditional, Madison Avenue, US-based agency, but through a series of gratuitous circumstances, this man ended up working there. Eventually, while I was still working for him, he wrote a book. The book was about his life as the first Japanese national working on Madison Avenue. That book has never been translated. It was only published in Japanese, but it was a somewhat successful book in Japan. In particular, it became something that was picked up and read by a lot of young, aspiring account people at Dentsu, which, of course, is my current place.

So there are these points along the journey. Everyone has them. Points at which one can look back and see an indicator or a coincidence that relates to a place we land later. This is clearly one of them. At the time, and perhaps even later, one can never really understand how these came about or what they might mean. This story is just one of these points along my journey and these points lined up in a certain direction that I would never have understood in my young twenties.

Tuten: So you started at a small shop, but then you had the chance to move. Tell me more about that and Kaz Kudo.

Fidoten: Yes, I made the move from the little retail ad shop where I got my first job in advertising to AC&R Advertising at 437 Madison Avenue. I had really had a hard time moving because I had worked there for a year and a half or two years, and at the little shop I was kind of a jack-of-all-trades. In a real agency, nobody does everything. This was exacerbated in that at the small shop, nobody was really giving any credit to what I was doing. Plus, I couldn't point to any of the clients as being anything anybody would actually pay any attention to! I mean, they were little retail accounts from all over the country, but [nothing] anyone would actually have ever heard of. So getting that break and getting that first interview with the type of agency I wanted to work with took some doing.

I had had a couple of interviews at this place on Madison. They said, "Okay, we're going to bring you back and have you meet with a man named Kaz Kudo." When I arrived, he was in a client meeting. So I was waiting there for him to come back from the meeting, and he finally showed up. I was ushered into his office. I remember it still—the office was everything you could imagine. It was a big executive office. Kudo had a kind of very imposing character about him. And, of course, this was at the time reflected now in *Mad Men*. Everybody was still smoking all the time. He lit up a cigarette, looked at my résumé, and started to smoke the cigarette. He didn't say a word. He didn't say a word to me for what felt like forever. I'm sure it was probably only maybe two or three minutes, but I think two to three minutes of silence in an interview has got to be a frightening kind of experience to anyone. He didn't speak and I didn't say a word. *I didn't say a word.* I waited for him to speak first. It was that action that actually got me the job! I mean, there were other things as well, but the fact that I had the patience to sit there, which immediately represented a cultural understanding to him—one that I didn't even know. I had never dealt with anybody who was Japanese before. I don't even think I had ever even been to a Japanese restaurant. And the fact that I had that patience, just sitting there and waiting, when I think most would have tried to fill up the time with some nervous chatter.

I remember the next day when I got the call. I was offered the job, and the guy, who was sort of the intermediary, said, "You did very, very well with Mr. Kudo." And I thought, "What did I do?" It's only after I came to know him very well, not only as a mentor but also as a friend, that I understood. There are things like this experience that have played major roles in my career, again many points further down the road. Sometimes I'll be in a situation with a group of Japanese executives and some other Americans, and afterwards I'll have understood the context of the meeting, even though half of it's in Japanese and half of it's in English. I'll be sharing the context with the other Americans, "This is what happened. This is what's going on, this is what somebody said." They'll say, "You must speak Japanese." But I have to explain, "No. I don't speak Japanese, but what I do understand is from a cultural point of view and from a business point of view. I understand the dynamic of what's important in the room."

Tuten: How did you learn to understand these kinds of cultural nuances?

Fidoten: Culture is more important than the language itself. The Japanese language can be exceedingly difficult and complex. But in terms of those connections between how we do business, how the Japanese look at it, and how to connect the dots, all of it literally goes back to that moment when Kaz was smoking the cigarette in his office.

Tuten: Are you still in touch with Kaz Kudo?

Fidoten: Yes. He's not a young man, and he makes his home in Japan now. We still correspond periodically via e-mail. He still remains a significant figure in my life.

Tuten: Does he know how important he is to you?

Fidoten: I think he certainly does. He has contacts at Dentsu, and I think he periodically touches base with some of them and gets word of what I'm up to. Hopefully, I make him proud.

Tuten: I'm sure you do.

Fidoten: He was a tough boss and I know he did his best to teach me well. I think as can only happen in the Japanese mentoring system. I can't remember the Japanese word for it, but there is kind of this Japanese sensibility of the mentor and the mentee.

Tuten: Sensei.

Fidoten: Well, *sensei* certainly, but there's another expression for it as well, and I think I've always had that relationship to certain other people who have been my mentors, and it's always been the same. No matter where we are in life, what our titles are, what our ages are, the nature of that relationship never changes. I think obviously, people have that relationship with their parents, but I think they also realize that with mentors and people who are significant in their life, that never changes. But I always think in my mind, "Is what I'm doing making them proud in terms of the influence they had on me?"

Tuten: Well, if you'd like, we can send him a copy of the book.

Fidoten: That would be nice. That would be really nice.

Tuten: Tell me about your favorite campaign. Do you have one that is especially meaningful to you?

Fidoten: Our agency had an opportunity to pitch for the Maxell business. Most people will know a very famous campaign for Maxell audiotape. It was a campaign done by Scali, McCabe, Sloves, and the concept was of this guy kind of sitting in his chair and getting blown away by the power and clarity of the music. That wasn't what we were pitching for. At that point, Maxell was introducing a whole new category of products—computer products. This was during the very early stages of the PC, when the central form of memory was floppy disks. None of your readers are going to remember this [laughter].

Maxell was introducing its series of floppy disks and it was going to be a new competitor in the market for computer storage devices. Now, in the excitement of the category at the time, where PCs were changing all the time and the category was in its first big boom, nothing could be less interesting or less utilitarian than computer memory. It was my first opportunity to not only win the business, but to actually understand the power of a brand. It was my first opportunity to bring a brand into a category where it was so hard to distinguish one brand from the next. Literally, the only thing that would distinguish one brand from another in this product category was the name placed on the box.

How do you get people to understand the power of something that was actually one of the first digital recording mediums? We won the business and we had a few campaigns. I don't know that any of them were very distinguished. But then, we really hit on this idea that we would separate the product by claiming it. By identifying it on the packaging, by creating this notion of the gold standard, creating literally a seal, making it part of the box, making it part of the campaign. We introduced the brand as the gold standard, in a product category where there was no standard. There was no way of distinguishing one from the next. This concept meant that when a prospect looked at the packaging, immediately it was clear that there's something about this brand that's different than the others.

Once we established that standard, we built a campaign, which to this day I still love. I don't know if I could ever find any examples of it. We came up with this notion of what's the ultimate computer, and if a computer could speak, if a computer could be discerning, why would it choose one product over another? Why would it choose Maxell over another brand? And the computer that we decided was the ultimate computer—and, again, you've got to realize how long ago this was—was a robot. We actually created a series of robots and created a campaign that was, for all intents and purposes, wordless. Imagine the contrast. Where every other brand was spouting specs and talking about this versus the other thing in what was then a very technical world, we had an ad that represented something entirely different.

See if you can imagine this. It was a beautiful ad. It was a gold robot staring right at you, sitting in this really elegant club, and sitting next to him was a partner, and they were having the ultimate business lunch. As they're sitting at the table, there's a waiter, also a robot, but done sort of in a black tux kind of coloration, unveiling the main course on one of those silver platters with the big silver domes. Sitting on it is the Maxell floppy disk. There was not a single word in it except "Maxell," a tagline, and the gold seal. It was a huge hit. These things were running in magazines when magazines were still a source of information, like *Fortune* and *Forbes*.

The ads tested through the roof, and in a category that had no real interest, against some of the other things we were selling. That was my first real visceral understanding of the power of creating a brand and the power of creating a difference using communication and powerful creative to cut through and make a statement. Also, the power of a visual, in that case to say much more than one hundred words could have said, much less what one thousand words could have said. And here it was still really just my second real advertising experience. For many years, that agency, AC&R, was my home. Unfortunately, it doesn't exist anymore.

I can really remember that moment as a real turning point in terms of understanding the business I was in—what we were doing, how we can make a difference. When you first get into the business, it is an apprenticeship. No matter what you've learned in school, you've got to learn the ropes. You've got to learn the craft. You've got to learn how agencies function and what the rhythms are and what the energy is and how people deal with each other. You can only learn this in the real world. You'll never learn that in a classroom. Obviously, I never had the ability to learn these things before my first jobs. I never did an internship in the business, and so I didn't even know the basics until I got into it. Even at my first job, that little shop with only four or five people, I never really understood. Because there, everyone did everything.

Tuten: Tell me about that transition—from your first experience in the industry to feeling like you understood how agencies work.

Fidoten: I never really understood what the real roles were. You can be in any agency of any size, and actually sooner or later you'll realize that you meet all the same people. They're different—their names are different and they look a little different, but in fact they play similar roles within the structure of the agency.

What I understood when I got my first break was how to get a job done. I was brought in to my first job to play multiple roles. I was young account guy, media buyer, and courier, you know, all rolled up into one. I might call some of these roles "traffic," even "production," these days but I was all of those things. It was not a fun job. I'm glad I didn't do it too long, but it did give me something that I could package and offer as experience to come in to another agency. I was invited to join another agency because they really were looking for somebody who could do that on a unique piece of business and kind of use my ability to get the job done. I used my ability as the promise of, "Okay, but I want to get into a more mainstream role and I don't want to be doing this forever."

Often times I think to myself, you know, that happens all the time now. I mean, still to this day I have people come work for me that start in an internship type of position or assistant coordinator, whatever. And I'll say, "Look, give me a year. Give me a year of your life doing what I need, and then you go on to do what you want to do." I've always hired like that. As a matter of fact, anytime I've tried to hire what I'd call a professional assistant, where that's kind of their role in life—that really they just want to be, you know, that executive assistant—it's never really worked for me. I've always wanted to work with people who come in ambitious about the business, and see it as a starting point. The starting point might be as an assistant! Maybe it's just because of the way I grew up in the business and it just feels the most comfortable to me.

Tuten: What does your current assistant want to be?

Fidoten: I think Melissa wants to go into strategic planning. So I think I've got maybe another six to seven months, and that's about it. Before Melissa, I had another guy. He almost gave me a year, and then he got lured away as an account person at a great agency in Los Angeles. So my desk, or near my desk, has always been a pathway to something. The industry is filled with people I've watched move on to great jobs and great careers and do great stuff. I'm fine with that. I always feel good about it. I hate losing people, but I know this is an industry where, if you don't move, you don't learn what you need to learn. If you don't look for the next step on the ladder, you're not going to grow.

Tuten: As a photographer, it seemed that you would have come up through the creative side. But yet you've ended up on the strategic side. How did that happen?

Fidoten: Good question. I think first of all, to be honest, until I got into advertising, I didn't understand the creative side. I didn't even understand how the creative side works. Now you would think, okay, I was working with a commercial photographer, how could I not get that? But I wasn't intro-duced to any of the things that many of us would take for granted now in terms of what the concepts are behind advertising, how the creative side thinks about kind of the underlying strategy, and then how to express that in art and copy. I really came at it from such a different direction that all I really knew was we were trying to illustrate something that an art director had scribbled, usually on a napkin. I only saw it as a visual sort of puzzle to be solved and even then I only saw it as the end result of the photograph.

I never really saw the full context of it, and I didn't really know the roles of copywriters and art directors and creative directors and all the people that were involved on that side of the business.

I remember one of the first shots I did years ago. Every American Express ad had, in the corner, a shot of the card and some little object that was significant to the ad. The name on that card—I don't know if this is still true—but the name that was on the card in the ad was always C. F. Frost, who I later learned was actually an account person who worked on the account and must have sold his name to American Express for a dollar to use in the ad. We were shooting an ad that was meant to get cards to students who were just graduating. The goal was to get these new graduates their first American Express card. I shot the inset shot, which was the card and a pen. Later, I was given the completed ad. I must still have the ad somewhere, but this was literally the first time I understood that there was a main visual, there was body copy, there was a headline, there was a concept, and there was a point being made. Seriously.

By the time I got into advertising and started understanding what was involved, my inclination seemed to move more to the account side because I seemed to have a facility to work with clients, to understand what they were doing and what they wanted. I didn't really understand the training that was necessary on the creative side, and I hadn't gone through any of that training.

Once I got into a larger agency and roles were more clearly defined, I was already going down this account-work road. What attracted me to account work was really strategic thinking. There's obviously a lot of work that's not strategic, that is just the kind of running the business and getting it done. But being on the account side, it didn't keep me from being involved or perhaps overly involved on the creative side. Over the years—and probably different creative people will weigh in on the positive and not so positive side of this—I've always felt comfortable working very closely with creative people, understanding what their challenges are, being able to talk to them in a way that maybe account people in the past weren't. Account people were always known as, are still known as, "the suits." You know, nobody wears a suit anymore, or rarely. [But] understanding early on in my career the challenges creative people have with the work that they do and also understanding what it means to sell the work has been a benefit.

Because if you didn't really appreciate the work and understand what it took to create the work, you could be very dismissive of it. The minute the client looked at it and said, "Well, I don't think that's what we want," you're really not going to be in a position to be very effective in arguing for it.

What I discovered along the way was in order to truly be effective with clients and as an account person and as somebody who is a representative for the agency and the agency's point of view, it's incumbent on you to really understand the client's business as well or better than the client does.

Tuten: It's important to know the client business, but how can we do that from our position within the agency?

Fidoten: [You do your best.] I learned that lesson, many times, and I learned it very early on. I've often said for years to the account people working for me that I expect them to be as conversant in the technology and the issues that the clients are facing and understand the product as well or better than their clients do. Because if they don't, there's no way they can be credible. There's no way they can speak with authority and defend or recommend anything. Clients see right through it.

On the other hand, when you've been on the front lines, when you've been out there with them, at the counter, selling the products, being involved with the engineers or being involved with the salespeople, you carry so much more credibility. You can do it at any age. I think one of the reasons that at a relatively young age I was in a position to lead accounts and have significant positions in my agency had more to do with my knowledge of the category and the business that the clients were in than it had anything to do with even how good I was, let's say, at advertising.

When I was at AC&R, I did a lot of technology work. I understood the category. I understood what was going on. My creative people worked with me because they knew I could help them and the clients worked with me. I'll never forget, I spent close to a decade running the Foot Locker business, on the agency side, not the client side, and had great clients there, many of whom had kind of grown up in the Foot Locker system. That was a company where if you wanted to come up through the ranks, you started in the store selling shoes. Otherwise, you never had credibility in the company, in those years.

I was out with a guy, terrific friend of mine [at Foot Locker], Brent Hollowell. Now, he's vice president of marketing with Woolrich. Brent and I were having a big challenge in Texas. There was competition down there, and it was really kicking our butts, and no one understood what to do. Brent and I got on the plane, flew down to Texas, and started visiting stores, talking to the managers, store by store, "What's the issue? What's going on here?" We walked into one store, and Brent looked at me and said, "Doug, let's put on the stripes." We went to the back of the store, took off our sport coats and our ties, put on the stripes, and went out on the floor, and for the rest of the day, we were busy selling. Now for him, this was second nature because this was where he had come from. To me, this was a first.

We came up with a great campaign for Texas, with a lot of good ideas, and we went to sell it at headquarters. We walked in to present to these guys who had all started in the stores, selling on the floor. We started talking about why we wanted to do this and where this was coming from and what we had done to understand the situation. The minute I said, "Yep, I was on the floor. I was selling shoes," everybody was listening. For the rest of the time I spent working on that company, it completely changed how we did business together.

At one point, a lot of their marketing money, a lot of their advertising money was supplied by the shoe companies. They had the ability to sort of roll it all up into one big fund and use it as they wished. The biggest, most power-ful shoe company at the time was Nike, and Nike changed its mind and said, "No, we don't want our money being commingled with other vendors'. It can only represent Nike products, and therefore we'll be happy to do the advertising for you and we'll be sure to feature the store and feature our shoes." Given that this sum represented a huge percentage of sales, what I saw was the end of my agency's role as a leader in the communications strat-egy. I thought about it from a strategic point of view, and I remember having a meeting with Foot Locker and saying, "Ladies and gentlemen, you're giving the store away if you go along with this. Right now you are a branded house. People come to Foot Locker because it's Foot Locker, and then within it, they find the things they want."

"It's your expertise. It's your sense of collection. It's your sense of curation that makes this place what it is. If you just turn over the reins of control to all the different vendors, then you're just going to be a house of brands. You'll be like a department store, but a very small version of it, and all of your communications will be essentially run by outside companies." I remember putting together a presentation on this and looking at the store displays at the lease line. I could see the store displays as a valuable property to be sold carefully, not as a property that simply kind of displayed everybody's stuff and gave it equal weight. Malls were really huge at that point and where the majority of sales were.

I said, "Let's treat the lease line, that last eighteen inches between the mall and interior of the store, as the most valuable thing in the world. Let's make them pay for the privilege of being there, being featured and support us with more money, to help us drive sales, which is going to benefit them and benefit us. And therefore we remain a branded house." We went out to Nike—and I won't mention all the names, but most of the founding elite were in that meeting. We presented this idea and got huge pushback on it.

Tuten: I'll bet.

Fidoten: And I can tell you where most of those guys are today, but I won't [laughter].

Tuten: [Laughter.]

Fidoten: We got huge pushback on it. Let me tell you, that was a long flight back to New York. We weren't deterred. We said, "Fine, let's go to Reebok." We flew up to Boston the following week. At that time, Reebok had originally launched a shoe called the Pump, and it had not been successful for a number of reasons. They were about to relaunch it, and we got up there and said, "Let's make this a Foot Locker launch, a Foot Locker exclusive launch. Let's do this kind of program." Reebok bought into it. We did a terrific campaign that launched the product at the Foot Locker stores.

There used to be a huge show—I don't know if it still exists—called Super Show, where all of the sports and athletic guys would gather in Atlanta, and at that time, the head of Reebok was showing the launch to Wall Street as an example of the way they were going to do business moving forward. By the time we got over to the Nike booth and went into a conference room, the Nike people were ready to talk a very, very different story. We called this form of advertising "vendor supported marketing," and I think that practice, that process, still exists to this day. I don't know if it's an inflection point in the industry, but certainly, it's an example of where strategic thinking and adversity and the ability to realize what's important both for your client and in a sense for your agency leads to really a breakthrough in thinking. The creative had to be great because, obviously, the best stuff being done in the world at that point was advertising for athletic products.

Every generation has its own product categories where there's an opportunity to do great work, and Foot Locker was an opportunity to do great work, but it was also an opportunity to understand what the dynamics of the business were. We have a fundamental need to understand what are the drivers of the business. That, to me, is the world of strategy and the world of an account person. It's really what the agency has to understand.

More than ever, you read stories today about how agencies should be in the business of helping their clients not just build their brands, but build their brands *and build businesses*. Now that may mean new business models. It may mean new ways of increasing revenue. It may mean understanding dynamics that have nothing to do with what is considering traditional advertising, whether it's store design, whether it's the layout of a hotel room, whether, you know, it's the important aspects of travel that have nothing to do with typically getting you from point A to point B. I mean, all of these things are important, but fundamentally you must be in touch with the business.

When you're not in touch with the business, you find yourself a disposable commodity. This is a tough business and we often say, "We're only as good as our last campaign."

Tuten: Is there any way for the industry to change this view of the work?

Fidoten: It can be true, but I think it's not true *if* you're really fundamentally partners and advisors to where the client business can go, what's possible, and how you can help. I mean, we're not supply chain experts here. We're not sourcing experts. We don't have a lot to do with basic R&D, but advertising has to do with a lot more than just the outer shell of communication.

If that's all you do—advertising—then, honestly, you are only as good as your last spot. You shouldn't just be judged with questions like, "Was that a great spot? Was that a great campaign?" More and more now, I think agencies are being judged and rewarded not just on paid fees and retainers and things, but also on performance.

As long as the measures are fair—because we don't control a lot of things—but as long as the measures are fair, it makes sense given the role that we play.

Tuten: Are you as involved in the client work now as you want to be?

Fidoten: No. As president, a lot of things that come to my desk aren't directly involved with campaigns. I mean, it has to do with personnel issues and making sure we have the best people, keeping the people we do have happy, and all of the things that go on in the overall running the business. But what I try to do—I can't say whether this is good or bad—but I try to stay involved in areas where I can be involved and areas where I can really add value. I just finished a nearly yearlong project, and I was in a lot of meetings, very actively involved and very hands-on. I did it because I love it. I did it because it's an area where I felt I could bring value and understanding because it was a complex assignment. I did it because I knew how important it was to the client in terms of their success. And I also did it because this is why I'm here. I mean, you know, without that kind of involvement, I think it's very easy to lose touch with what we do.

On the other hand, I'm also reluctant because I know what this is like to be at the other end. I have a lot of good people here and I want to give them room. I want them to have freedom to run businesses, control the work, and not feel like somebody's micromanaging them. That's one of the wonderful things about this business—that at a pretty young age you can be given a lot of autonomy.

That's a good thing. I think it's up to us to be guides, to be mentors, to make sure we're helping and guiding and directing, but give people room. Give people room to grow, and give people room to take ownership, because that's the only way they're going to be passionate, and they're not going to be passive because if somebody's telling you what to do, you're going to be passive. You're going to do it because you were told to do it. But if somebody's giving you the room and saying, "This is where you've got to get to. Now you've got to figure out a lot. I'm going to help you, but you've got to figure out how to get there." I think you take ownership—or the right people take ownership.

Tuten: Right.

Fidoten: Those are the kinds of people you want to have around you, but you also want to have people who know when to ask, when to get you involved, and, even when you don't have to get involved. That's the ideal. It doesn't happen all the time, but on the flip side, I think if I got too far away from the day-to-day or from things that were important to my clients, I think I'd lose touch and I'd lose value. I don't think you can just become an administrator.

Look, there are people in very senior executive positions who have lots to do that doesn't have to do with any particular client, but I think that even those people pick up the phone, call senior clients, talk about the business, talk about what's going on, know what's going on because that's what clients care about and that's what they're paying for. And, the rest of it—frankly, the rest of it is overhead, and no one's happy about that. No one's happy about paying for overhead. They want to be paying for people who are paying attention to their business and helping make a difference.

This is true, what I'm about to tell you. Well, it may not be true in all businesses, but it is true in advertising. I've talked to a number of people and I think I have enough evidence that this is true. No matter how many steps you take from the first time you're sitting at a desk to years and years later, you don't actually shed any job. You just collectively wrap them up. So, as an account person you begin as an assistant account executive. You're schlepping the bags around. You're making sure the decks are ready. You're doing copies for meetings. You're making sure that the PowerPoint is working or Keynote is working, that the computers are going to work. You make sure you're not going to get there and find out three cables are missing. Fast-forward twenty years, and you're an executive vice president and all the rest of it, and frankly, you're worrying about the same stuff, all of that plus everything else that comes with it.

Tuten: You have an ability to tell stories as though you had just experienced them. Did that come from your experiences in advertising?

Fidoten: It's important. Frankly the entire notion of a campaign came out of storytelling. I know everyone thinks about brands and branding, but ultimately, behind all of it, it's storytelling.

Tuten: What if you were telling the story of your life? If you wrote an autobiography, what would it be called?

Fidoten: I always say that if I wrote an autobiography, it'd be called "A Life in Advertising: Just Worry About It." That clearly comes from my character. I do worry. That's who I am. I get anxious about things. I worry. I consider it to be actually one of my greatest weapons in this business. I'm always concerned. I'm always thinking, what did we not think about? What did we not look for? What did we leave out? In this business, you can never take anything for granted. To take things for granted could be the worst thing that could befall a person in advertising.

It's not an easy life to be a worrier. But I just read last week's issue of *Time* magazine and the cover story was about how anxiety is actually good for you. Obviously, too much anxiety isn't good for you, but a little bit of anxiety in this business is what drives us. I think we all talk about it as we get closer and closer to deadline, how we become more and more productive. And I just think there's a lot of that in this business and a lot of need to really be thinking about what's next, what's wrong, what didn't we think about, and not use it in a negative way, but use it as an energizing way as kind of keeping you focused and concerned about your clients' business. I've often told my clients—and this is from long before there were cell phones—that I'm available 24/7. I mean it.

There are a couple of wonderful stories about that. I'll tell one story, which kind of says something about balancing advertising and life. I was doing a commercial many years ago, and it involved a superstar baseball player. We had been struggling to connect with him and his agent to make sure that he would do the commercial. He was in a baseball all-star game that was taking place in San Diego, on the West Coast, and my client at the time was out there at the game and had told me, "I will track him down. I will find him after the game. And I will get confirmation that he's actually coming." I don't know what time the baseball game ended on the West Coast, but it was probably, New York time, three o'clock in the morning. The client goes running for the phone saying, "I'm going to call Doug. I'm going to let him know I talked to this guy and he said he's going to do it." And somebody says to him, "What? It's three o'clock in the morning." My client said, "No, no, no." He said, "You don't get it. Not only is Doug waiting for this call, but he'll be thrilled if I wake him up and tell him because he's been worrying about it all night." And you know, sure enough, he calls me at three in the morning—and it was the best call I got. He was exactly right.

Tuten: It's wonderful you are available 24/7 from a work perspective, but what does that do to your ability to maintain some balance between work and home life?

Fidoten: I'm very fortunate that I'm married to a woman, Beth, who has been in advertising almost as long as I have—maybe longer—not in account work, but largely on the media side. A media maven of her own, actually. She's been named, "Woman of the Year in Advertising" and been nominated for a number of honors. Even "Mother of the Year in Advertising." She's really compiled her own wonderful record in the world of advertising. First of all, I'm probably more proud of her career than my own, but I think her work and understanding of the industry have always made my work possible. We both understand what we do.

If we didn't understand, it would never work. We both did a lot of these crazy nights and long hours and weekends and for anyone who isn't in the industry, after a point, this life is just really not understandable. We are in a service industry. That's a part of it. The nature of advertising is just second nature to both of us. Obviously our love of the industry and shared passion has been a huge glue in our relationship. We have three kids too, which is kind of amazing when you consider our work schedules. When she was Mother of the Year, it was when our twins were, I think, probably all of three or four. Many people when they have children decide to move out of the city and commute in. But Beth insisted, absolutely insisted that we stay in the city. We live and work in Manhattan. Living here has made it possible for us to not only have a work life, [but] to be with our kids as they grow up. They are city kids and they have their own experiences, but they can see us and see our work and we can participate in their lives and still be part of this business. I don't think any of them will end up in advertising [laughter].

Believe me, I know many people who work crazy hard and their families are hours are way. I'm not saying it can't be done. People do it. People do it well. I'm not saying everyone should live in Manhattan, because it comes with its own issues, but it has made our life possible.

Tuten: Is your wife still in advertising?

Fidoten: She was until very recently. Now she's returning to school to become an art teacher. You always return to what you know and love, I guess. My mother was an artist and teacher. My wife and my father, too. After my father retired from his first career, he ended up teaching communications at Slippery Rock, a school in western Pennsylvania. It was only after teaching there in communications that he had an appreciation for what I actually did. Prior to that it was hard to explain. We often joke, what is it we do in advertising? Even after I'd been in advertising for years, he'd say—what is it that you do? Do you write the words? Do you take the pictures?

I'm not sure *Mad Men* has made it any clearer what it is that we do! [Laughter.] The only show that came close was *Thirtysomething*. My wife and I used to watch that and it was the most painful but funny thing because it was like reliving your day all over again. I don't know if the show would resonate now as it did then, but when we watched it, we'd say it was the closest thing to what our day was like. A far cry from *Bewitched*! Definitely a closer look at what the day-to-day experience is like [laughter].

Tuten: What's still ahead for you?

Fidoten: I have many challenges in the business I'm in. We have a lot of things we want to do with the agency. There are things we can do in advertising now that we never even dreamed of before. The tools we have have changed. The markets are changing. The market is fragmented. There are more challenges and we have to figure out how to take all of these tools, things, and marry them to what we know is true. We have to continue to be effective and continue to create work that we can proud of. This business continues to be exciting.

I have a lot more I want to do in mentoring others and sharing successes. There are so many people involved in everything we accomplish. These people are like a cast of characters. We have stars, we have people with charisma, people who are on the front lines, people who have to carry the heavy load. In our case, it may be two to three weeks that we give these people to bring a campaign together. There is a great deal of pride when we are able to come together and create something wonderful. We can feel enormous pride about a campaign that we worked well on and know when we accomplished what we set out to do. We share the success as a team. As a group. That's what it's about. Whether you are in a big organization with thousands of people or a small group of five that just started up as an agency, sharing what's produced together is what brings an agency to greatness or pulls an agency down to where it vanishes overnight.

I may want to find more time to teach, too. I love to teach. I've been teaching on and off as opportunities have arisen. I've lectured for Dentsu all around the world in Tokyo, Bangkok, Singapore. I love that. There is such an energy to thinking about what's important, sharing it with people, and getting them energized about it. It's just like a client presentation. You are sharing with a group what they should be excited about. I enjoy teaching just like I enjoy making a client presentation. So far there hasn't been much time for this, but I hope it happens more in the future.

I'll tell a final story. A very close friend of mine whom I've known since I first came to New York got me an amazing birthday gift. He's an inspiring teacher in his own right. He spent his own life teaching kindergarten because he believes that's where the foundation of education begins. He knows of my passion for photography and that other than taking pictures of my kids, my photography has taken a backseat to my career.

It was one of my cornerstone birthdays and there was a seminal exhibit of Richard Avedon's work at the museum. Avedon was an amazing photographer, known for his work in fashion, portraits—such a gifted photographer. Anyway, my friend went to the exhibit and then to the bookstore to get this book for me as a gift for my birthday. He got there just at the close of the museum, bought the book, and sat down on the great stairwell in the museum. As he was sitting there on the staircase, Richard Avedon comes down the stairs! My friend stood and explained that he had just bought this book for me and he'd so appreciate it if Avedon would include an inscription. He told Avedon of my great love and talent in photography, but that my life and career had taken a different direction.

When my friend brings me the book, I open it up and inside, Avedon had written, "Doug, it's never too late to begin. Richard Avedon." And, you know, you just have to say to yourself—that it's true of everything.

Here, I have a terrific career in advertising. I have great relationships. I have been a part of wonderful campaigns that have made a difference for clients and made a difference in their businesses. But you have to keep looking at your life like that: it's never too late to begin, whatever our talents are, whatever our motivation is. And, you know, to get something from somebody like that—someone who is at the pinnacle of his life and talent, it's nothing short of inspiring. Avedon died fairly shortly thereafter.

Tuten: Are there other famous people who've made a difference in how you view your life?

Fidoten: It's tough to top the impact of Richard Avedon's message other than to say that recently I met Martin Scorsese. I've met celebrities. I've met athletes—scores of athletes. Very accomplished people from all walks of life. But recently I've had a couple of opportunities to meet Marty Scorsese for a project we were involved in. He's on the cover now of *Wired*. There's actually a story in there definitely worth reading, a story about creativity and maintaining creative spirit.[2]

Scorsese is nearing seventy. What I found remarkable about talking to him was the passion and intellectual curiosity that he has still about everything— about his phenomenal knowledge of film, about the way he could bring up one thing after the other, about the way he made references to the cave paintings of Lascaux, the single-point perspective of the Renaissance, the panels of paintings that were done pre–Renaissance. I mean, he has this sense of the world in which he works, what's important about that world, and all of the aspects of the world. That's what keeps him current and creative. And I say the same thing about our business of advertising. You know, it's about knowing your craft, knowing the history in a way that's important to what we do today because it does matter, and then understanding that there's always going to be a new challenge. We can learn a lot from Martin Scorsese. Here's a man at nearly the age of seventy who tackled his first children's film, his first 3D feature [*Hugo*], and a lot of other new creative work with the same passion and intensity that he tackled his student work at NYU.

In some ways, meeting and getting to know Scorsese represents another one of those series of connected points in my journey. A lot of my personal attraction to New York and my love of the city first started with his films. From that story I told you about the Staten Island ferry to right now, meeting him connects more points on my path. I'm still here, living up on the Upper West Side, and he's still here somewhere in Manhattan. I don't know exactly where, but he doesn't live in Hollywood. He lives here.

Tuten: How does knowing someone like Scorsese shape your own plans for the future? What's ahead for you?

Fidoten: I want to be able to do the same thing, but in my own field. I want to be able to tackle the next campaign, the next thing I do with the same passion and freshness that I had when I first came in. I want to keep the same curiosity and interest I had when I was trying to figure out how to move my first mechanical around the agency and get it out the door.

---

[2] Philippe Stark, "Creativity, Money, and Sex," www.wired.com/epicenter/2011/12/starck-creativity-money-sex/, December 21, 2011.

And not just passion—also with the same bit of self-doubt. A little bit of "I'm not sure." A reminder to me that I will never have it all figured out. Not that I ever do feel that way! And I know others don't. Sometimes you do wish that you could have it all figured out. But it's better to be on the problem-solving side. We should be always learning and always doing more with something than we thought we could before. We need more seminal experiences.

David Oakley

Creative Director

BooneOakley

David Oakley is president, and creative director at BooneOakley (booneoakley.com), the agency he co-founded with partner John Boone. The agency, based in Charlotte, NC, has done well since its inception in 2000. In a relatively short period of time, the agency has brought home a Webby, a Cannes Gold Lion, and multiple Clio and Addy awards. Under David's leadership, BooneOakley has been named an Advertising Age "Southeast Small Agency of the Year," and David and John were named a "Hot Creative Team" by Creativity magazine. The agency web site was honored in the Google Creative Canvas for 2010.

David started his advertising career as a copywriter at Young & Rubicam in New York, where he crafted campaigns for major brands including Certs, Dr. Pepper, and AT&T. From there, he went to TBWA/Chiat/Day to help develop the Absolut Vodka campaign—voted one of Ad Age's "Top Twenty Ad Campaigns of the Twentieth Century." After seven years in the Big Apple, David followed his Carolina roots to super-regional agency, Price McNabb, where he worked on several award-winning campaigns. In 1997, David and John Boone opened a satellite office of The Martin Agency in Charlotte. There, David served as associate creative director for Wrangler, Alltel, Kellogg's, Saan, and the Charlotte Hornets.

David Oakley: I'm telling you, blunders happen to us. That happens a lot to BooneOakley. It seems anytime we go in for a presentation, either something about the AV equipment doesn't work or—I don't know. It's just been our history. It happens, so I just kind of laugh because it happened to somebody else.[1]

Tracy Tuten: BooneOakley has the Bojangles account. How is everything at Bojangles?

Oakley: It's really interesting. Bojangles is doing a lot of interesting consumer research right now. We are in the process of learning more about the customer base, which is always a good thing. A lot of the work that we're going to be doing in the coming months is going to be based on the findings.

Tuten: Who's doing the research?

Oakley: It's a company called Bain and Company. I think the research firm is based out of Massachusetts. Bojangles actually was purchased last summer by a holding company called Advent and the holding company, fortunately, is willing to do some spending for good consumer data, which is a good thing. It's something that we really wanted to do before, but Bojangles never had the budgets to do it.

Tuten: Interesting. I had Bojangles this morning for breakfast.

Oakley: Really? You did not.

Tuten: I did. Seriously!

Oakley: What did you have?

Tuten: I had a chicken biscuit.

Oakley: A Cajun fillet biscuit? Very good, very good. I'm very impressed.

Tuten: I thought about you while I was going through the drive-through. I said, "David would be so pleased to know that we have this interview today and I'm here frequenting his client."

Oakley: It's Bo time! [The tag line for Bojangles' campaign.] You were probably going through the drive-through while I was sitting at corporate headquarters. Actually, it's not known as a corporate headquarters. It's known as the support center, right? That's what it's called. It's not called corporate headquarters. It's called support center because they're there to support all of the individual franchises and owners.

---

[1] David Oakley here is referring to the fact that I did an initial interview and on the "save," my computer crashed and I lost it all. I had to ask him to do the whole thing again. He graciously agreed.

Tuten: What led you to advertising as a profession? Did you grow up wanting to work in this field?

Oakley: Both of my parents were potters, which was great. It was a really creative background to have. I actually didn't realize until I got in college that I'd had a very unusual upbringing, being the son of two craftspeople. It was really a great childhood. We traveled to craft shows up and down the Eastern seaboard when I was a kid. We would go to Florida or we'd go to Virginia Beach and we'd show our wares. But it was also a lot of work and growing up that way taught me that while I wanted to do something creative in my career, I did not want to be a craftsperson. I really didn't want to be a potter. I saw my dad and my mom, and they always had mud all over them. They had clay all over them, you know, just from making pots. It's a really hard business being a potter, and they worked really hard. I wanted to find a way to be creative and not be dirty all the time. That sounds like a really weird thing because I'm not exactly the cleanest person around, you know? I take a shower once every couple of months [laughter].

Tuten: Are your parents still living?

Oakley: My mom is still living. My dad passed away seven years ago, but the business that they started out in Creedmoor, North Carolina, which is north of Raleigh, is still going strong. My sister runs the business now. My sister is a glass blower. She has a great, glass-blowing business there, and there are still four potters who make pottery at the Cedar Creek facilities. It's awesome. The business my parents started is forty-four years old now, and just this year it was recognized by the Department of Transportation, or the Highway System, or whoever does the tourism signage. Now, there are signs on the highway that say "Attraction: Cedar Creek Gallery and Pottery." So it's kind of like a state treasure now.

Tuten: That's fantastic.

Oakley: Yeah, it's really cool, I'm really proud to be a part of it. And that was a great place to be from.

Tuten: Does BooneOakley do the advertising for the gallery?

Oakley: We have done ads for them, yes, in the past. But, you know, they're just a little too small for us. You know, they don't have the budgets that we want [laughter]. No, I'm just kidding. We do everything—we do a lot of stuff for them for free actually. It's my sister. We talk about ads and marketing all the time.

Tuten: Is your mom surprised how you turned out? At how you ended up using your creativity?

Oakley: Yes, she actually thought I'd be successful instead [laughter]. Instead, this happened. This ad thing happened. No, she's really psyched. She's really proud of me. Like any mom. I'm kind of embarrassed by that question, but the answer is yes, she's very proud, of course.

Tuten: It just occurred to me when you were talking about growing up, for her to be a potter and to see how you channeled creativity in a different way. It must be a source of pride for her.

Oakley: At the beginning though, things were different. I have to be honest. When I was finishing school at Chapel Hill, I really thought that I would go back to Cedar Creek and run the Cedar Creek Gallery. I thought that would be my work. And even though I wanted a different creative route, I thought that I would probably become a potter, too. Even though that's not really what I wanted to do. The hardest thing I ever did was really decide to leave that opportunity, that sure thing, and go out on my own and figure out a different way for myself. I just needed to *do* something. My parents were very supportive of me moving to New York and going and getting my first job in advertising. They thought that was really cool. But, still, it was a big decision.

Tuten: Did you go to college to study advertising? How did you discover advertising as your creative field?

Oakley: No, I didn't plan to study advertising. I really went to college pretty much to meet girls [laughter]. I went to North Carolina because I heard that it was like sixty-three percent women. No, I went to North Carolina and I really went there because they had a good basketball team. That's really why I went there. And because I was able to get in. I loved my time at Carolina. I took a lot of business courses. I was a business major.

See, it's like this. When sons and daughters of bankers go to school and they rebel, they go into the arts. When the son of an artist goes to school, they rebel by going into business. I was kind of like that at college. I really wasn't a great student. I was an *okay* student. I was really more into the whole college experience than I was into learning. When I was about to graduate, I was over at a girlfriend's house on a Sunday afternoon, and I was doing my economics homework, and she was doodling or drawing these little drawings of—they looked like stick figures. She couldn't draw for anything. But I asked, "What are you doing?"

She says, "I'm drawing the Pillsbury Doughboy."

I'm like, "Why?"

She said, "I'm writing headlines for Advertising 170."

I'm like, "Wait a minute. You get college credit for doing that? That's so easy. Anyone could do that."

She said, "It's not so easy." Blah, blah, blah.

I said, "Well, wait a minute." It never occurred to me that people could make a living, you know, doing print ads or writing commercials. It never, ever occurred to me that people actually did that for a living. So she told me about a professor, and his name was John Sweeney. She said, "He's awesome. He worked at an agency for seven years and he's been a professor here for four, and you really should go talk with him if you're really interested in this."

I was the kind of student [for whom] it was really unusual to go to class, let alone to go talk to a professor. That was beyond my capabilities. I mean, seriously, it was like a big deal to go see a professor at random and say, "I want to take your class."

I went to his class. I went to see him the next morning. I introduced myself. He said, "Well, great. What year are you, freshman, sophomore?"

I'm like, "No, I'm a senior."

He goes, "Oh, so you're graduating in two months?"

I said, "Yeah."

He said, "Well, I suggest you probably go and get a job, you know? That's probably what you should do."

I'm like, "Well, yeah, I want to do that, but I want to get a job in advertising. That's what I want to do. It just hit me yesterday. This is it."

John Sweeney said, "Well, there are a lot of people graduating every year, and it's a really hard field to get into, and you probably should just get a job in whatever—what's your major, David?"

And I said, "Industrial relations."

And he says, "I think you should get a job in whatever kind of job, whatever kind of career you go into with an industrial relations business major."

And I'm like, "Okay, well, I'm not sure, but I know that I want a job in advertising."

Anyway, basically, he said that his class was full and I was really bummed. I graduated and then that summer I saw that he had another class. He was teaching a summer school class, so I went back to him. And I said, "Hi, Professor Sweeney. Do you remember me?"

And he says, "Yeah." He kind of remembered me.

I said, "I'm David Oakley."

He said, "You graduated, didn't you? Didn't you graduate?"

I said, "Yeah, I did, but I'm still here in Chapel Hill."

And he asks, "Why?"

I said, "Continuing education. I just hadn't left Chapel Hill. So I really want to take your class."

He said, "No, you can't take my class. It's full, and there's a fifteen-person waiting list to get in it."

And I don't know what made me say this to Sweeney, but I said, "I know you're like the most popular professor in the advertising track. I know you've won Professor of the Year for the last three years, but I also know college students, and I guarantee you that every single one of your classes, at least one other person will skip, and when that person skips your class, I'm going to be in that seat." And he just looked at me like I was crazy. I said, "I will be in that seat." And I walked away.

So I went to his class the first day, and it was literally packed with people. Then somebody got up and left, and I sat down in the seat. I went every single day. Every day there were open seats, so I just kept going even though I wasn't enrolled in his class. Eventually it came time for the mid-term exam and I came ready to take the exam as though I was actually enrolled in the class. Professor Sweeney must have been thinking, "This guy's a psycho." [Laughter].

Up until that point, four weeks into the class, he had barely acknowledged me. But that day he came up to me, looked at me and he just threw a copy of the test on my desk, and he said, "Okay, you're in." That was that. He officially added me into the class. I ended up staying at Chapel Hill another year and a half and working as a waiter and oyster shucker. During that time, I took three more classes with Sweeney. He helped me put my portfolio together, and to make a really long story short, I took my beginning advertising portfolio, and I moved to New York.

Sweeney introduced me to some people in New York, and I kind of networked my way around and ended up getting my first job at Young & Rubicam. Twenty-five years later, Sweeney is still a really good friend of mine, and he's been my mentor since the beginning. He is a great professor. But you know what? He really wanted me to prove to him that I wanted a career in advertising. Once I showed him that I really wanted it and I was committed, he was like, "Okay, we'll go. You'll get it." So that's how I started.

Tuten: You are exactly the kind of success story from students that keeps professors going, keeps us teaching every day. There are plenty of those other ones who—well, like you were before you met him.

Oakley: Just going through the motions, going through the bars, hanging out, coming into class hung over. Something clicked when I realized that I really wanted to do advertising. It was a crazy decision, and, it's been a crazy career, and it's still young. I still feel really young, and I can't believe that was like twenty-five years ago. It feels like it's gone by in twenty-five minutes, and I guess that's because I was having a good time.

Tuten: What was your first job at Young & Rubicam?

Oakley: My first job was as a copy cub. Basically, it was a junior copywriter position. They called copy trainees copy cubs. I was hired with four other junior writers from around the country. They hired a guy from Winthrop University whose portfolio basically consisted of poetry that he had written. They hired a guy from University of Illinois. They hired a woman from University of Missouri. We all started together. It was like this melting pot of different people. We all became friends because we started together and we went through this six-week copy-training program. Through this training program we were introduced into what a big ad agency was all about. After training, we were split up. We were all put into different groups.

Of course, we were the low person on the totem pole in our respective creative departments. When I was there at Young & Rubicam—this is around 1987—there were fourteen hundred people in the office. It was crazy. It was almost like going to a small college inside this giant ad agency. It was just ridiculous how many people were there.

Tuten: What kinds of campaigns did you work on there?

Oakley: Let's see. I did a really fun print campaign for Certs breath mints. It was the first time they'd ever done a sugar-free version of Certs, and it was interesting because it was such a big agency, and everybody wanted to do TV. So people really didn't care about the campaign. The more seasoned creative types didn't really care about doing print advertising at the time. Y&R was known then as a TV shop, so I couldn't believe that one of my first assignments was to do a full-color magazine advertisement for Certs. I ended up getting lucky. I was assigned to work with an older art director.

I was like twenty-four and my art director was sixty-two. This art director actually drew his comps with a paintbrush, and watercolor, and paintbrushes. He didn't use markers. He didn't use a computer. He drew all of his comps with a paintbrush, which was like crazy. I couldn't believe it, and

I really kick myself because I don't have any of his comps. I wish I had saved them. At the time, he would do them and throw them away. But, anyway, we did a campaign for Certs that ended up winning all these awards. It won at the One Show and it won Clios. The funny thing was that this Certs campaign was the only thing that won awards out of the entire New York office. I was still pretty new at Y&R and it was just kind of ironic that this little print campaign that no one wanted to do ended up winning the only awards of the year.

Tony Carillo was the art director. While we worked, he would sit there and tell me stories about his daughter. He would talk about his tennis-playing daughter, who was this great tennis player. He'd say, "Yeah, she's from Flushing, she's from Queens. You know, she was junior partners with this kid. You probably know him, John McEnroe." So he's telling me about going and hanging out with McEnroe and I'm like, "What's your daughter's name?" And he says, "Oh, Mary, Mary Carillo." So the tennis announcer that you see now, Mary Carillo, is his daughter.

So Mary Carillo was John McEnroe's mixed doubles partner, and they won the US Open together. It was like, holy shit! Y&R was a very, very amazing place to work actually. It was like a school. It exposed you to so much.

Tuten: What's the most important thing that you learned while you were working there?

Oakley: The most important thing that happened to me is that I met my wife, Claire while I was at Y&R. She was an accounts person. I fell in love with her, we got married, and we celebrated twenty-one years last week.

Tuten: Congratulations.

Oakley: Well, thank you very much. Thank you. What was the most important thing I learned? I kind of knew this from my parents, but it was reiterated at Y&R. The lesson is to always to believe in yourself and keep your eye on the prize. Y&R was my first step into advertising. It was really cool and I learned a lot, but there were also times that I didn't like what I was producing. The Certs campaign was really one of the few things that I produced there that I really liked.

Y&R was a bureaucracy, and I really learned to keep my eye on the prize because I wanted to do the type of work that some of the other agencies in town were doing at the time, like Chiat/Day or Scali, McCabe, Sloves. They were doing unbelievable work. I was also keeping my eye on a couple of the agencies in North Carolina, one was McKinney, and LKM—Loeffler Ketchum Mountjoy—in Charlotte at the time, and also The Martin Agency, which was doing great work. I just really watched other agencies, and I knew that I wanted to work at a smaller agency. But Y&R was the best place you could ever start a career. I'll put it to you this way. It got me in, got my foot in the door. It was my first job, and a lot of great things came from it. I can sit here for hours and tell you Y&R stories, but if you really want to know all of the good ones, you have to buy the book.

Tuten: Your book?

Oakley: Exactly. Whenever it's ready in 2028.

Tuten: I'll be your first sale. Tell me about this bureaucracy issue at Y&R.

Oakley: When you're a junior writer, there are just so many levels to work through to get your ideas approved. You have to be very guarded with an idea. When you come up with a good idea, it's almost like it's your baby, and you have to shepherd it through. You don't want these different cooks to come in and put different things into it. Sometimes you'll have a creative director or a supervisor that can add things and make it better. There are some who are gifted at that. But there are also a lot of people who aren't so gifted at that, and sometimes what they add to an idea, well, it's like they just want to put their fingerprint on your idea to put their fingerprint on it.

So when you're a junior writer, you have to go through the senior writer, and then you go through the associate creative director, and then you go through the group creative director, and then you finally get it to the executive creative director before it goes out to the client. An idea has to go through like five levels before it actually gets to see the light of day. It's very, very hard to get it through all these levels. It's much easier to do great work by having an idea, working through a creative director, and then going to the client. The bureaucracy of it all was frustrating. It was frustrating to have such a long, difficult road to work with ideas.

Tuten: So you said that Chiat and The Martin Agency were doing the kind of great work you wanted to do while you were at Y&R. What kinds of things were they doing? What was different at those agencies than Y&R?

Oakley: Chiat/Day had done a campaign for NYNEX, which was the telephone system in town at the time, and it was a print campaign, and it was all over the subways. I'm completely blanking on exactly what the executions were right now, but I was in love with this campaign! I was like, "This is the best thing that I've ever seen." And then there was a great campaign for Smith and Wollensky Steakhouse that I thought was written brilliantly. The work appealed to me in a different way. Y&R was more akin to formulated packaged goods stuff. Y&R did ads for Efferdent and Rolaids. I worked on the Rolaids account. I met Tommy Lasorda, the Dodgers' manager, and I did radio spots with him, and I met Rollie Massimino, the Villanova head coach, and did radio spots with him. The work was fantastic and fun, but the creative was just kind of formulaic. It just wasn't really anything breakthrough. It wasn't what I wanted to do.

Tuten: Was this the "Rolaids: How do you spell relief?" campaign?

Oakley: Yes [laughter]. Yes, I worked on that campaign.

Tuten: I still use that campaign as an example in class. To point out the value in repetition.

Oakley: When I was there, they started giving out the Rolaids Reliever of the Year award for the best relief pitcher in baseball. I did a print campaign for that. It was good. When I look back on it, Y&R was pretty awesome, and I met friends, not only Claire, but friends that I've had for life. People who are still in my life today. Y&R was kind of like this mini-graduate school that I was in, and I was there for three and a half years.

Tuten: And then what happened?

Oakley: There were a lot of changes going on during that time at Y&R. A new group of creative directors came in. I saw people get laid off at Y&R, old people who had been there forever. People who had been there during the "mad men" days, you know, and I'm there in the late eighties and people who had been there for like thirty years get laid off. A new guy would come in and just lay everyone off. They didn't lay me off because I wasn't making enough money to save them any money, I guess. But what was your question? Why did I leave?

Well, I had been working to make my portfolio better and I got an opportunity to go to TBWA. This was right before they merged with Chiat/Day. TBWA was right across the street from Y&R. I literally just walked across Madison Avenue and started a new job. I got to work with some incredible people there. I worked on the Absolut Vodka campaign. It was about two years or three years after the campaign had just started. I got to come in. I was lucky. I was still really junior. I had only been in the business for three years. It was just incredible. I was at TBWA/Chiat/Day for four years.

Tuten: Is the Absolut Vodka campaign the only one that you worked on there?

Oakley: No. Absolut was an interesting thing because it was a print campaign that really became iconic, if you really think about it. Imagine if you said to a creative team, "Hey, here's what I want you to do. I want you to put the product *really big* in the middle of the page. I want the product to take up the whole page. I want the name of the product to be in like 2-inch type at the bottom, and I want there to be one other word on the page. That's your assignment." The creative team would vomit! Seriously, we would vomit. That would have been like the worst assignment you could ever have. I mean, it's terrible. But that's exactly what that campaign is based on.

Geoff Hayes was the originator of the campaign. He actually saw the genius in the package design of Absolut Vodka. The taste of Absolut vodka is no better than any other vodka. It's the same stuff, basically. I mean, if you put out five glasses, I could never tell you which one was Absolut—even then, even when I was working on it! What Absolut had was an amazing package. I think Absolut was the first to actually spray the type and label on the bottle instead of using a paper label. Spraying the label made the brand seem so much more classy, chic, cool. It really made the brand seem more high-end. I thought that was pretty amazing.

What Geoff Hayes was able to recognize is that they should really make the package the king. The bottle should be king. He had this idea to feature the bottle and make the package the hero. Geoff looked at it and said, "This bottle is perfect. This is perfect." And then he just wrote, "Absolut Perfection" and put a little halo over the bottle, and that's how the campaign was born. It was just one execution, and the legs on this campaign were unbelievable. It went on for fifteen or twenty years. I think they've changed it now, but it did go on for a long time.

Tuten: So what's your favorite one?

Oakley: My favorite one is an evolution that happened right as I was getting to TBWA. A team named David Warren and Tom McManus worked on a campaign. They had the insight to branch the campaign out and do a city campaign. Michael Roux was the head of Absolut and he wanted to do something that recognized certain cities. Roux said something like, "I'd love to do something that we could run in *Chicago* magazine or *New York* magazine that would be specific to that town." David and Tom took Michael's request and came back with this idea that a city icon could be reflected as the bottle. What if you took an overhead shot of a swimming pool and made a swimming pool look like a vodka bottle, an Absolut bottle? They named it "Absolut LA."

In that same meeting, they brought in an overhead shot of Central Park that they had altered to look like the bottle, and it said, "Absolut New York." And it was just like, "Holy shit. That is like unbelievable, but it doesn't have the bottle, so we're not going to be able to do that." I mean, they clawed and clawed, and I have to give them major credit for being persistent, but they were able to get that to Michael Roux. I think that he was skeptical at first, but he decided to go for it. Roux bought those two ads. They would run specifically only in New York and Los Angeles, and they got Steve Bronstein to shoot them. They had models made for the shoots.

There must have been rocket fuel added to that campaign because when those two ads hit the market, that's when people started tearing them out of magazines and collecting them. From that point on, it just opened up this whole thing. I was lucky to work with those guys because they kind of took me under their wing and invited me to really help them come up with more ideas for the campaign. They'd say, "Okay, Oakley. Help us think some more." That's how, as a young writer, I got to work on an iconic campaign. I did the Absolut Boston ad, which was the parquet floor of the Boston Garden. I'm such a big basketball fan. I really wanted to do Absolut Chapel Hill, but, you know, we decided to do it for Boston [laughter]. We did Absolut Louisville and Absolut Seattle and Absolut St. Louis. We did these city ads all over the place. There were some ads that never made it.

Tuten: Do you have a favorite ad that was never produced?

Oakley: There was one that didn't make it, which I think would have been one of the best of all time. It had a political leaning to it, and this was in 1992. It was the political season of 1992. It was a spread and the ad had the Absolut bottle way on the left side of the page and it said, "Absolut Liberal," and the other side of the spread had the bottle on the right side, and it said, "Absolut Conservative." It was left-right. It was one quick visual pun. Everybody at the agency loved it. We were like, "This is going to be the best one we've ever done, blah, blah, blah, blah." We presented it to Michael Roux, and he was just like, "No, no, no, no. I do not get involved in politics. No politics, no politics." And we were like, "But you're appealing to everyone now. You're saying it doesn't matter your political affiliations. This is the vodka for you." He wouldn't do it. Four years later, in 1996, they took that ad back out to those guys because Absolut under new leadership, and they tried to sell it, and the same thing happened. They could not sell that ad. So anyway, that one didn't happen.

Tuten: That's a great idea. I love it.

Oakley: Well, thanks. That was a good one. There are a lot of ads that never made it, never saw the light of day. Oh well.

Tuten: Is it heartbreaking?

Oakley: It is, especially when you're starting off in your career because you put so much heart and soul into coming up with an idea and the ideas can get killed for so many odd reasons. The stereotypical reason is like, the client's wife didn't like it. That sounds so lame, but it's happened. It's happened.

Tuten: So how do you deal with it?

Oakley: With one that doesn't make it? For every ad that's made it through the pipe, there are ten that don't make it through, you know? It's kind of like sperm, I guess. God, I don't know why I said that! [Laughter.]

Have you ever heard the saying, "The one that makes it through is a good one"? It makes me think of Luke Sullivan, and I think you said you were interviewing Luke Sullivan, right?

Tuten: Yes, I did.

Oakley: Okay. His book, *Hey Whipple, Squeeze This,*[2] was a huge, huge influence on me. There is a principle in that book that I will never forget and I tell people all the time. It is just a simple thing: "outlast the idiots." Meaning if someone kills your ad, go back to the drawing board and come back with a better one—and if they kill that one, go back again, suck it up, and come back with a better one because eventually there's going to be a deadline, and they're going to have to buy it. So if you give in and just say, "Oh, screw it. Here, take this. Is that what you want?" then you're going to have to produce that ad. It takes just as long to produce a bad ad as it does to produce a good ad. So you should really outlast the idiots, and eventually, the deadline will happen, and you'll have to produce something really good. Anyway, thank you, Luke.

Tuten: I bet he'll be happy to see that you learned such valuable lessons from his book.

Oakley: He's a great guy. He's been a huge influence on not only me, but a whole generation of writers, really. You know what, I wrote a blog post a few months ago, and it was entitled "Luke Sullivan's Mistake."[3] It was really funny because I put it out there knowing he would end up seeing it somehow. Someone would forward it to him.

In the original printing of *Hey Whipple, Squeeze This,* there's a picture of Absolut Magnetism, which was an ad I did. I had heard that ad was going to be in the book and that meant I would be mentioned in the book. I was so

---

[2] Wiley, 2003.
[3] David's blog, Stories of the Oak, is at www.davidoakley.com.

psyched. I was like, "Wow! Luke Sullivan's writing a book," you know, because he was winning every award you can imagine at this time in advertising. He was like a god, and here he's writing a book about it, about how he does it.

Someone said to me, "Hey, your ad is in there. Oakley's 'Magnetism' is in there." So I run out to the bookstore to buy the book. I get it. I'm flipping through the book to find the ad. I find it on page twenty or whatever page it's on, and there it is. I'm like, "Oh my God. It's here." I flip immediately back to the credits to see if my name is in it. It lists me as the art director. And I'm like, "Fuck! I'm a copywriter. This is the greatest copywriter ever, Luke Sullivan, and he thinks I'm an art director. He thinks I'm an art director!"

He got it backwards—my art director was listed as the copywriter. So I wrote this whole thing about he made this big mistake in his first book. But anyway, you have to read it. He was really nice about it. He wrote me like three e-mails, saying, "Oh my God. I cannot believe I never knew that, you know?" He says, "I'm changing it in the new edition. I will make sure it's right." I'm like, "No, it's really funny. I'd rather be known as the art director. The art directors did more on that campaign than any copywriter ever did."

Tuten: The new edition is supposed to be a complete new edition to incorporate social media and digital.

Oakley: Oh good. Well, he doesn't, he doesn't know anything about that [laughter].

Tuten: Should I let him know so he can stop work on the book?

Oakley: Yeah, definitely stop him.

Tuten: So it sounds like you had a great experience at TBWA/Chiat/Day.

Oakley: Oh, I did. Claire and I got married during this time. And after three years of being married, we had our first kid, Sydney. We had a little tiny apartment and after about six months, we decided that we were either going to move to New Jersey or we were going to move really out of Manhattan. I got an offer to come down to Charlotte, and I really had only been to Charlotte a couple of times. We moved here. We just up and moved. I didn't realize what a traumatic experience that was going to be—moving with a little baby to a place like Charlotte in the mid-1990s from New York City. Even though I'm from North Carolina, it was a huge culture shock to me. For Claire, who had spent her whole life in New York, it was like, "Holy moly, where have you brought me?" It was very different. Looking back on it, it was the best thing we could have ever done, but at first living here was an interesting experience. Anyway, I'm getting off track.

Tuten: Who did you work for when you first came to Charlotte?

Oakley: I worked for an agency called Price McNabb. It was founded by Charlie Price, who's from North Carolina, and at the time I think he had an office in Raleigh, Columbia, Asheville, and Charlotte. And I met John Boone there, and we started working together. I spent about two and a half years at Price McNabb. I loved that it was small and the layers of bureaucracy weren't there. It was just one creative director. We got a lot of great work done in the time that I was there, a lot of good stuff produced.

I got an opportunity after that to go to The Martin Agency. I got a call from Mike Hughes, who was the creative director at The Martin Agency. This was like getting a call from God. I mean, Martin was just, was *it*. Luke Sullivan worked at Martin for a long time. I mean, it was, "Wow. Mike Hughes has noticed my work and he's interested in it," you know? I got the job offer to move to Martin in Richmond, but I turned it down. Isn't that crazy? Claire was expecting our second baby. We were expecting Lucas. So I talked to Mike Hughes and said, "You know what? I really don't want to leave Charlotte, and I can't believe I'm saying this to you, Mike, but I'm not going to take the job offer. I cannot believe I'm saying this, but it's not—the timing is not right, you know? I can't believe I just turned down that job."

I went back to Price McNabb and I worked there for another six months. Lucas was born, and it was awesome. In the meantime, John Boone had been freelancing. He had left Price McNabb and was freelancing at The Martin Agency, and they offered him a job, and John, almost jokingly, said to Mike Hughes, "I know that you had offered David Oakley a job a few months back. He's in Charlotte and I'm in Charlotte. I know he didn't want to move to Richmond. Why don't you just open an office in Charlotte and you can hire both of us, and I know he would take the job." John came back to Charlotte and told me about it. And I'm like, "You did what? You said that to Mike? Wow! That's pretty cool." And then a week later, Mike Hughes called and says, "We'd love for you to work for us. God knows why you want to live in Charlotte, but, if you want to live in Charlotte, we'll do it. We'll get you guys a little place and we'll hire you." So that was that. We opened up an office for The Martin Agency here.

Tuten: So how did BooneOakley come about? Why isn't it The Martin Agency Charlotte?

Oakley: That's a good question. We worked with Martin for maybe three years. Three years seemed to be about my limit before I needed something new. We got to work on Wrangler jeans. We did a ton of fun stuff for Wrangler. I thought it was a great account. We pitched and won the

Charlotte Hornets. We pitched Performance Bike. John and I were kind of autonomous, but we also worked on some of Martin's bigger brands, like Kellogg's and Saab and Wrangler out of Richmond. We were really just a creative output and we spent a lot of time in Richmond. I personally started to get bored. I just kept thinking, "You know, this is kind of boring." I don't know if sitting and looking at John all day was boring. I don't know what it was. He was probably more bored than I was, but I really wanted to break off and start our own agency.

Honestly, Martin thought the Charlotte Hornets account was too small for them. And I was like, "You know what? It's not too small for me." Also, I didn't want to travel as much at the time. I was doing a lot of traveling for production, and I had two small kids and I wanted to be in Charlotte with my family. I talked to John and we came to an agreement: "Okay, we're going to start BooneOakley." But then we had to talk with Mike. We went to Richmond. I sat down with Mike Hughes and told him, "I really have always wanted to open my own shop. There is only one place I'd rather work than The Martin Agency and that one place would be working for myself. The Martin Agency was like my dream job. Everything's been great about it. I'm going to do it [open my own agency], but I'm really honestly scared out of mind because this is like jumping out of an airplane—or jumping off a trapeze without a safety net below."

And the Mike Hughes said the coolest thing. He said, "This is your safety net right here. You can always come back to work for me." That's what he said. I was like, "Wow. That is so amazing. Mike, are you serious?" And he says, "No." He just started laughing, but then he said, "Yeah, I am serious. If you guys get tired of it in a year or two years and you realize what a pain in the ass running your own agency is and how hard it is, you can call me and come back. He was serious when he said, "I will take you back," which I thought was one of the greatest things ever. If I can ever offer that to someone who works for me, I will. I would always want to be like Mike Hughes. He's the best boss ever.

Tuten: Do you ever think about going back?

Oakley: Every day. Every day I think about it. I do! Running your own business is really hard and it's a lot more than just doing fun, creative work. It's so much more than that. It's much harder than I ever realized. At the time, we were this kind of cocky creative team. *Creativity* magazine had named us "hot creative team of the year," and this was in 2000. We were full of ourselves a little bit. We were like, "We don't need those account people. We don't need those support people. We don't need big Martin. What do they do? We can do all of this on our own." And we struck out on our own, and it was like, "Holy shit. You know, they did a lot of stuff. They did so much stuff, and it's not really all about the creative." Running your own business is probably the hardest thing I've ever done, but yet it's probably the most rewarding.

Tuten: Have you ever called Mike to ask him if you could come back?

Oakley: Yeah, it was a couple weeks ago. I did talk with him. I said, "Remember when I came to talk to you and you said if we ever wanted our jobs back we could? Can I have it back?"

And he just says, "No. I was lying. No, you can't have it back."

I'm like, "Oh, man, come on. You said that I could come back."

He says, "I was kidding." But he was just totally joking. He's the type of guy that if I called him today and say I wanted a job, he would give me a job. It might be as a janitor. I don't know what the job would be, but he would help me.

Tuten: How did you launch BooneOakley? What did you do?

Oakley: The first thing that we did for BooneOakley was to put a billboard out on Highway 485. It was in the year 2000. It was about two weeks before the presidential election. That was the year that Al Gore was running against George Bush. We put a billboard up that had a picture of Governor Bush and it said, "Gore 2000." This was a big, fourteen by forty-eight [foot] billboard. When we had the outdoor company print it, they're looking at it like, "What is this? This is a mistake." I'm like, "Don't worry. Just print it and put it up."

So we put it up, and within an hour, we're getting calls from CNN, Fox News, wondering, "How in the world could you have made such a horrible mistake and how did you do this?" I respond, "Well, you've got to understand, um, um, um, it's our first day, our first week in business. You're not really going to write a story on this, are you? You're not really going to?"

This one guy from Fox kept saying, "This is the biggest political campaign blunder in history. Of course we're going to write a story on it." But then he says, "So tell me: who are you working for? Is it the Democrats or the Republicans?"

And I don't know how to respond. I just say, "Um, we've been instructed not to say." I just said it like that. He says, "Oh! You've been instructed not to say? They don't want you to tell us who you're working for? Oh, okay." He was all over me. And I'm like, "That's all I can say. I would really appreciate it if you would just let this drop."

"We're not letting this drop."

That afternoon, it was the lead story on CNN.com: "Ad agency bungles campaign billboard." It was kind of a worldwide story. This was on a Friday, but on Sunday, I'm online, Googling the story, and I'm seeing pictures of this billboard everywhere. I'm seeing it in, you know, in Chinese. They had written about this story in China. I'm like, "Oh my God."

I remember telling Claire, "No, I can read this. Look. It says, 'Those idiots don't know the difference between Bush and Gore. What a bunch of idiots, losers, whatever.'" Anyway, that's basically what it said. We had to pretend all weekend that we didn't know anything, except that we had just really screwed up. On Friday afternoon, we had said, "Well, we're going to get it changed as soon as possible. We'll get it taken down, but the outdoor company has left for the weekend. They don't work on Saturday and Sunday. You know how unions are." [Laughter.] I'm saying that—like there are no unions in North Carolina. But, anyway, we had said, "They don't work on the weekends. We'll change it Monday morning." Then on Monday morning, we sent out a little press release saying, "At eleven o'clock the Bush-Gore billboard will be fixed." That's basically what we said. And at eleven o'clock, there was an NBC News helicopter literally filming live while we put a sign across the billboard. The sign said, "Today's job opening: proofreader for 123Hire. com," which was a jobs listing site. Someone had needed a proofreader. Obviously, there was a proofreader who was needed because there was a giant mistake!

The news story was carried on CNN and everywhere. It ran all over the news outlets again. The story was, "Well, you thought it was a humungous blunder, but what it turned into was an amazing, amazing publicity stunt for 123Hire.com," and we got nationwide coverage again. On Wednesday of that same week, there was an article in *The Wall Street Journal* about it, and we were interviewed for *The Wall Street Journal,* which is a pretty darned good way to start a business. That was a good thing.

The president of Continental Tire North America, which is based in Charlotte, drove by the billboard that weekend and came into the office on Monday morning and told his marketing team, "Find out who did this billboard. I want them to pitch our business." Continental just happened to be in the middle of an agency review, and they asked us to come into the review. To make a long story short, we ended up winning that business two weeks later. That billboard really catapulted us and got us going.

Tuten: That's a great idea. How did you come up with that?

Oakley: John and I were talking one afternoon about all the political signs that were in the neighborhood. It was primary season, probably in August of that year. You know, there were like tons of Pat McCrory signs in our neighborhood, and John was saying he couldn't believe how many were in his neighborhood. One of us happened to say how weird it would be if there were a mistake or, you know, what if one was printed wrong? Then I remembered this story about Yonkers Raceway. I don't know if you've ever heard of this, but there's a horseracing track up in New York, probably in the Bronx, I guess. Yonkers is in the Bronx. When they opened it, if I have my stories straight, it was in the 1940s. They were almost bankrupt by the time they finished it, but they put giant letters up and they spelled it "Yonkers Raceway," but they spelled it "wya." They misspelled it, and the next day, it was on the cover of *The New York Herald.* I think the *Herald* was the paper of the time, but the *New York Post* and *The Daily News* had it on the cover. The Raceway had free publicity from this giant screw-up, but then all of a sudden, everyone knew that Yonkers Raceway was opening that weekend. They were idiots because they spelled it wrong, but they had gotten the publicity that they had wanted. They had a sellout that weekend. Everyone came out to the race to laugh at the sign, and it got them started off successfully.

We thought, "Man, wouldn't it be wild if a political billboard was done the wrong way like that?" We had a friend from 123Hire, and we were talking to him about using our new agency. We honestly had this idea for 123Hire before we even had them as a client. But we called Brian Parsley, who was the owner of 123Hire. We were like, "Look, we've got a great idea. We want to come present it to you." We brought it to him, and said, "There's no way anyone's ever going to do this. It's so risky. You're talking about the president, the future president of the United States," and we're thinking copyright infringement, and this and that. Somehow though, Brian just says, "That is awesome. I love that." He went on, "It won't cost that much to print this. I already have billboards in Charlotte. I'll just take one of my old ones down and put that one up." So that's how it happened.

Tuten: That's perfect.

Oakley: It worked out really well. I will tell you. It was scary that weekend. I was not prepared for the media onslaught, but I was able to kind of get through it somehow.

Tuten: Are you usually the voice of BooneOakley? Are you the primary spokesperson?

Oakley: Yeah, pretty much. I just have that personality. When I was in the eighth grade, I won an award at the end of the year. The Kaopectate Award, for basically having diarrhea of the mouth. I'll never forget my eighth-grade teacher giving me that award in front of the whole school. It was great, yeah.

Tuten: Teachers live for moments like that.

Oakley: [Laughter.]

Tuten: BooneOakley's web site is very unusual. Can you tell us about that?

Oakley: It's basically a series of YouTube videos. I wish I could take all the credit for it, but all the credit really goes to a junior team that was working here, Jim Robbins and Ryan Holland. We had given them the task of redoing our web site. Our web site prior to this one launching about a year and a half ago was basically built-in flash. It was really cool. It had astronauts on it. We were dressed as astronauts. It had gotten a lot of attention and won industry kudos for being a cool web site. We wanted something new, but also to do something else that was very attention-getting. Well, Jim and Ryan had come to us with an idea to include a talkbot on the site. Basically, the idea was that a visitor could type something into our site and the site would give an answer. Anything you typed in, we would have an answer for it. It seemed like a really cool idea. We were working on it for a while, and then another agency did something similar, so John and I killed the idea. We said, "We can't do that. It's too similar."

Jim and Ryan did just what Luke Sullivan talked about: they outlasted the idiots. We killed the idea and they came back to us a week or two later and said, "You know what? We noticed this thing on YouTube where you can do annotations in the videos, and you can click on the videos to go to another video." They were showing it to us, and we were like, "Wow. I didn't know that. That's crazy. I had no idea you could do that." It was a brand-new technology.

We started talking about the agency, asking things like: What is BooneOakley's story? What are we all about? We were about really doing daring work and doing things that are outside the, very unusual, creative stuff, so let's tell our story and maybe tell our story in a series of videos. We talked with Jim and Ryan about what we wanted to say in the videos, and then they went back and illustrated the ideas with stick figures. It almost took me back to my friend, Laura Bowen, and the first time I considered advertising as a possible career. They were just really crude drawings.

They put them together on file cards and came in and showed the first video one afternoon, and I almost fell off my seat. I was like, "Holy God, this is good! This is so funny." We spent like the next two months coming up with other videos and other things to link them all together. Really, the whole web site was just a vehicle to show our work and to show what we did, what we had done, and to make it very interactive and easy to get through.

Tuten: You got tons of publicity for doing the web site that way, but are there any cons?

Oakley: We got a lot of publicity. We've gotten a lot of new business inquiries through it. One of the cons, though, is using YouTube. A lot of corporations block certain sites, like porn, I guess, and YouTube! That means many people cannot access YouTube at the office. We didn't realize this, so in some respects, we shut ourselves off from consideration by companies. At companies in which YouTube is restricted, when someone types in booneoakley.com, the site comes up as "restricted." We have had a lot of new business leads, but the biggest con is that not everybody can look at YouTube at the office.

Tuten: What do you think you'll do next with it?

Oakley: You know what we're going to do now and we're in the process of doing it? We're going to keep the YouTube site. We're going to keep it because I think it's great, and we're able to update it and add things. It is a little bit of a problem that people can't view it from some companies, so we've done a very simple site. We direct people to that site if they have problems navigating the one on YouTube.

Tuten: I read recently on your blog about a pitch that you lost.

Oakley: Which one?

Tuten: I don't know which one it was.

Oakley: I'm joking. But I'm also laughing because I feel like we've lost like our last three pitches.

Tuten: Oh.

Oakley: It's very fresh in our mind—losing. The hardest thing is losing. I hate, hate, hate losing, absolutely hate it.

Tuten: It's surprising then that you blogged about losing.

Oakley: Well, I just felt like it was almost cathartic. I wanted to send the message out to our people that maybe sometimes when you lose, that's what was meant to happen, and you have to accept it and move on. Maybe we weren't right for that client, even though we really wanted it. And, you know what? We weren't right. We weren't right for the client if we lost the pitch. In that blog post, I told a story about a pitch I was on when I was with The Martin Agency. We went down and pitched Alamo Rental Car. While we were waiting to give our presentation, I found the pitch that the agency that had previously pitched in the morning had left by mistake in the rehearsal room. I'm looking through the pitch thinking, "Oh my God. This stuff is terrible. This is awful. Oh my God. There's no way we're going to lose to this." I brought the other pitch with us, and we did our presentation.

Our presentation basically was [laughter] received by crickets [dead silence]. When we presented, it was like crickets. We were in Ft. Lauderdale, Florida, and we all loaded into the van that would take us back to the airport. I was like, "I can't believe the stuff that Foote, Cone, and Belding presented. It's terrible. It's got like Bobby McFerrin singing and changing his song to 'Don't Worry. Drive Happy.' I can't believe anyone would actually present that. If we lose to these guys, I'll be vomiting all the way home."

John Adams, Martin's CEO, and really, really a brilliant guy, was with us on the pitch. He said, "If we lose to these guys, I'll be okay with it."

I'm like, "What? Are you like crazy?"

He goes, "No. If we lose to these guys, we weren't right for them. They don't want the type of work we do, and it wouldn't have been a good fit. So it's better for us to lose now and move on to something else." He goes on to say, "If we were pitching against Chiat or Wieden+Kennedy or Goodby, I would really, really be upset if we lost to them, but I won't be upset if we lose to FCB because it wasn't meant to be. They don't do the same type of work that we do, and if they win, they will have beaten us at a different ballgame than what we're playing. Obviously, the client wants something different." Well, we found out a week later that they went with FCB, and that actual campaign I had found in the rehearsal room got produced.

I really didn't believe John Adams. I'm like, "You're full of it. Don't you want to win?"

He said, "I don't want to win if it's not the right fit for our agency. You have to take a step back and realize that you're not meant to win everything. Sometimes it's better to lose than to get into a bad relationship."

Anyway, that's what I needed to share with our people here. When we lose, it's meant to be. We just weren't the agency who produced the kind of work that that prospective client wanted. Sometimes it's better to lose.

Tuten: How did the employees take it?

Oakley: They told me I was full of shit. No, I don't mean that. I think they really appreciated it. I wrote it more for them than anything. I wrote it for the people who actually worked on the pitch. I wrote it for the agency. And I wrote it for me, too. Because even though I know what John Adams taught me is true, it's still really hard to lose.

Tuten: How do you handle it as an agency when you lose? Do you have a meeting about it? Do you talk through what you did right and what you did wrong?

Oakley: We always bring everyone together. We're very transparent about things. We're a small agency, and I'm not a great poker player. People can read me. They know when I'm really psyched, and they can tell when I'm really bummed. When I get that phone call after the pitch and the first thing I hear on the phone is, "Unfortunately, we've decided to go with another agency," you know, I'm not going to be able to walk around the rest of the day joking and everything. I'm going to go to the guys and say, "Here's the deal. We didn't win. We gave it our best. I'm really proud of everyone. We went all the way down the field." It's almost like being a coach. You've got to keep your team excited and up, and you can't let them get too low. I think that's one of the things about running a business that you end up becoming. You become a coach.

Tuten: You've had three losses recently?

Oakley: Yes.

Tuten: What's that like? That's got to be a whole new level of coaching, coaching past it.

Oakley: It is. It's really hard because I'm right in the middle of it. I want to win, but we just have to be patient and find the right next piece of business that's good for us. It's really difficult and you have to keep your head up. It's not that different from any sports team when you go on a three-game losing streak. You just have to get up the next day and go to work, and eventually, things will fall in place. I've been through periods of time where we won like crazy. The work's coming in like crazy. Of course, winning creates another set of problems. It's a funny business. It's very much a roller coaster business: you're up, you're down, you're up, you're down. It's a wild, wild, fun ride.

Tuten: Can't take it too personally.

Oakley: You definitely can't take it personally. It's just like when you're a junior writer and your creative director's telling you, "No, that idea sucks," or "That idea's not good," or "But maybe you should do this." You really can't take it personally. You just have to keep going and coming back with new stuff. You kind of have to go home and lick your wounds a little bit and then come back the next day and be ready to go after the next piece of business that might be available.

Tuten: Is that the best piece of advice that you'd give to someone who's somewhat new in the business?

Oakley: Well, I think you really have to learn to have a thick skin, and figure out how to deal with obstacles put in your way so that you can get around them. Figure out a way to get around them and make things happen. That's the best way. In this business there are always different obstacles and different ways to get to a solution, and you've got to find a way to make it happen.

Tuten: What's next for you? What dreams and aspirations do you still have?

Oakley: Well, actually, it was just doing this interview, so I've pretty much peaked now [laughter]. But seriously, I'd like to grow into someone more like Mike Hughes. I look at Mike as like the best boss I've ever had in terms of being a real, genuine, nice, good person, who has great instincts and is great with people and is fair in his judgments and people respect him. Yet he was able to let the people who work for him grow and do the work and become better. That's what I'm hoping that I'm able to do, that the people who work for me become better people and definitely better creative people, but more than anything, better, and maybe one day they'll go off and start their own place.

Tuten: Do you want to grow BooneOakley? Is it as big as you want it to be?

Oakley: No, I'm not really that concerned about size for BooneOakley as long as we're able to make a decent living and continue to do the type of work that really makes me happy and makes John happy, the type of work that gets noticed and gets talked about, and really creates a reaction for our clients. I mean, really—it's not fun—advertising sucks if you're doing boring work. It's like beige wallpaper. No one even notices it. I just want to be able to continue doing the type of work we've been doing and doing it on different canvases. I'm really excited about things that are happening digitally. The developments in digital represent such a new, interesting way of talking with people. That's what I'm excited about. Oh, and writing that book.

Tuten: Are you and John still creative partners or too busy managing the business to be a creative team anymore?

Oakley: We are occasionally creative partners, but over the last couple of years, basically, we've been creative directors on different accounts, and we've been—we haven't done that much creative together recently. He's an awesome, awesome art director, great creative mind, and a brilliant guy. Yeah, we haven't really, honestly.

Tuten: Do you miss it?

Oakley: I definitely miss it. But, you know, I feel like there are different things that I am destined to do right now versus doing copywriting or, you know.

Tuten: What are you destined to do?

Oakley: I'm destined to do interviews [laughter]. No, I think I'm destined to be Mr. Client Relationship guy. Not really. I don't know. I really want to be someone who is—I'm trying to think of how to say it—fostering a den of creativity. I want to be someone who creates a place where people come to do creative stuff and do it for our clients. I don't know how to explain it, but someone who's created this environment where really cool things happen.

Tuten: I'll look forward to seeing what you do to make that happen.

Anne Bologna

Managing Director
MDC Partners

Anne Bologna serves as managing director of MDC Partners (www.mdc-partners.com), a holding company that contains several advertising agencies, including Crispin, Porter, & Bogusky. Prior to joining MDC Partners, Bologna was the managing director for Cramer-Krasselt's New York office. Between 2005 and 2010, she was founding partner and CEO of the independent agency, Toy. Over its nearly five-year run, Toy New York garnered numerous industry accolades and attracted clients such as Amazon, Budweiser, Virgin Mobile, Macy's, and Google. One of the agency's most celebrated campaigns, "Elf Yourself" for OfficeMax, achieved unique notoriety when it spread virally to over 200 million people in less than six weeks.

Prior to that, Bologna spent much of her 25 years in the advertising business at Fallon; first as director of strategic planning for its Minneapolis office and later as president of the New York office, where she nearly doubled the agency's billings and transformed the outpost into one of the top ten most awarded agencies in the world. During that time, she contributed pioneering thinking to a number of global brands, creating the "brand bible" that gave focus to Starbucks in the late 1990s and helping develop the global brand strategy for Citibank's award-winning "Live Richly" campaign, considered the most successful in Citibank's history.

In 2008, Advertising Age named Anne Bologna a "Woman to Watch." She is a guest lecturer at Columbia University and one of an elite group of industry leaders who co-authored the book The 22 Irrefutable Laws of Advertising and When to Violate Them (Wiley, 2006). In 2009, Bologna received the "Changing the Game Award"—an honor given by Adweek and Advertising Women of New York to honor women who've reinvented their businesses to meet today's challenges. She's happily married to her college sweetheart and has one son, who lives in Brooklyn.

Tracy Tuten: Let's begin today with how your career evolved. Did you grow up wanting to work in advertising

Anne Bologna: So, the thirty thousand–foot view of my career? It is not an exaggeration to say I am probably one of those limited number of people who have a blessed career. I've only worked in four agencies, one of which was my own, before starting at MDC Partners, and all of those agencies were sort of at the peak of their life stage when I was there, which was purely a coincidence, of course.

First of all, I was a television reporter right out of college, but it wasn't my calling and so I got into advertising by having dropped out of the reporter business. I went back to my alma mater and took these interest inventory tests, and all signs pointed to advertising, which was not at all anything I had ever considered. But it turns out that those tests must be good because the person who was counseling me, she said, "I think you'd be great in advertising. You should go do some information interviews."

After my first interview, I was hooked on advertising. I thought I really feel like hand-and-glove fit with this industry. Then with my second interview, I was actually offered a job. I spent ten years at an agency called Campbell Mithun in Minneapolis. I spent ten years there, which I call my MBA in advertising because it was an agency that had a number of blue chip packaged-goods companies, like General Mills, Pillsbury, and ConAgra.

One of the things that Campbell Mithun did that was very noteworthy during that time, was having launched Healthy Choice from scratch. The Healthy Choice launch was obviously a tremendous success. It's still around and it still is a robust business. I worked there for ten years as an account person and then I became an account director.

I started to get a little bit bored because all the assignments seemed to be the same to me. I was looking for new challenges, and so I walked across the street to Fallon. I started at Fallon as a planner, an account planner, which is on the strategy side of our business. I was a senior planner even though I had no idea what I was doing exactly in that particular discipline, but a handful of years later, I became the head of the planning department, and I had as many as twenty-five planners reporting to me. I did that for ten years.

At that point, I left Minneapolis and I moved out to New York City. This was in the early 2000s and at that time I wanted to make the switch from running a department to running an agency. I was the president of Fallon New York in the early 2000s. My primary goal at Fallon New York was to turn around the agency's creative. It was a big challenge. At that time, Fallon New York didn't even have a reel. In our business, the reel is obviously a catchphrase for having a body of work that is a calling card to clients. I found a creative partner, Ari Merkin, and together we reinvented the office. By the end of that third year there, we were proud to be able to be able to say that little New York office of Fallon was among the top ten most creative agencies in the world. We were very, very proud of that.

It was right at that point that the industry started to shift. There were startups in New York, like Mother and Taxi and Strawberry Frog. You could see things changing, and at the same time, Fallon didn't necessarily need a New York office. It seemed like a good time to start an agency. That's just what we did and we called the agency "Toy."

Tuten: Where did the name Toy come from?

Bologna: Basically, Toy was a metaphor for ideas that are as engaging as a new toy. That was basically the idea, which I think kind of sums up what was happening in the advertising industry. In other words, we need consumers much more than they need us. If our ideas are not engaging, as engaging as a new toy, we won't be able to communicate effectively with our consumers. So we founded an agency based on that philosophy.

Tuten: What was it like to compete as a new agency in this world of powerhouses?

Bologna: We did some things that we are really proud of. We launched the Kindle (for Amazon) and developed the "Elf Yourself" campaign for Office Max. The "Elf Yourself" campaign attracted 193 million visitors and was called the best viral campaign in the history of the Web. More than 123 million "elves" were created and shared online.

But my hindsight learning was that we started the agency too late in our careers. After five years, we closed. We were an amazing threesome, the three partners—myself, and Ari Merkin, who's now at Crispin Porter, and David Dabill, who's also at MDC. We needed another five or six years to reach the level of scale that we needed. At this late stage of our lives, it just didn't feel like we had the luxury of doing that. After five years, the timing was right with our employees and with our clients for us to say, "You know what? Let's transition all of our clients and we'll all kind of move on." We tried to treat our people well in that transition and now here we are.

Tuten: What was it like, giving up an agency that you essentially birthed?

Bologna: It was pretty emotional stuff. I call it "the exceedingly rational business decision with profoundly emotional consequences" because it was difficult. It was like giving up a baby, really. And it still is. It will always be one of the best experiences in advertising that I will ever have had because there's nothing like having your own. It certainly is one of the most unique experiences, but it lives on because it is actually you. One of the best things that came out of it is it strengthened the partnerships and the friendships, frankly, that I had with my two business partners at the agency, David and Ari. That's something I'll carry with me forever, as well.

We did some good things and we left a little bit of a creative legacy. "Elf Yourself" is still one of the most significant successes in viral marketing. I think it reached one in five Americans, after just six weeks. So funny. And, of course, launching the Kindle was a something that we were proud to be a part of. It felt like it was a wonderful and precious little moment in time, but for all kinds of reasons it was time to move on.

Tuten: And then you joined Cramer-Krasselt as managing director of the New York office.

Bologna: Interestingly, Peter Krivkovich, who is CEO of C-K, was one of the first people that I spoke to after we decided to close down Toy.

Well, the transition was astoundingly seamless because C-K honestly shared all the same values that I have, which range from a strong work ethic to a humble sense of self. For instance, I don't talk much about myself. I always say, "I'm from Minnesota. I don't talk about myself. I just get the work done, you know?" And that was similar to C-K.

C-K is at heart a Midwestern agency, in terms of their home base. They have a very strong work ethic and a philosophy of being humble: don't pound your chest too hard and talk about yourself too much. Just focus on the work and focus on the client and good things will come. That's the culture, but it's also an agency that is essentially smart. It isn't really fair to summarize an agency in one word, but if I had to do it, I'd say that C-K is smart. It attracts smart people. It's run by smart people, and the CEO and the chief financial officer and the chief operating officer are all incredibly smart people and they focus on business strategy and consumer strategy. They spend a lot of time on getting the foundation, which is often termed "the strategy."

And if you played a reel of all the agency's work beyond just television, you'll just feel the sort of intelligence that's baked into it. I value putting intelligence into marketing, because I think the marketing lasts longer and it works harder. That's what led me to being a strategic planner in the first place. C-K does that—it puts intelligence into everything it produces.

Tuten: It seems in this industry we tend to think that creative work can be creative or it can be effective, but we might not see many examples of both. When creative is smart, it can achieve both?

Bologna: Exactly. You see a lot of clever but kind of "dumb," or not clever but creative—but still dumb—advertising on the market. Consumers can feel when it's this kind of creative for its own sake as opposed to being smartly creative, you know? I really appreciate effective and smart creative, and I appreciate that consumers get it.

Tuten: Has it been hard to integrate into a new agency? How is it different from creating a new agency from scratch?

Bologna: When you start an agency from scratch, you have this ability to attract people who want that. People who are eager to see what the agency can become. I've always had that experience, though, whether it was grow- ing up or working at developed agencies or beginning my own. I am spoiled because I grew up with a very, very wonderful family. I always say I won the gene-pool lottery. So I was lucky that way, and I was lucky to work at both Campbell Mithun and Fallon with smart, nice people. I've just been spoiled by that.

Tuten: What's a typical day like for you?

Bologna: Well, every day's different, which is one of the things I love about advertising. We basically learn new things for a living and because all of our clients' problems are new, not only across clients but within clients, you've got to learn something new every day in order to exist in this business. But I would say the general manager's job falls into less than a handful of buckets. One big part of my job is setting a vision, and setting a mission, and creat- ing an environment in the agency where people can do the jobs that they need to do and do them well. Setting the bar and maintaining high standards, which is the leadership piece in its purest form.

Beyond that, I deal with a lot of the soft issues, like people issues, growth and development issues, and opportunities. Frankly, I just deal with a lot of the people-people-people stuff. That's one big bucket.

Tuten: Are you involved in client work?

Bologna: That is another bucket of work—client relationships. I try to forge very strong trust-based relationships with each one of our clients. I'm almost an activist in that regard. I'm very proactive in being involved in enough of the detail so that I actually know my clients' businesses. I have to be involved in client work. I figure the minute I become only a figurehead, then I should be fired. I should fire myself.

Do you know why I think that? In advertising, we are really simply a service business. We service our clients. We make things, but at the end of the day, we are an extension of our clients' business problems and their brands.

I think if you get too far away from being deeply involved in your clients' businesses, if you get too far away to add value, you're over. Frankly, clients are paying for leadership from senior staff and if they're not, they should be. Those that aren't usually will end up regretting it. Why? Because I have a lot of experience to bring to bear on behalf of my clients. That's what senior staff does. I really like doing that. You could think of client relationships and adding value to clients as kind of a whole bucket in the role of a managing director.

The third bucket is new business development. To work on developing new business means that I'm constantly out in the marketplace meeting people, networking, and making sure that people that I know—or people that I could or should know—know what the agency is doing. I send e-mails and notes and letters. I contact people and let them know what's happening, and now that there's social media, I can post things on Facebook and Twitter about the things the agency is doing. Definitely new business is another bucket of tasks related to my job.

The final bucket is really just the general, operational part. There's just a lot of business stuff. I run a business here, too, as well as an agency, and that's a lot about the numbers for everything ranging from how well we're running the place to what kind of light bulbs should we have. It's running the infrastructure; decisions that nobody really cares about, but yet can't be neglected.

Tuten: People oftentimes struggle with maintaining a balance between work life and home life. One might suggest this is harder for women than men and also harder in a business like advertising than it might be in some other professions. How do you manage maintaining balance? Or do you?

Bologna: That's a good question, and I have a little bit of a different answer than you might expect. I didn't do this consciously, but as I look back on my career and my professional and personal life, I never really balanced. I never said to myself, "Gee. I've just got to get more balance."

I did say, "I wish I could spend more time with my child." I don't think any mother, working mother, ever feels like she's spending enough time with her child. But I've always integrated my work life with my personal life. I don't know if that's unusual, but I've always blurred those lines. My business relationships became my personal relationships, and my personal relationships became my business relationships. That's still the case. It all felt satisfying to me because I just never drew those dividing lines. I've been called a "workaholic," but I've never felt like a workaholic. I feel like I love what I do and I like all the people that I do it with. This is why I'm extremely careful about choosing who I work with. When you're working with people that you don't see eye to eye with or people who are just big energy drainers, which is poison to me, that's when work starts to feel like work.

Tuten: How did you grow from your early work as a planner to serving in leadership roles?

Bologna: This goes back to the fortunate part. If you look back over my career, you could say that the majority of my career has been spent at Fallon. My experiences there totaled twelve or thirteen years. I always have said the culture of Fallon is simply an extension of me. You have to consider too that not only did I feel so consistent with the culture of Fallon, but I also worked there during my most formative years. I was there during my early-to-mid thirties through to the mid-to late forties. It just felt like I was there forever. Those are really formative years. During that time I rose from just being an employee to being a manager to being a leader. I grew up there. It's like you're birds of a feather. Toy was more of the same. During my time at C-K, likewise. I have felt that I worked with people that I would want to spend time with. I'm so fortunate to be able to work with like-minded colleagues and like-minded clients.

As for leadership, people either take to leadership or they don't. I did and I do. Even if becoming a leader is difficult for someone, even if a person doesn't take to the leadership role initially, growing into a leadership role is really about serving others. There comes a point in a leader's tenure when they have to reconcile the fact that leadership is nothing more than being the best possible version of yourself in service of others. Basically, that's what leadership is. To lead, you've got to get comfortable with that.

Once you step into that role of leadership—well for me, at least, it's not like I miss being in the actual day-to-day practitioner roles. Why? Because once you have a certain role in the agency, it's not like you ever really stop. I still do account planning every day. I still do account management every day. I kind of pretend to be a creative every day. It is more satisfying to me to help other people to be the best version of the roles they are playing, which is what they are, than for me to be doing those roles, though. In that way, I guess you can say that I've crossed over to the side of facilitating and developing people more so than doing the work of the agency.

I'll tell you this, if I wasn't around account planners, or around account planning such that I could at least contribute, I probably would miss it, but I'm still around it. And I'm better off, because I think there are people that are better than me now doing account planning. I can add value, but the people actively in those roles are current and practiced in their respective crafts.

Tuten: Do you have any rituals that are important to your ability to work effectively? Things you do to gear up for work?

Bologna: That is an interesting question. I do a couple of things. One of my rituals—really more of a practice than a ritual—is to nurture diversity. I'm really, really big on diverse people. I love getting a group of people who have different points of view together in a room. When you do that, chances are the room is not going to be a comfortable place for anyone there! But good things can come out of a room full of different people with different points of view. I even hire that way. Companies need to fill themselves with diverse people. Agencies need diversity to grow and succeed. Pick people with the same values, and you'll get the same outcomes. So I'm really big on that. I also try to foster debate and discussion. People tell me that I create tension. I call it "creative tension." I call it "healthy tension."

First of all, I think when you are disagreeing with someone, the act of disagreeing must always be managed with utmost respect for the individual. I won't tolerate people treating others in a disrespectful manner, no matter the nature of the disagreement. But healthy discussion and debate, I think, is how you get to places, to more creative solutions.

The other thing I believe in and that I use as a practice for effectiveness is to be "in touch." When my son was young, I really felt like I was in touch. If you have children, you know that's how you stay current. Just look at the children and you know what's happening! You look and see what they're doing, and that keeps you fresh. This is really key for creativity. Creativity comes when you combine two things that aren't generally combined. That's why I talk to a lot of people—I find stimulation in talking to a lot of diverse people. And I read a lot. I keep myself in touch with whatever is new and fresh. I'm sort of an early adopter of new technologies and new things because I think that's how you make connections between things that might otherwise not be made. So my unwritten rules are just the whole embracing of a sense of diversity and outside influences and bringing those things to bear to solve the problem at hand.

Tuten: If you had a magic, fairy wand and with it you could change one thing about advertising, what would you change?

Bologna: I would abolish all fear. There is so much fear now. Too much fear in the business world and particularly today, with the economy the way it is. One of the things I lament about is the way fear limits us from making advances forward. It's not like I'm pointing fingers because the clients are under pressure. Still, the business world in general has a lot of legacy and fear and we have to stand up to pressure and adversity. These are just words when I say them—it's easy to say these things, of course. But it can be amazing when you stand up in the face of pressure and adversity and you just take a stand for something and you decide you're going to take a risk with something. That takes personal courage, and I think we need more of that today than ever.

And in the agency world there's a fear of change. On the client side, there's fear of being the champion for an idea that has longer-term potential than just next quarter. So I would eradicate fear.

Tuten: Is there a way to do this?

Bologna: Well, first of all, I think humor can be very useful sometimes. It can be useful to think of people from the perspective of a parent. I would say everything you needed to know about humans you learn as a parent. If you're not a parent, I would say think about what it was like for you when you were a child or when you were a teenager. You never wanted to do what your parents told you to do. In fact, if they told you what to do, you wanted to do just the opposite. Everybody is still that way.

If you want to get people to do things, you've got to take note of human nature and you've got to do a bit more cajoling and allow people to have ideas of their own. Nobody wants to be told what to do. You need to inspire people and to help direct and guide people to make good decisions on their own. I deal with fear the same way I would deal with any challenge. I brought up the humor thing because sometimes humor can be the great leveler. It can cut through a lot of tension. I remember I've done that since I was a kid. I'm a pretty straightforward gal, and I try to deal with things head-on. I don't let things fester and I'm also not big on subterfuge. I always say I'm too stupid for politics. I just don't get that stuff. I just say what needs to be said. But I'm direct and yet respectful of people's humanity and people's sensitivity. I deal with things straight on, but I also use a liberal amount of humor and empathy.

Tuten: It's easy to forget how powerful simply showing empathy to others can be.

Bologna: Oh yes. Besides the fact that human beings can be far more fragile than they appear, there's also this fragile thing called ego. Sometimes you just have to be mindful of the fact that ultimately everyone needs to feel all right about themselves. I remember I heard a terrorist negotiator once say that the secret to successful negotiation is to allow your opponent to save face. I think people forget that. People forget that nobody wants to look stupid. No one wants to look wrong, and certainly not in a big meeting when the stakes are high and others can observe your shortcomings. People don't want their dignity challenged. You've got to be mindful of those things as you handle difficult situations. It takes a deft hand.

At the end of the day, I would say the one thing that I've always found that transcends things and makes difficult things very easy besides a liberal amount of humor is just simple honesty and integrity. Those two things will get you a long way. Even recently, I've had to face some very difficult conversations with clients. Conversations involving very sensitive situations with clients. Whether they knew they were doing it or not, situations in which clients were treating some of our people with disrespect. Those are hard conversations, but they are conversations that must be had. You can't let those things go. As a leader, I have to bring those things up, but such conversations have to be managed in just the right way. If you do it with integrity and honesty and treat them the way you want to be treated, it's going to be okay. I can't think of any situation where this approach has gotten me into trouble or even gotten me an adverse effect. Frankly, if it has, it was probably meant to be anyway, whatever the outcome was, even if the agency got fired or they asked me off the business, whatever. Probably in the end, it was the right thing.

Tuten: *Mad Men* has reintroduced a lot of stereotypes about advertising. Do you see any truth to those stereotypes in the industry today?

Bologna: Well, I think a lot of stereotypes still exist, I just think they're a lot more hidden today than they used to be. They're a lot more under the radar. There are things that happen and things people believe or don't believe, but these kinds of things are kept more covert. I try to ignore all that, I guess. When you watch that show, I think the things that definitely still exist in the industry today are the characters. In fact, there are a lot of characters in the business, which is one of the things I love about it. Sometimes the quirkier you are, the better. I think human beings are characters, and I think sometimes we hide our quirkiness, which is not a good thing.

There's a lot of drama in agency business. Whether you're making a show about it or not, there's a lot of drama in agency business. I think it's because we deal with the most fragile part of the human condition. We use our imaginations for a living, which means you have to have an idea. That means you're putting yourself out there—way out there—all the time, every day. It's a very insecure place when you're doing that. You're dealing with a lot of human drama in the whole business.

Even beyond creativity, pitching business is the lifeblood of the agency business. We're constantly pitching. There is no high like winning, and there's very few lows like losing. It's an emotional rollercoaster. I always say that managing an agency is really about managing energy. You can help build that energy and fuel that energy in a positive way, or you can do the opposite. If you lose a pitch, an agency feels terrible, just terrible. . If you lose several in a row, which happens to all agencies sometimes because that's just how it goes, it can be extremely demoralizing. There is an ebb and flow to the industry. Agency leaders have to figure out how to just keep people up.

The other thing, that's not as prevalent in the industry today that *should* be more prevalent, and that did exist back in the *Mad Men* era, is the ability to get to the point. This might sound funny. But watch an episode with a pitch in it. If you watch their presentations, Don Draper will spend about two minutes just setting up the situation, something like, "Well, okay. You came to us and you said you want to sell hotels." Then he says about a minute's worth of explanation on creative strategy and then he shows the ads. That's it. Agencies have gotten into this really bad habit of spending forty-five minutes or more, and one hundred and twenty slides to explain the most obvious things. We explain things the client knows. We explain what can be assumed. And in the process, we make something that should be exciting and interesting, boring. We have made things a lot more complicated and time-consuming than they need to be.

Tuten: I see that kind of inability to focus in many areas today. Do you ever say that to the team you are working with as you prepare presentations?

Bologna: I do try. I think if you ask people here one of the things that I am notorious for saying is, "Excuse me. Do you have a point? So what's your point?" It's like, "Get to the point!" People do not want to hear you drone on and on. A good metaphor is PowerPoint. On a slide template, there is a headline and then there's a whole body of text. The client doesn't need to hear all the text. Get to the headline! Then move on to the story. We tend to overwhelm clients with too much information that's not really leading to a solution. That's something that has become prevalent throughout the industry—the overkill of information. *Mad Men* has that right. That's how presentations ought to be and that's a lesson that the industry has forgotten.

You know, this isn't really rocket science. We are in a very human business, whether people like to admit that or not. If you look at some of the best advertising ideas of all times, they are so incredibly simple. Now, the business world has gotten very complex. How to reach consumers is complex. I'm not issuing a call for oversimplification. I am, however, issuing a call for simplicity.

Tuten: But everyone has bought into the same approach. What if one agency goes in with simplicity and another goes in with overkill. There's the fear you mentioned earlier—what one agency loses from an impression of lack of preparedness.

Bologna: Yes, right. We're our worst enemy. You know why? It's because agencies are so competitive. And the times that we do that most is when we're pitching. You keep thinking to yourself, "Oh my God, my competitors are probably going to come in with more ideas and a better strategy." Agencies tend to react to that by presenting more and saying more and going deeper into the details when, in practice, you should do the opposite. You should have better ideas and explain them less [laughter].

Tuten: What changes in the industry have you found surprising?

Bologna: One of the things that is most surprising to me is that things are really not as different as we think they are. Consumers aren't that different. What's different is how they're behaving and what they're interacting with. But the basic motivations? They are the same. Five years ago, I did not get the majority of my news on Twitter. I still got the news. My need for news is the same, but where I go to get the news is different. The point though is that human nature has remained very much the same. As an industry, we tend to forget this. The other thing about advertising is that we're in a "back to the future" situation as an industry. We are actually returning to some of the approaches we used long ago. Remember, the soap operas were invented by advertisers. That was branded entertainment. Now, years later, we see brand-sponsored entertainment as one of the most rapidly developing areas of advertising.

I was reading a piece that was published in *Harvard Business Review* in the early nineties. [It] was published almost twenty years ago. The article was about launching brands without mass media advertising. The article was all about the importance of sponsorship and promotions. It talked about Swatch, Häagen-Dazs, and The Body Shop. Since then, of course, there's been Starbucks. The idea is that consumers aren't watching as much television anymore, and we have to respond with sponsorships and promotions.

But, you know what? When advertising *started*, consumers weren't watching television! Brands infiltrated popular culture then and when brands infiltrate culture and consumers' lives now, we think how it is all brand new. It's really not! What's new is the range of vehicles and technologies. We just have to use some of those old-fashioned principles of getting your brand in front of consumers in a relevant way without just pouring money into thirty-second TV commercials. My short answer to what's surprising to me is that things are actually not that different. Once you look beneath the massive changes in vehicles and technologies to the way consumers actually interact with messages in the media, the fundamentals are still the same.

Tuten: Share a campaign that is personally meaningful to you. Is there one that stands out? A favorite?

Bologna: Do you mean from my own personal career? I have one that comes to mind. One from my history that is near and dear to me is Citibank—the "Live Richly" campaign. It launched in 2000, I believe. What I loved about it is that it was like a good movie. When you go and see a really good movie, the movie stays with you for not only days, but you remember it for years. That's what happens with a movie that really resonates with you. The same thing that makes a movie great is the same thing that makes an advertising campaign great. It's not easy—but a lot has to go right.

With the Citibank "Live Richly" campaign, everything went right. First off, the clients were wonderful people. Anne McDonald and Brad Jakeman were the clients, who are now still professionals in marketing. Anne and Brad are really very talented, visionary people. They decided that they wanted to do the best work in the world, not just in banking, which, by the way, was not known for great advertising. So they set an enormously high vision, an aspirational vision for the campaign. They did their homework. They didn't even do an agency search until they had their own ducks in a row. So they really set an aspirational vision, and then they got their act together.

One thing that's become too uncommon in the agency business is that sometimes a client needs to kind of get their own house in order before they do an agency search. So Citibank did that. They got their house in order. They spent a couple of years figuring out their own internal politics and their own product and they put together a really thorough visionary brief, and then they decided to do an agency search. In a nutshell, they were brilliant people who set a high aspiration and did their homework and they briefed the agencies really well.

In the agency business it is a little bit like garbage in—garbage out. The work is only ever as good as what you put into it. I always say that one of the dirty little secrets in the agency business is that agencies really are *pleasers*. Agencies want to do a great job, and when you give them a huge challenge and then you get out of the way and let them do their jobs, agencies will go beyond the call of duty. Citibank did that. The pitch included seven or eight agencies, and Fallon ended up winning it. We made history together.

We launched this campaign called "Live Richly" and it ran in thirty-three countries. It was their most successful marketing campaign ever. In fact, after the first six weeks, the increase in checking accounts was something like three hundred percent just because the campaign struck an emotional chord. It was an incredibly successful campaign. It touched people in ways that no one would have ever imagined. It was just an emotional appeal, but it moved the business and we, everyone who worked on it, had not only continued successful careers after that, but we all became friends. We're still very close friends more than ten years later.

Tuten: What made it so special? The work or the people with whom you were working?

Bologna: It was all of the above. Back to the point that everything went right. All those things that went right are the same things that are so satisfying. The campaign theme was smart and emotional. It was successful. We made friendships. We were like a band of brothers. It's satisfying to be a part of something.

Tuten: Any special moments from your current role?

Bologna: I wish I had a story here to share, and I'm sure I will at some point. But since you've asked such a big question, I thought I'd better go back into the archives of my history.

Tuten: What's still ahead for you? You've started your own agency. You've risen through the ranks at two of the top agencies in existence. What still awaits you?

Bologna: That's a great question. I think I kind of alluded to it earlier when I was saying how satisfying it is to me, having crossed over into the realm of leadership. Really, I would love nothing more than to help create the conditions for greatness for other people. To help create the right environment for successes like the Citibank "Live Richly" campaign to happen for those working on my team. I work with a wonderfully talented group of people, and many of them are in that sweet spot age of between thirty and early forties. Everyone should be able to have the kinds of opportunities that I've had. I'd love to be able to give these folks the opportunity to have the same kinds of experiences that I've had, to be honest. If I can do that, it will be very satisfying for me at this stage in life. It's the whole giving back day to day. Frankly, I don't think you have to go to Africa to help the world, right? You can help people in your own backyard. That's one thing I want to do. It's important to me.

And then, when you think about the struggles and challenges we have in the world. But one of the realities of the world in which we live is that the entire world is challenged. Things are not great in the world right now, starting with our own economy. Our economic situation is pretty dire. I heard a statistic the other day that's very upsetting, which is thirty-seven percent of the children in America are living in poverty. That's terrible. That's here. Right here in the US. When I talked about how I blur the lines between my personal and professional lives, well, I'd like to blur the lines between doing business and doing good. I haven't quite figured out how to do that yet, but it's something I will do and I look forward to doing.

CHAPTER 11

Jayanta Jenkins

Global Creative Director
TBWA/Chiat/Day

Jayanta Jenkins is global creative director with TBWA/Chiat/Day (www.tbwachiat. com), the agency known for the iconic 1984 Apple ad, where he is responsible for managing and creating the global integrated marketing communications for Gatorade. A graduate of Virginia Commonwealth University (VCU) with a BFA in fashion art and advertising, Jenkins began his advertising career at The Martin Agency in Richmond, Virginia, and then went on to work at Wieden+Kennedy in Portland, Amsterdam, and Tokyo, where he created and produced integrated campaigns for Nike Basketball, Nike Running, EA Sports, Powerade, Lebron James, and Amazon.uk. His work has been awarded at Cannes, One Show, and the Communication Arts Annuals, among others. His portfolio and blog live at www. freshistheword.com.

Tracy Tuten: Jayanta, how did you end up in advertising? Did you grow up wanting to be in the field?

Jayanta Jenkins: No, it was completely by accident to be honest with you. I grew up in a family that definitely wasn't on any particular side of creativity. I mean, my father wasn't in advertising, nor was my mother or my grand-parents, for that matter. My uncle was a lounge singer, and I always found it interesting going as a kid to watch him sing. I guess if there's any form of creativity in my past, it was from him. And, as a kid, I loved to draw. I loved to take pictures. There is one thing growing up that I think did have an impact on me. We lived probably about twenty-five minutes west of Washington,

DC, and I always ended up at the museums because my father worked literally less than a block, a quarter block away from the Smithsonian Mall. I do remember quite often spending a weekend at least once or twice a month just hanging out at the museums all day. This happened from the time I was eleven until I was eighteen. Usually I would end up at either the Air and Space Museum or the National Gallery of Art. Those were my favorites.

Tuten: So with advertising you are able to integrate your love of art with your career?

Jenkins: That was definitely the beginnings of my interest and love for art. In terms of how specifically I got into advertising, I would say it was really by mistake. When I went to undergraduate school, I went into school wanting to be either a painter or a graphic designer or a photographer. Ultimately I ended up studying fashion photography and photojournalism, and I got my major—those are my minors—my major was in fashion art and advertising. But I remember the kind of pivotal thing that happened while I was in school. There was a guy named Jerry Torchia, who was a creative director at The Martin Agency. He had an advertising class at VCU where I got my undergraduate degree. Basically in this class, he taught about advertising, and the creative process used to come up with ads.

In the class, we would create ads and we had to bring in work that we'd done for critique. I hadn't done any ads whatsoever. All I had was photography. So I brought in photos that I'd taken. He looked through it all, and then he looked at me and very convincingly said, "You should be an art director." And I'm like, "Okay. What is an art director? It sounds cool. Yeah, sure." And I remember him giving me an art director's annual, a *One Show Annual*. I started going through these things, and I don't know what happened, but I completely locked into it.

I had definitely wanted to be a creative in advertising because what I had noticed and saw at the time was just the ability to do all of the things I'd ever loved as a kid and as a teenager. Everything I loved was at my disposal as an art director: photography, illustration, film, music. Once I fully understood that I could in some way or shape connect to all these people and collaborate—that was it. I absolutely dug my nails in and I haven't looked back since.

Tuten: That was the pivotal moment, for your teacher to turn to you and say you could be an art director.

Jenkins: Yeah, absolutely. Because again, I had no clue what an art director was. I didn't even know how ads were made at the time. We're all surrounded by advertising from the moment we're born until [we] die. Growing up where I grew up, there's no reason I would have known or had any insight as to how ads are made or that people even actually came up with them, you know?

Tuten: Did you think, "People get paid for that? You've got to be kidding."

Jenkins: They get paid, and in some instances you get paid very well. It's crazy just how well. More importantly beyond money, you get to inspire and challenge yourself daily.

Tuten: You finished out your fashion and fine arts degree. You didn't switch over to a degree in advertising at that point?

Jenkins: No, I went back to school after I got my undergraduate degree. At the time, the big school for advertising was called the Portfolio Center in Atlanta, Georgia. All the people that I'd seen in these One Show annuals had gone to the Portfolio Center. It was highly recommended at the time. So I applied and ended up going to the Portfolio Center for two years to get my advertising skills sharpened.

That was a great experience as well because I went from VCU, which was kind of very broad and general, to a very highly disciplined program. I was surrounded by kids who had the same ambition, and I learned and grew and was taught by other advertising professionals. Those are really great experiences, and it really helped me prove to myself that I actually should pursue a career in advertising. Up to that point, it was a desire for me, but I hadn't made any ads! Like I said, I had just been doing photography—and Portfolio Center was a good training ground for me to finesse my skills and create a portfolio.

Tuten: What was your specialty? Did you stick with photography or did you branch out at that point?

Jenkins: You know, at that point, when I got into Portfolio Center, what I really fundamentally began to understand about all creative—photography, illustration, film—is that it has to be guided by a powerful concept or powerful idea. Whatever message you have has to be guided by a powerful, powerful idea. It was part two of my "Aha" moment in advertising. To be good, you must come up with really great ideas. Photography or film or whatever is going to be the medium that you may use to execute that idea. And then you must execute brilliantly. Illustration, same thing. Television, same thing. Design, the same thing. Even product packaging! All these things are guided by the key component, which is having a great idea. So that was the thing that I focused on in my time at Portfolio School—creating ideas. It wasn't like photography or illustration, but it just was making sure that no matter what the delivery device was for the message, that it had a brilliant, beautiful, big idea.

Tuten: In your role now, as the global creative director, are you still generating ideas?

Jenkins: Absolutely. I mean, ideas are like oxygen! We require ideas to breathe. Ideas are definitely the thing that drives business. I work on Gatorade now, and my work, it's all about ideas, one hundred percent.

Tuten: You're actively involved in client work?

Jenkins: Oh yes. I've been involved on a daily basis. When I first got into the business, [I had] no concept of the client work. It's a skill that can't be taught in school. It's just honed over time. It's one of the things I love doing—interacting with our clients and helping sell ideas and working together collaboratively to make things come to life. It's one of my most favorite things about being in this business—the collaboration.

Tuten: Can you share something you're working on now? Something that you're excited about?

Jenkins: Now that I'm doing global work, what's really exciting is taking the platform that we started here in the United States. We're basically transforming Gatorade from a hydration company to a sports nutrition company and creating that imprint around the world.

We're creating a global language that will unify the brand, not just as an American brand, but as a global brand. You don't really get too many opportunities like that in your career to lead brands like Gatorade in a really big way. It's very exciting to me, and it's something I've always wanted to do. It started when I was working on Nike in Portland at Wieden+Kennedy. I was working on basketball, and I had the opportunity to launch Lebron James in Asia. It was just really exciting to strip away language and again come up with ideas that could connect with people universally. Once I started seeing ways of doing it, being able to participate in the process, I recognized that I wanted to be the global guy. I didn't just want to be the guy that worked on a brand and spoke to people within our borders. I wanted to really develop ideas and platforms that really spoke universally because we are a global community. That really excites me about being a communicator in advertising. It's being able to express ideas universally to people, you know?

Tuten: What is a typical day like? Do you have one?

Jenkins: You know, I'm glad you asked that question because this is one of the things I love about advertising. It's a different job every single day you walk into the door. My father worked for the government. His job was the same exact type of job every single day of his life. I mean, that works for some people. Some people like that very systematic routine. But advertising is such that literally the complexion and the complexity changes every day, sometimes for the better, sometimes for the worse. Sometimes something happens that you don't like, but no matter what, it's a different organism every day you walk into the office.

Tuten: How much time are you spending traveling?

Jenkins: A ton. I probably spend a good fifty-seven percent, if not a little bit more, presenting work or on production. Travel is a big portion of this job, which is also fun. I love going to different countries and seeing things and learning about different cultures because that helps to inform the work that I do on Gatorade, and other things I get to do as well.

Tuten: Now, with Gatorade, you mentioned that company shifting its focus to nutrition.

Jenkins: Yep.

Tuten: So repositioning the mission of the brand even. Did you help come up with that idea? Did you help direct the path?

Jenkins: I was part of the team. I work with some really amazing strategic people here at Chiat Day. One guy in particular is Scott MacMaster. He's a brilliant strategist. A couple of other guys I work with are Nick Drake [global managing director], Brent Anderson [global group creative director], Patrick O'Neill [executive creative director], and Steve Howard [global group creative director]. We have a really amazing team of smart, passionate people on Gatorade who love the brand. Our clients are passionate and have a really strong vision for the brand as well. You've got to put all these heads into play as you look at things to roll out, like the tagline we just came up with, or the positioning of going from a hydration brand to a sports nutrition brand. There are a lot of players involved in the work.

Tuten: Do you usually specialize in sport, given your background at Wieden? Did you come into Chiat to work on a sport brand?

Jenkins: Yeah, yeah, I did. But the thing for me that's interesting is that I was never a big sports person growing up. I didn't really play sports as a kid, but the thing that I probably bring to this whole game that helps tremendously is my love for culture, popular culture and sports culture. And, you know, not being that typical—not that there's anything wrong with being a jock, but I was never that numbers kind of jock person, you know what I mean? I was never in the gym all the time, but I loved the culture behind sports. That's been the thing that's really helped me carve out a little path for myself and find my own voice within this whole experience for sure.

Wieden was my first entrance into dealing with a sports brand. My very first job was with The Martin Agency, ironically because the guy who got me into this was from The Martin Agency. But when I got up to Wieden, I was assigned to Nike. I just immersed myself. That's what you do. You immerse yourself. What makes the stories that people tell special, whether those stories are told through commercials or some other channel of communication, what's special is that the stories they tell are told through their own lens, their own filter, their own take on things. What's brilliant about what comes out of Wieden and absolutely what comes out of Chiat or any really great advertising agency is the ability to tell stories and to tell them from a unique perspective. You're coming at the story from a different angle. It's about getting people's points of view that come from their own experiences. That's what makes everything really unique, I think, in most cases.

Tuten: I would think your background, not being a jock, would really be a huge benefit to you to speak differently, to have a unique voice in the world of sport, and help you understand people who also come to sport from a different perspective.

Jenkins: Yeah, absolutely.

Tuten: So, tell me about the path that led you to your current role. You started at Martin. You would have worked under Mike Hughes at that time?

Jenkins: Yep. Mike is awesome. Mike was one of those people who really helped me take flight. The Martin Agency was an amazing place to start for me. Obviously, they have an amazing reputation, an amazing legacy, and they continue to do amazing things. But one of the things that I learned really, really strongly, one of the things that made an imprint on me at Martin was their ability to do print. They were doing print advertising back in the eighties to nineties that was just head and shoulders above anything that was being done nationally. Maybe even internationally. I learned the craft of print advertising from those guys, and they really took me under their wing and helped nurture me and give me a real good runway to take off because my second job was at Wieden+Kennedy.

Wieden is where I really found my voice. I learned television and I learned how to take an idea and blow it out to many different forms and to communicate the idea on multidimensional levels. It was an amazing place to grow and to be nurtured and, again, to find my voice. I grew up at Wieden.

Now, Chiat has just been amazing. I've been able to take all that I've learned over the last—let's say eight or nine years—and throw it away to a good extent because every place is different and has a different approach to things. With Chiat, I've developed a degree of maturity that has aligned with all my past experiences and has allowed me to really become more than I had ever imagined I would become in this business. I'm still growing. I'm still defining myself, but Chiat has given me an amazing platform to lead brands and to do things in a way that I never dreamed of at Wieden or at Martin. It's been an amazing career so far actually, when I sit down and think about it.

Tuten: Well, when I consider the path, the hierarchy of the agencies, going from Martin to Wieden to Chiat. That's impressive.

Jenkins: Thank you. I don't know if anyone else has talked to you about this, but you begin to wonder what's next, you know what I mean? You reach a point where you wonder what the next challenges are. Each place that I've been at so far has really given me the ability to stretch and grow into roles and to define myself and to access things that really career-wise have been amazing. Really, really amazing.

Tuten: So what do you think you want to do next in terms of a personal goal or professional development?

Jenkins: [With] the pursuit of a career in advertising, what's been great is all the things I've been able to achieve. But I've left some things off, and that's been personal relationships. I've never been married and part of the reason is because I've been really chasing this thing. I've been totally dedicated to developing my career. Personally, I'd like to get to a place where I can just feel good about where I am and maybe be married and have a family.

Professionally, it's looking for the next challenge and maybe the challenge isn't through creating a TV commercial. Maybe it's something else. Maybe it's a movie. Maybe it's working on product development. I don't know what. I just think the lesson I've learned, that I've been learning over the last ten-plus years, is it's all about the power of an idea. The vessel is what you use to deliver that idea.

Tuten: You have me curious. I'm going to follow you and find out what you end up doing.

Jenkins: Me, too.

[Laughter.]

Tuten: Do you think about opening your own shop?

Jenkins: No, I don't think about opening my own shop. A good friend of mine just recently opened his shop. For me, it's not really anything that's ever crossed my mind. I can't explain why not, but it's not something that I've actually wanted to do, to be honest with you.

Tuten: Just because you like to focus on doing the fun stuff and not the other stuff?

Jenkins: Yeah, exactly, exactly.

Tuten: Well, I've talked to a mix of people with this book. Some people at major agencies like you, and some people, like David Oakley, who have started out on their own, and consistently, they all said, "We had no idea what we were getting into."

Jenkins: Yeah, that's kind of the beauty of this business or businesses like this. That unknown and that question mark really helps foster and create a lot of this magic that happens. I don't know that anyone who begins an agency really knew where they were going to end up. They just have the passion. And I think that's the common theme with everyone you've spoken to. They're very highly motivated, passionate people who have had the luxury and the blessings of being able to land themselves with brands that need people like them to help communicate their stories. They've had the opportunities to work with great brands that want to put good into the world.

You know, I've never worked on cigarettes. I don't want to. I don't drink anymore so I wouldn't put my energy toward that kind of product either. But it's really been a blessing to be able to align myself with brands that promote the common good among people. That kind of work is inspiring, amazing.

Tuten: Is there a brand that you want to work with? One that's like a dream?

Jenkins: Yes. There is a brand that I would love to work with: Prince.

Tuten: Prince the musician?

Jenkins: Yeah. I think it would be amazing to work with someone like that in developing marketing for a record or for a tour, you know, whatever he put his pursuit toward. That's someone that's actually been a really big influence on my career. Prince is an iconic individual who has taken an industry and, through his point of view and music, has defined himself and the category. And not just music, but film and however many other different things.

I always imagine that if I could approach my career in advertising the way that Prince has approached his career in music that it would be a never-ending journey of fun, amazing, great things. Can you imagine what it would take? I don't know if you follow Prince or musicians like Prince, but just imagine what it would take to reinvent yourself, to stay part of the social consciousness, and to do it your own way. I think that's amazing. It's that same quality that I admire about Dan Wieden and David Kennedy. That's what I admire about Mike Hughes and also David and John at BooneOakley, and Rob Schwartz, Patrick O'Neill, and Lee Clow here at Chiat. These are people who really helped define things on their own terms, and a lot of people agreed with them or came along for the ride, you know? I think that's beautiful.

Tuten: Do you actively try to plan for your life and your career following in Prince's model? Are you doing that?

Jenkins: You know, I think—yes, to answer the question. I mean, I don't know if I'm anywhere near that trajectory, but I know that's been my motto for sure, absolutely.

Tuten: When did you come to a place where you recognized that would be a model that would be appropriate for you?

Jenkins: It was long before I got into advertising. I think this was probably when I was a kid, you know, a teenager, when I was listening to his music. I think to a lot of people back in the eighties, Prince's music was just highly sexual. It wasn't the sexuality that attracted me to his music. What I definitely saw was someone who was creatively a genius. I was really moved by the approach and the music and just the style of the music. His personal style. To this day it still really blows me away and it motivates me in a really huge way.

Tuten: Do you know him?

Jenkins: I don't, and it's funny because I've been to like seventy-five-plus concerts and I've definitely followed this cat for a while, but I've not had the opportunity to work with him yet.

Tuten: I bet you will. I can just see that happening. You've put your wish out into the universe, and I think it's going to come.

Jenkins: Yeah, I hope so. That would be a good one to come true.

Tuten: Do you have something that you worked on in the past that never made it, that never got produced, but something that you loved when you were working on it?

Jenkins: You know what? Here's another thing that's really been cool because I was talking to a good friend of mine, Melanie Myers, who is a global recruiter at Wieden+Kennedy. We talked a few weeks ago about creatives who get into these funks where they don't produce things for a year or six months or however long. Going dry that long can be a mental death if you're a creative person. The conversation made me think back on my career and productivity. Ever since I started at Martin, I've been consistently producing work. There's probably work that someone might wish would get produced that doesn't, but I think I've been really blessed, knock on wood, that every year that I've been in this business I've been able to put something out there to be judged or contribute to the greater good. I can't say that there's anything that's been killed or a brand that I've wanted to work on that I haven't been able to put my hands on yet.

I will say that I never could have imagined that when Jerry Torchia told me to be an art director that I would have worked on brands like Nike and Gatorade. I couldn't have imagined then that I would be able to say I'd be a global creative director helping lead a bunch of people in the business. I mean, that's just mind-blowing. So I don't spend much time thinking about what I haven't done or what I wish I'd done. I'm just very blessed at the moment where I'm at, and hopefully where I'm heading.

Tuten: What do you do to nurture your creativity?

Jenkins: I take lots of pictures, I'm on Instagram, and I just try to stay connected and *present.* In advertising, time can go by very quickly. The downside of working in advertising is the social aspect. Socially, the focus tends to be on alcohol. Which is just not good. It puts you in a place of being unconnected and not present and *not in the moment.* I think these days what I tend to try to do is give myself a creative outlet. The outlet is staying connected to the culture, and just doing things that kind of again keep me in the moment. When I first got into advertising, I got caught up in the external part of advertising. The part that people think is really cool. Drinking is a big part of socializing in the advertising industry.

Tuten: The *Mad Men* portrayal.

Jenkins: Yeah, yeah. Everyone's different, but I'm definitely in a happy place right now. I quit drinking almost a year ago and I'm really happy about that. It changed my whole point of view [about myself] and being in this business, and I think it's made me a better person, you know?

Tuten: How did that come about?

Jenkins: Well, this business, for me, it's been about relationships on a very personal level, being able to communicate with people and being able to be a nice person. This is what I'm getting at. There were times when I wasn't "in the moment" like I am now. Times when I would come to work and I was just so hazy and so cloudy from drinking the night before that I wasn't able to be one hundred percent—I wasn't able to contribute one hundred percent. I was only contributing about, let's say, forty-seven percent, which is actually—I was doing damn good at forty-seven percent [laughter]. Which is why it's even more of a blast to people to be doing my thing at one hundred percent now. But I don't know, I just feel a lot more together and my head's screwed on a little more tightly, without all that other nonsense.

Tuten: You said at Chiat that you came into your own and developed your maturity, and I can hear that maturity in what you're saying. It a big step to take, I think, for anyone.

Jenkins: Yeah, it is. You know what's funny about being a creative in advertising? The idea is that you want to stay a young person at heart. You need to feel that you can connect to people and feel you're not passé. I've been able to maintain the sense of connection without having to go off on the deep end. I don't need to drink and act like a complete lunatic, which I think some people think you have to be to be a creative in advertising. Again, maturity is the word. Chiat, my work here, has matured me for the better. I love it.

Tuten: Do you have a mentor now?

Jenkins: You know, that's funny. Yes, I do. Jimmy Smith has been my mentor probably for the last twelve years, and that's actually a very interesting story if you have time to hear it.

Tuten: I certainly do.

Jenkins: Jimmy Smith was a creative at Wieden+Kennedy. And after Jerry Torchia told me to be in advertising, I started going to annuals and looking at work religiously. I saw Jimmy Smith's name. He happened to be at Wieden+Kennedy. After I started looking through these annuals over and over again, I started recognizing the work of Wieden+Kennedy and places like Chiat, Fallon, and BBH London. Very soon after I discovered I wanted to be in advertising, I also discovered I wanted to work at places like Wieden+Kennedy, by all means. Jimmy is another African American, and I just cold-called him. He asked me to send him my portfolio, and I did, and he didn't like it. That's when I'd gone back to school, to the Portfolio Center. I'd stayed in touch with Jerry Torchia, who was my first mentor in advertising.

Then Jimmy Smith became my mentor. Jimmy would give me pointers here and there, but to make a long story a little bit shorter, I ended up, through Jimmy's guidance, getting the job at Wieden+Kennedy. Jimmy talked to Dan, and Dan saw my work, and then Jimmy helped to continue to nurture me from the point when I joined Wieden. The very cool thing that happened was Jimmy went from being my mentor within my fourth year of working at Wieden to becoming my partner. At the time I didn't think about it much, but my mentor became my partner. We worked together for a number of years, and then we became business partners, and then he became a family friend and today he is probably like a brother to me, like more than a brother to me. That cold call turned into this relationship that became something much bigger and broader than I would ever have imagined. To this moment, he's still one of my best friends and continues to inspire and to give me pointers. And, he tells me when I'm fucking up. He's been a huge force in my life as a friend and professionally as well.

Tuten: Did he play a role in your decision to mature and to stop the haze?

Jenkins: Yes, yes, yes, he did. He absolutely did. In fact, he also played a role in me coming to Chiat. Chiat had gotten Gatorade and spoken to Jimmy. Jimmy had left Wieden in probably 2005 and I'd stayed behind. Then Chiat asked me to come too without knowing that Jimmy and I were connected. It was cool because we were able to reconnect again. He's actually gone off and started his own business called Amusement Park Entertainment. He's doing his own thing now in a big way. When I look back on it, it's a really cool relationship that I've stumbled upon because of advertising.

Tuten: Are you helping to mentor anyone yourself now?

Jenkins: I am, definitely. I mentor a guy who basically just cold-called me out of the blue and then showed up in Portland! I've been mentoring him for probably the last five or six years. I've at least tried my best to help him along and do his thing. The thing that's interesting about when you mentor people is that sometimes people will show up for a split second and then basically they'll get discouraged and go off and do whatever. But then you have a small few people who really value your time and your input and actually end up finding their own path. They may need a little bit of assistance, but they're doing amazing things. This guy is starting to do that for sure for himself.

Tuten: He's at Chiat?

Jenkins: No, he's not at Chiat. Actually, he works for the Food Network, as an associate creative director.

Tuten: Interesting.

Jenkins: Very different path.

Tuten: That must be very fulfilling for you to have had someone who helped you so much and then be able to do that for somebody else.

Jenkins: Yeah, it's cool. It's definitely very cool.

Tuten: What's it been like being an African American in the advertising industry, where we hear so much about issues with developing diversity in staff and that kind of thing?

Jenkins: That's a great question. You know what? It's been crazy. It's been absolutely crazy. And it's been crazy because there aren't a lot of black creatives in the United States, and definitely not in positions like mine. Overall I would probably say less than one percent, right? And then even outside of creative, industry wide, there are just not a lot of African Americans in other positions either. And funny enough, at The Martin Agency, I was the first African-American creative they'd ever hired in the department since they opened the doors in 1977.

Tuten: Seriously? Wow.

Jenkins: Yeah, straight up. But let me get to your question. I think the reason it's been somewhat crazy from time to time is that I'm sometimes in situations with people who aren't used to socializing across ethnicities. What am I trying to say? It's just very interesting as a black person in this business, navigating. Not that it's been hard or there's been racism or there's been doors shut in my face. There is simply just a lack of women and a lack of diversity in the ethnicities represented behind advertising doors. Diversity can really help businesses open their eyes and see the world differently. And I don't think it's because of anything that was purposeful, and the industry has definitely changed a lot since I got into the business.

And I've talked to Jimmy about this too. It's changed dramatically since he started working in advertising, probably back in '86 or '87. But for me, I think the thing that's been really great is being able to have a point of view and have a voice that's helped change things and change people's perceptions and help brands grow.

Maybe my voice has helped more African Americans be hired in creative departments. If you look at the landscape of this country, it's not just all white or all black or all female or all male. Having different points of view in agencies really helps brands to stand out and carve niches for themselves, and not just black ones or white ones, but ones that represent a mass of voices, you know?

Tuten: What do you think can be done to encourage more diversity in the industry?

Jenkins: I think kids need to know. When you first asked me how I got into advertising, I said, "by accident." There aren't a lot of black-run agencies that are in the United States, right? So there aren't kids that have neighbors or uncles or whomever who are in these places, so they wouldn't know about advertising as a career path, right? That's probably one thing. And I just think more education in school because this is an incredibly, incredibly fun job, right? I come in every day, I sit around with other people and come up with ideas, and I get to work with some of the most talented people on the planet to execute ideas. I think if more kids knew about advertising, like really they knew about the roles within advertising, the creative directors, the writers, the art directors, even the planners or the account management, I think it would probably open things up.

It's funny because my friend Jimmy, the reason he knew about advertising was *Bewitched*. He said to himself, "Wow, that guy has a beautiful wife, awesome home, and a fun job. I want to do that." So that's how he discovered advertising. You know, of course, I was aware of *Bewitched*, but I didn't connect to it like Jimmy did. I've actually done a lot of things in communities where I've gone to schools and talked to kids about what I do to help inform and inspire kids to consider a career path in advertising. Again, it's all about creativity and having a point of view and having the skills to develop that.

Tuten: Those skills can be used in lots of different industries as well.

Jenkins: Oh absolutely, entertainment—across the board. Absolutely.

Tuten: If you had a magic, fairy wand and with it you could change one thing about the advertising industry, what would you change?

Jenkins: I would completely eliminate alcohol.

Tuten: That's interesting.

Jenkins: Like hands down.

Tuten: Because nobody's better with it?

Jenkins: No, no, no. Not at all. I think if there's one thing that definitely becomes a huge waste of a person's time in general is alcohol abuse, but I think in this industry, it's so ever-present. Alcohol does nothing good for any person in this entire business, period.

Tuten: But some people might say that it's a creative crutch, something that they use to get their creative juices flowing.

Jenkins: What I would say to that is it's definitely an illusion. I think alcohol creates an illusion, and you know illusions are make-believe. We can contribute at a higher level by expressing through the one creative intelligence that exists in and around all of us.

Tuten: Has that been hard for you since it is so much a part of the culture of the industry when you're out meeting with people, doing the relationship-building thing? Has it been difficult for you?

Jenkins: No, not at all. It's been great because I've been somewhat of a beacon. When people come across a creative person who doesn't drink, the first question isn't, "What's wrong with him?" It's instead, "Oh, that's refreshing."

Tuten: You might inspire other people.

Jenkins: Yeah, absolutely.

Tuten: Now, you said that there's one other thing you wanted to change. What is it?

Jenkins: Well, now this is a very personal thing. I just became, within the last two years, a vegan. I'll tell you, another thing people do, not just in advertising, but in general, people don't pay attention to diet, I think. When I corrected the way I ate and eliminated alcohol, my clarity and so many things came together in such a beautiful way. In this business, the way we work, it's a lot of late nights, lots of pizzas, lots of crazy food.

And you see a lot of people in this business who are very unhealthy. Imagine, you get into this business in your early to mid twenties and then for ten years, you are just eating shit. Then imagine being our age. Your body just can't sustain the energy level that it's going to take to start a business or go to the next shoot or whatever. Obviously, I've been thinking a lot about sustainability as it relates to my career and beyond my career and to the traps of alcohol or eating poorly. It doesn't really add up when you look at the big, big, big picture. Those are simple things, too. You know what I mean? They're very simple things to adjust in your life.

Tuten: It's simple, but when you're talking about the culture of the late nights, the rush, the travel, it's simple, but it wouldn't be easy to do either.

Jenkins: No, it's not because it comes down to a personal choice, because being vegan and the way I travel is extremely hard. But, again, on the other side of it, I have much more energy now and I can do things in a way that I wasn't able to do eight years ago, and I'm not super old. I'm only forty-one. And my energy level has gone up in the last two years as opposed to plateauing.

Tuten: You mentioned spirituality a little earlier in our interview. What role does that play?

Jenkins: Spirituality's playing a huge role in my personal life and it's informing my career definitely. By spirit I don't meant breaking it down to being Christian or being Islamic or being Jewish, or whatever. What I mean is having the presence of mind to know that there's more than yourself. The spirit that helps you get through the day. I've really been deeply connected to spirituality in a way that I wasn't before because of bad habits or just—I don't know—I won't say "stupidity," but just ignorance. And I think it's helped inform the way I interact with people I work with. Being spiritually centered, I feel that I'm just a nicer person, you know. Without getting too philosophical about it.

Tuten: How did you grow into that?

Jenkins: I hope to grow even more.

Tuten: How did you nurture that aspect of your life?

Jenkins: Well, I come from a family background that's highly spiritual. My father was Buddhist—which is how I got my name—and went through a lot of different philosophies and religions as I was growing up. My grandmother was into metaphysics, which is, you might know, its own thing altogether. My other grandmother was Christian, Baptist specifically. Those aspects of my family definitely informed my journey, my path that I'm on.

Tuten: So you had the foundation already. You just had to return to your roots.

Jenkins: Yeah, yeah, definitely. And I never allow faith or religious views to inform my work directly, but, at the same time, there's left and there's right. I try to allow the good principles to inform my decisions as I create things or as I communicate with people or as I walk this path.

Tuten: I respect everything that you've said. I'm really impressed with the thoughtfulness that you've applied to your personal life and your professional life.

Jenkins: Thank you.

Tuten: Your family must be really proud of you.

Jenkins: Oh, this is funny. This is my favorite story about me in advertising and my family. So I'd been working at Wieden and I was home visiting for the holidays, and my grandmother says to me, "I was at church the other day. Everybody was asking about you." And I'm like, "Oh, that's cool." And she said, "[I told them] Jayanta's in Portland selling shoes. He's a shoes salesman now."

That's hilarious because my grandmother's perception of what I do is like Al Bundy from *Married with Children*. But she got it half-right, because I guess I was selling shoes. She's never had a concept of what it means to be an art director. No one in my family gets it. I brought my father out to see a shoot. I brought my cousin out to see a shoot so he could see behind-the-scenes work of what it takes to put a thirty-second or a sixty-second commercial together. Even with the visits, what they understand is simply enough to know that I'm wildly happy, so they're happy to that extent, but they definitely don't get it.

Tuten: That's really funny, and, you know, you're right—I mean, she's right. When it comes down to the bottom line, that's what you were doing. You were selling shoes.

Jenkins: Yep.

Tuten: Do you get to see them as much as you'd like to?

Jenkins: I go home once a year and hang out. It's always interesting going back home because so much has changed for me personally, just things that I've exposed myself to. When you go home, it's just—it's representative of things from the past most of the time. I don't know if you're from North Carolina or if you're far away from home or not, but it's always interesting to go back home. It's always very interesting.

Tuten: Actually, that's something that I've been dealing with quite a lot for the last two years because I was in Richmond. I was actually out at Virginia Commonwealth. I taught advertising in that program.

Jenkins: Oh, awesome.

Tuten: I probably taught the class that changed your life while I was there. And then I re-met someone that I went to school with from fourth grade to twelfth grade and we fell in love, and I moved back to my hometown. For the last two years, after spending twenty years away, I have been going through on a daily basis just what you're talking about. You know, some things are the same, and some things—you just can't put the toothpaste back in the package.

Jenkins: Yep. That's awesome.

Tuten: How do you see the advertising industry changing over the next few years?

Jenkins: I think what's really awesome is the technology. I love technology. I've always loved technology since I was a kid. I love that the whole way we interact with each other socially has changed forever and forever changed the way advertising will grow and evolve. I remember when I was getting into advertising, a big deal was banner ads. Because the internet had just started.

To do a good banner ad back in 1999 was a big deal. The whole social aspect of the way we communicate is going to continue to change and evolve advertising. The thing that's really interesting to me is teenagers don't necessarily look at TV to get all of their cultural references. The kids today aren't connected to television the way we were when we were teenagers. I think smartphones and mobile devices are playing a big role in that, and obviously computers play a big role. It's interesting because you've got to think there's a wonderful question mark on what this will be even five years from now. Because of Facebook, because of Twitter, because of things that we don't even have names for yet. All of this will evolve over the next five years to a decade.

I honestly wish I were a teenager right now because this would be the most mind-blowing time from a technological standpoint to be a teenager. Again, if you think about when we were kids, a Walkman was a big deal! It was a big deal because a Walkman meant personal music was portable. I mean, a cassette versus an eight-track, an eight-track versus an LP. I'm very envious of what will be when I'm probably in my seventies because things are going to change so dramatically. It's exciting. And I think it will give us different ways to understand to each other.

From a global standpoint, we'll be connected to each other in a way we really never have been before. That's super exciting. Brands that are smart and the people who run them will get on board and take a stake in this, and not in a way to show and to sell things, not be a huckster, but just to find ways to push things forward and to allow people to grow in really beautiful ways.

Tuten: Do you think brands are ready for the labor commitment that social is bringing in terms of communication? I mean, it's really not mass communication anymore.

Jenkins: What did you say, the labor commitment?

Tuten: Yeah.

Jenkins: What do you mean by that?

Tuten: Well, when I think about what it means for a brand to speak to consumers, I mean, they might be responding to individual posts or trying every day to engage individuals, to come up with fresh content.

Jenkins: Oh, I see.

Tuten: Just the amount of production that can be involved for social communication is so much more involved than the amount of production that might have been involved for three television commercials we're running as part of a campaign.

Jenkins: Yeah, that's true. I hadn't really thought about it that way, but you're right. I don't know. I think in a world where a lot of this stuff is user-generated, brands will probably piggyback on that a little bit, and the real big brands will always have the resources to do really interesting things as well. The GEs, the Proctors, the Nikes—those types of brands.

Tuten: Actually, this reminds me of your web site. It's called Fresh Is the Word?

Jenkins: Yeah.

Tuten: So what's that?

Jenkins: Fresh Is the Word is—there's a group that I loved as a kid called Mantronix, and they had a song called "Fresh Is the Word." It was a song I used to breakdance to. Actually I was shocked I was able to get that URL because I thought someone would have taken it. But Fresh Is the Word basically emanated from that song. I also try to hopefully apply it to my work and to my own life, and that's always just kind of a reminder to look at things from a very fresh perspective, which is really hard to do. It's easy to not do it. What's easy is to follow the status quo. That's exclusively where that came from.

Tuten: That's your slogan, your personal slogan?

Jenkins: Yep, absolutely.

Tuten: So what's next for you?

Jenkins: What's next for me? I feel very fortunate to Martin, Wieden, and Chiat because it's been such a great progression. I've really started at a medium-sized place and then I went from a medium to a large place to a behemoth. And at all three of these places, I've still been able to be creative and to grow and to learn things on a daily basis.

I'm at a point in my career where I want to really be able to contribute in a very holistic way to the culture of the *place*, and not just to an account. The culture of a place is what seems to me to drive the work. That's why places like Martin thrive, because of the culture. Wieden, because of the culture. And this place, Chiat, because of the culture. I wonder how I could contribute to the culture of the agency in a way that would really affect brands and the agency and its work?

Tuten: When I talked with Marshall Ross, of Cramer-Krasselt, he had said that his mission for C-K was to create a creative environment, a culture there that would allow consistently best-in-class work. He defined best in class as what comes out of Goodby or Wieden. You were at one of those agencies. You were working at a place Ross identified as a goal for C-K culture. I also talked to Eric Kallman, who's with Gerry Graf's new shop in New York.

Jenkins: Yeah. See, that place seems very interesting, but keep going.

Tuten: Eric basically said what you said. That's why he went to Barton F. Graf 9000—to have that chance to create something bigger than himself there.

Jenkins: Yeah, I mean, that guy, he is brilliant, genius. Eric is a monster. When he made that move coming off of all the work he'd been doing at Wieden, it wasn't a "What the fuck?" If you're dialed in enough to your own thing, you understand why people make moves like that. I'm very envious of that guy in the most beautiful way possible, completely envious.

Tuten: Do you know him?

Jenkins: I don't. I don't know him at all. I know he was at Chiat New York for a while, and I know his work. I've always heard good things about the guy. It's very rare that you hear "super nice guy" and "advertising person" in the same breath, and this guy has had that throughout his whole entire career.

Tuten: Anything you want to tell me that I haven't asked you about?

Jenkins: No, but this conversation's been really good because you've allowed me to sit and pause and think about some things in a way that I haven't in one setting for a long time, so I thank you. Just for the opportunity to talk to you and to share some of my experiences and contribute. I hope it helps influence and inform the next generation of really awesome, talented people, and not people who are disillusioned about why they should get into advertising.

I think that when you look at a *Mad Men* or you look at some of the ways advertising has been represented, there are some other ways of doing things out there, and I commend you for your efforts in talking to people who have beautiful outlooks on the industry and the future, and can do things for the right reasons.

Tuten: I hope that you're right that young people will read this, read these interviews, and be inspired, and believe that something's possible.

Jenkins: One thing I will often tell kids and young people who want to get into advertising is that this business, any business really, depends on and will grow and flourish on people bringing fresh points of view and insights of themselves to that business. When I sit down and talk to kids, I'll look at two kids and talk about the way one's dressed versus the way the other one's dressed and how each person's individuality helps feed the creative process. It helps people distinguish themselves and it helps brands distinguish themselves and, it helps people associate themselves and identify with who they are and who they aren't.

Tuten: It's interesting to me that you can connect the nodes of people who know each other throughout the book. Everyone is somehow connected and at the same time, they all have had, every single person has had, something so profound to say and something different from everybody else.

Jenkins: That's one thing about creativity, and advertising suffers from it a little bit, is how to be really distinctly different, having a fresh point of view. One of my old instructors would always say to look at album covers from the sixties. He would point out how there was so much music produced, but every album cover was beautiful and interesting and unique. They were all different, and no one was trying to copy each other. What you said, that you've talked to people with distinctly different points of view and something profound to say, reminds me of what my old instructor said about albums. It's a really good sign in terms of where this industry is going. I think that's an awesome sign.

Eric Kallman

Executive Creative Director
Barton F. Graf 9000

Eric Kallman is executive creative director at the relatively new agency, Barton F. Graf 9000 (www.bfg9000ny.com), headed by Gerry Graf and based in New York. Prior to joining Barton F. Graf 9000 (BFG), Kallman was a copywriter at Wieden+Kennedy in Portland, Oregon, where he worked with Craig Allen on campaigns that included the Old Spice campaign, "The Man Your Man Could Smell Like." Kallman was partly responsible for game-changing Skittles and Starburst campaigns during his tenure at TBWA/Chiat/Day. Before going to ad school and joining TBWA, Kallman studied journalism and was a local NPR host in California.

Tracy Tuten: Tell me about this new role you are playing with BFG. You're in a different situation than the other people I've been interviewing because you've just like jumped off a bridge into a new agency. Tell me about it.

Eric Kallman: Well, it's Gerry's thing. I didn't know what apparently everyone else had known at the time, which was that Gerry was starting his own agency. I didn't know if it had started or was starting or what really was going on. The first round of Kayak[.com] commercials done by the agency hadn't come out or anything.[1] I was in town [in New York judging the art directors' club show] and we are old friends, so I went to visit him. He was at his new offices. We sat down and he told me what he was doing and that

[1] Barton F. Graf 9000 New York, "Creativity Online," http://creativity-online.com/credits/barton-f-graf-9000-new-york/2405/2.

he had just won Kayak from Goodby. Gerry explained his vision for the agency and what he wanted to do, what he was hoping to build. It sounded awesome and something I couldn't say no to.

Tuten: You went to visit Gerry having no idea you were getting a job offer?

Kallman: Yeah, he offered me a job! It wasn't worded harshly, like, "Leave your job now and join me," [laughter] but yeah, he offered me a job. It sounded so exciting. I couldn't say no.

Tuten: Tell me about the vision for Barton F. Graf 9000.

Kallman: Well, I feel corny using the word "vision." Gerry had worked at a number of large agencies his whole career. I had only been at larger agencies. He knew he wanted to do his own thing and build it the way he wanted to build it. Most importantly, Gerry wanted to work with the type of people and clients that he wanted to work with. People who wanted the type of work that he liked to do. Ultimately, what Gerry wanted was right in tune with what I would want to do as well, so I decided to join him.

Tuten: Can you tell me what that kind of work is? Is there a philosophy to the work?

Kallman: Oh, good work, literally, good work. We want to hopefully work with clients who want to make good, creative advertising. Solid, creative advertising. Agencies get so big or they're so political or they're owned by bigger and more powerful places and the ability to make solid creative advertising can get lost in all of that. It can get to a place where you realize that you have to do a piece of work a certain way or you go into a project knowing its limitations upfront in terms of how good the work could be. We honestly just want to do the best work that we possibly can and want to work with people and clients who want the most creative and best work. It's pretty simple.

When you start something new, you cut out all the politics and you create the rules and the culture yourselves. I wasn't looking for a job when this happened, and I am not looking now, but it wasn't until I talked to Gerry that I could see what my next step would be. If I didn't work for Gerry, my next job would probably be at the management level at some big agency. I think it would have been like being a junior again in a huge pool of creative directors.

What I imagined about moving up to the management level at a big shop, is that it must get even less talent-driven and more political. Cutting out all the politics, and working hard, and making the best work possible is all we're going for.

Tuten: How many people are with the agency now?

Kallman: We're up to twenty-five.

Tuten: Are you worried that as you grow, some of the politics will sneak back in, or do you think you can create a culture that will ensure it doesn't?

Kallman: Well, I'm assuming that the more people working in an agency, the more politics will come into play in any situation naturally. But we're really careful with our new hires to make sure that they're kind and hard-working, straightforward, talented people. It's a quality-control issue as with any newer agency or any independent agency starting. So far, so good.

Tuten: Are the new hires coming to you or are you getting a reputation for poaching the best in the business?

Kallman: No, well, that's funny. Our president, Barney Robinson, who was the president of Bartle Bogle Hegarty [BBH], left to come over and be the president of BFG. He's fabulous at hiring these wonderful people with amazing, amazing pedigrees. Our head planner came from Google and the new account director on DISH worked at BBH and then at Coca-Cola. All of these people are wonderfully smart people with wonderfully smart résumés. He brings them over right away.

And then Gerry and I—we're slower. I think, we're being very, very picky. Our creative department right now is five people, and they're all juniors. We don't label them as juniors. It's not their title, but they're all recently out of school, mostly in their first jobs. They're wonderful, doing great, and hopefully learning a lot and getting better and better. Gerry and I need to focus right now on bringing in some senior creatives. I don't know why, but so far, it's not like I'm getting hundreds of books[2] in my e-mail inbox or anything. But then again, we're young. We only have a couple of clients. We're still a small agency.

Tuten: It sounds like a really exciting time.

Kallman: We're very excited.

Tuten: Were you scared?

Kallman: Not scared at all. And I'm not even saying that in any kind of egotistical way. I'm not scared at all just because I really, truly believe it's going to work. Everyone working with us is so talented. Everyone we've brought in really is so talented. I feel so lucky to get to work with this kind of agency. I don't think it would happen, but if for some reason we went under—I don't think we ever would, but if we did—everyone here could the next day find

---

[2] Portfolios of creative work.

not just a great job, but even a better job, probably wherever they want. In that aspect, there's no fear. Maybe I'm just too dumb, but I just haven't thought about us failing. So far things have been going good, so knock on wood.

Tuten: How do you spend your time at work? Are you mostly mentoring?

Kallman: No.

Tuten: Managing, creating?

Kallman: No. It's crazy. I go from getting a little bit of time to write—but that rarely ever happens—to calling the client to reviewing work. I've often heard creative directors feel like they don't have enough time to create for themselves.

I see that happens more and more and more for me. I used to have a little time here and there to write or work on my own or with Gerry. As we grow, I'm getting less and less time. The one time I do get to concept and write is when the other teams show me work. I'll get another thought from what they've presented. I'll sit there with those creatives and work with them and kind of think off of what they've brought to me or blow out a new idea. It's my favorite time to work. Obviously, creatives like to work and be creative. But besides that, this is really new. I'm not only managing for the first time, but I'm also at a new agency.

And I'll go from working with my creative team and then, right after that, we have to go look at something else. Like we'll look at the new glass walls in the new office or something. Do you see what I mean? We're like picking out desks or something random, and I'm like, "I don't know. You pick the desks. Let's just make work." It's a very unique situation. I'm very aware of how unique it is. Every two hours I'm in a totally different place, doing something totally different, and some of that time I'm doing creative work, or reviewing creative work. Still for me, the creative work is the most fun.

Tuten: How do you mentally prepare yourself for each day?

Kallman: I don't, actually. I don't really know when each day will start or end. It's one big kind of blur. The days just go on and on. I just kind of go and go until . . . That's another thing I learned. I'm younger than most of the awesome people you've been talking to for this book and obviously far less experienced in a managerial position. But what I've found is that I kind of have to pick a point to end my day, if that makes sense.

Tuten: That does make sense.

Kallman: Because there's so much to do, I could just keep going. I could always keep going and never stop on any given day.

Tuten: Do you just decide on spur of the moment, or do you start off that morning saying, "Today my day will end at eight p.m." or . . . ?

Kallman: Oh, no. I never put limits on stuff like that. So, yeah, I get in as soon as I can and go and go usually until well, I'm tuckered out. It's pretty much a constant and it's most weekends, too. But, it's been going well, and it's getting more and more exciting and encouraging with every day. This is more than a job for me. I don't think I could do this if I wasn't so personally invested it.

Tuten: Does it feel like it's your own shop?

Kallman: Oh, gosh. No, it doesn't feel like it's *my* own shop. Gerry's the boss, but I do feel more a part of it than any other job I've had. I don't feel like I'm working under Gerry because there are so few people here. It's a small amount of highly intelligent people who are all working together. Right now, that's the vibe, and there's no weird hierarchy. No one's afraid to talk to anyone else or express their opinions. It's a group of really smart people who get along really well. I just feel like I'm a part of something that's gotten off on the right foot.

Tuten: That's a good feeling.

Kallman: Yeah, yeah, it's great. It's hard to get. I feel lucky to say that I care about this agency, more about its future, this is all more than a job. I think that most people aren't that fortunate.

Tuten: What led you to advertising as a profession?

Kallman: In college, I studied journalism. I went to college thinking I wanted to be a sportscaster. First, because I love sports and [second,] because sportscasters seem like they have a ton of fun. "Yeah, that Craig Kilborn, he used to be an anchor on Sports Center, and then he got the show after Letterman." It seemed to be a little more entertainment or comedy infused than in most journalism. So, anyway, I wanted to be a sportscaster. I went to college and I worked like nuts. I interned at NPR, and I interned at NBC Sports.

Then after college I landed an awesome first job. I was the local morning host for NPR's *Morning Edition* in Santa Barbara. I did that for a while. But I guess what I was learning, throughout all my internships and then my job, was that journalism was not for me. I'm not trying to get over the top about it, but, really, when you broke it down, instead of doing something with your own life, you followed other people around all day and talked about what they were doing with their lives. When I interned at NBC Sports, I realized it I guess for the first time. I love sports, but I quickly realized that the job meant talking to other people about what they were doing—and what I wasn't doing. I hope that doesn't sound horrible. It was just important for me to do something myself, and not just observe others.

Does that make sense?

Tuten: It does.

Kallman: I had this realization about journalism and I quit my job. I moved home, to San Francisco, with my mom and grandparents. I was twenty-three or something like that. I had to figure out what to do. While I was home, I looked at my old college catalog and noticed the only class I didn't take as a communications major was Intro to Advertising.

And I thought about it. I was like, "Oh, maybe"—I literally thought, "Maybe. I see commercials on TV. Some of them are good, but most of them aren't any good. I bet I could come up with stuff at least half as good as that." So I went online and I found the AAAA, the Advertising whatever Association of America web site. And I looked up the agency list in San Francisco. At that point, I couldn't tell the difference between Goodby or Joe's Advertising on the corner [laughter]. I just went down the list and I called them all, one by one. I said, "Hi, I'm a recent college graduate, and I'm interested . . ." and then *click*. They just hung up on me, time and time and time again.

Finally, I got an in. Some account guy—I believe it was DDB San Francisco. Whoever does those Chevron ads with the claymation cars. I put on a suit, and I went in, and I met with this guy. He just talked about himself for two hours. Seriously, and he talked about the business side. And I said, "Well, what about the actual commercials themselves and the ideas behind them. I see that you work on Chevron. Who found the idea for the claymation cars?

And he was like, "Oh, that's the creative department."

I'm like, "Oh, where are they? How do you do that?"

And he goes, "You have to have a portfolio."

And I said, "How do you do that?"

And he said, "You do that in ad school." That was it! As soon as I got home, I went online and I found an online ad school in San Francisco. I went there for a couple of quarters. And then I went to a different ad school for a short while and put together a book. Eventually I went job hunting and luckily I got my first job with Gerry Graf, at Chiat New York.

Tuten: So it's like coming home again then to work with Gerry now?

Kallman: Yeah, coming back to the old boss! [Laughter.] Like I said, when I learned about the opportunity, I honest to God didn't know that he was going to offer me a job. I honest to God didn't know where he was with starting his agency. I was just in town and I was visiting my old boss. I thought I was just visiting him to say hi and then it turned into a job offer and, of course, more talks later and eventually, it happened. It all worked out.

Tuten: Once you took a look in that old college catalog and you saw Intro to Advertising and you started on that path, did you ever stop? You knew it was the right thing?

Kallman: No, no, no. Maybe. Well, it struck me as right. Then calling the places and getting to go to an ad agency, well then it struck me even more. I was like, "Oh, okay, now this is getting interesting." And then when I found my ad school, I sat in on a class there and saw what they did. Basically, I saw a bunch of students present concepts to a teacher. Then, I got really excited, like, "Wow, I think this is something I'm really interested in." And then if you combined all that with the fact that you're twenty-three or twenty-four and you're living with your mom and grandparents, you have a very strong, maybe more reason to figure something out and work harder.

But, yes, my curiosity was piqued by that catalog, but it grew and especially once I sat in on the class. And then I thought, "Oh my gosh. This is something I think might be right up my alley." Besides being a sportscaster, I couldn't really think of a job for people who get to sit around with their buddies and make jokes all day. Let's just say I was fortunate to find this career [laughter.]

I was also fortunate to work so hard at journalism in college to realize it's what I didn't want to do, if that makes sense. Otherwise I would have been trapped. I wouldn't have started pursuing advertising until so many years down the line, and I could have been stuck, if that makes sense.

Tuten: I think a lot of people do feel stuck. They would have to go through too much to switch.

Kallman: Yeah. I was fortunate.

Tuten: What advice would you give then to young people today who are trying to figure out what to do with their lives?

Kallman: Whatever you think you might be interested in, you have to fully investigate. That is really the best advice. I also think that generally people don't realize how willing other people are to help. You'd be amazed how willing people are to help others. If you're interested in something, you should fully explore and investigate it. If that means going to places you don't know or going to people that you care about or whose work you respect and asking if you can talk to them, I think people are very willing to help. Talking to as many people and doing as much of it as you can as early as you can will really help you figure out what you are all about. "Oh, I like this aspect or that aspect," whatever it is about the job. Those kinds of conversations can help you narrow down and find what's right for you sooner rather than later.

Tuten: Did you have a mentor who was instrumental in how you developed in your career?

Kallman: Creatively? My old partner, Craig Allen, is one of the first that comes to mind. He had been working already for a year, I believe, when I got a job at Chiat. What I learned from him while working with him was just instrumental for me—I learned so much. I'll always consider Craig not only my partner, but also someone I learned a great deal from, especially in my first couple of years.

Aside from Craig, I learned much from Gerry. Gerry's my boss, but now my relationship with him is a little bit more like a partnership, not like when I was a junior and he was ECD [executive creative director]. Every day, I feel like I'm learning. It's similar to when I first started working with Craig and I felt I learned a lot every single day I was working. With Gerry now, I'm learning about managing, about running an agency, about sensing out priorities, and so many other things. I feel like I'm learning so much as I work with him.

Tuten: Any lessons you can share with us? About creativity or about managing?

Kallman: An important lesson is how to approach new ideas. Once you think you've thought of a great idea, at least what you believe is a good idea, you should get over it really fast. Get over it. Because you need to think of a lot more ideas you think are really good until you actually have one, if that makes sense.

There are so many different lessons I could share. Different areas to think about. If we're talking about when "concepting" in general, though, the lesson is "the more ideas you think of, the more good ones you'll think of." And always remain open as you move along with an idea, as you're thinking out the idea. As the idea develops, it may develop in a way you didn't expect. Even as the idea moves on into being sold to the client, and then into production eventually, it's easy to get trapped in your own mind. You have to stay open to everyone and everything as the idea becomes an ad.

It can harm the idea's growth if you get trapped in your own mind, if you already have in your head what the ad should be like, what it is going to be. The idea may grow differently than you imagined, and in a good way.

It's best to openly collaborate. The more collaboration, the better. And that doesn't mean agreeing with everyone, but that means considering every idea that comes along. The majority of the time, I probably disagree with them, but something I guess that I've learned is that every possible idea shared on any aspect of a project coming from any one at any level is something you should really be open to and think about. Because there's going to be some good ideas and you wouldn't want to limit your project or the success of what you end up with by being so blinded by your own vision.

It's important to stay open not only in your writing or when you're doing the concepting part, but also with your production.

Lessons learned: the keys are hard work and staying open and sticking to what you're good at. Maybe I've not even ever fully experimented with this kind of commitment, but you should—when concepting and working, you should. This is probably like Advertising 101 and a "no, duh" truth of the business—but, seriously, you need to be true to yourself. A lot of times people can get caught up in what's popular at the moment. I see a lot of ads that are like a lot of other ads in tone or style. All the good creatives stay true to their own voice and are going to execute on a brief with their own voice. But, yeah, just be yourself.

Tuten: Do you have a way of judging the work either that you do or that your junior people do and come in and present to you?

Kallman: I do have a way of judging work and it's by this pattern. Everything a) gets weeded out according to whether it answers the brief or not and then, b) I look for the best ad. The best ad may not be humorous. Just because majority lot of the work I've done has been humor and the people I've learned from like Gerry do a lot of humor, looking for the best work doesn't mean looking for the funniest. It means looking for the best. For some people, looking for the best ad may sound so subjective. But you're just looking for the most unique, the breakthrough way, the way to answer a brief, to answer it in the right way, to answer the brief with a voice, to answer with a voice that you've never quite heard before. Uniqueness is what stands out and I think it's what breaks through in any finished ads that you see. The best ad is not only the strongest communication. It's often times the most unique or new. It's something I've never seen before.

Tuten: That would be hard.

Kallman: Yeah. But it's hard for anyone to come up with something that's a good ad.

Tuten: What was it like to be one of the guys who created "The Man My Man Could Smell Like"?

Kallman: Oh, man. It was fun. Looking back on it, it happened very fast [laughter]. Can I talk about this? Well, I don't work there anymore, so I can't get in trouble [laughter].

Tuten: That's right [laughter].

Kallman: I remember Old Spice wanted to do one more spot for the body wash, because it wasn't selling as well as they wanted. They wanted to do a single spot and then they planned to discontinue the body wash. We had a really short timeline, I want to say three days to write it. Somehow it happened.

Tuten: You had the idea already at that point?

Kallman: No, we didn't. This is actually a good example of how "staying open" to what everyone else does in a campaign and around an idea really pays off. Old Spice had already established the style and tone and humor in its earlier campaigns. We had done a few Old Spice projects already by that point. The foundation was already in place. The planner—I don't know who it was—found out that the overwhelming majority of male body wash is purchased by females. Of course, that makes perfect sense. The assignment was to keep that in mind while doing an ad in the Old Spice comedic tone. Basically, do an Old Spice spokesman ad that spoke directly to women.

Whoever it was, I don't know it if was a strategist at Wieden or someone at P&G, but whoever dug up the fact that the smartest way to sell body wash for men would be to actually sell the body wash to women should get half or more than half the credit for anything. Know what I mean? We had the assignment. We worked on the assignment. The script was written.

I remember the script seeming different than what Craig and I usually pitched. Usually we have a very strong sense of the visuals involved in a spot. When we're presenting a TV spot, as I would imagine most creatives would, we typically have fully envisioned what will be seen in the spot. In this case, we had a dialogue script, and we had shown maybe eight or ten other scripts to our creative directors. And then when we got to it, I remember we said, "We're not quite sure what you see yet, but we think you see a guy talking to the camera and we think you see all this other stuff happening." Anyway, we prefaced it, before we presented it, by saying, "We're not quite sure what you see yet." Because really what we had written, it was more like a radio script when we wrote it. It was only the dialogue.[3]

---

[3]Wieden+Kennedy, "Old Spice: Smell Like a Man, Man," www.wk.com/campaign/old_spice_man_man.

The creative directors liked it, and as we worked on it further, we figured out, "Yeah, you should just pretty much see what this guy's talking about." The visuals just followed the dialogue.

I'm sorry. This could end up being two hours if I take you start to finish on the whole thing.

Long story short, I think we presented two spots to the client. We liked the "The Man You Smell Like" more. The other one sold. There was a regroup with the creative directors and our ECD. We went back and sold in "The Man Your Man Could Smell Like," so the project almost died once there. The timing was all off too. When we went to make the thing, we did casting on Christmas Eve. You usually call in two hundred people for casting and one hundred and twenty show up. But because it was Christmas Eve, we barely scraped together twenty to forty people. The choices were horrific, and, then Isaiah walks in the door and delivers it exactly how you see it. Isaiah Mustafa, he's the actor.

That's a saving grace. When we went to shoot the thing, we had two days and we weren't anywhere near to having a usable take. The afternoon of the second day, it started raining something like a half-hour before the insurance ended for a weather day. So we got a third weather day with insurance or something like that. It was almost the last take on that third day that became the one that finally worked and that we used.

They weren't sure about the spot when we first presented it to them.

Tuten: They weren't?

Kallman: Here's what happened. We presented the spot over the phone. They had a link to the ad. They had a roomful of people there. They watched it. We hear the spot playing over the phone, and then there's silence. And then they came on and said, "We're going to put you on mute for a bit." They put us on mute for like ten or fifteen minutes. They came back on, and they said they weren't sure about it.

Now, these are wonderful clients and wonderful people. Everyone likes or doesn't like stuff that ends up being popular sometimes, so I'm not trying to diss the clients at all, because they're great clients. They just weren't sure about how good the ad was. That's how it ended up being aired after the Super Bowl. They had already done the media buy to start it on the Super Bowl and keep running the ad after. They decided not to run it on the Super Bowl. They started the day after instead. I wasn't involved in the discussions—but I believe that the higher-ups talked them into running it through the rest of the media buy, but not on the Super Bowl. Somehow it ended up catching on fire. It caught fire so quick that it ended up winning a one of those Super Bowl polls of what your favorite commercial is, even though it never aired in Super Bowl.

The whole deal was just up and down, a roller coaster ride, the whole way through production. After we had it filmed, we weren't like, "Yes! We've done it!" We had this idea and we went and made it. It had gone through so much and took so much effort. It was over the holidays and the process was so draining.

By the time we were done with it and especially because the first few people who had seen it weren't over the moon about it, at that point, I was just hoping it would be considered "ok." Every time you want it to be great, every time you make an ad or spot, you want it to be great. By the time it was about to hit air, I was just hoping people didn't hate it, honest to God. And then, it caught on and we were floored obviously. It was amazing.

Tuten: It won the top award.

Kallman: Yeah, yeah. It won the Grand Prix for film, the Grand Prix at Cannes.

Tuten: Do you ever feel like the magic might not happen again?

Kallman: Well, the Grand Prix is just as full of luck as anything. Luck is involved. Sometimes things have to come together. We thought it was a cool idea and was going to be a good spot. But the huge reaction was over-whelming. It was similar to when we did the online responses, when we did the "Twitter Response" campaign.[4]

Tuten: I loved that campaign!

Kallman: Thank you. When we went into doing that, literally, it was a team from Wieden, a bunch of technical and digital people who had the abili-ties and could do things and get them online so fast. There were people who weeded through all the tweets and were responsible for picking the ones that were not only the best ones to respond to as far as getting the "response" out there, but also people who had followers and whatnot.

---

[4]The first ad generated much buzz online and on talk shows, including mentions by Ellen DeGeneres. The "response" campaign came about when the team realized they could feed on the buzz. The campaign was built on the idea that the team would pick tweets and comments from social media, and the actor would then "respond" in short videos posted on YouTube.

Besides that whole team, there was Isaiah on his little set with a tele-prompter and then me and Craig on our laptops and our CDs [creative directors] there, too, on their laptops.

When it all started, either Craig or I or someone joked something like, "Welcome to the hardest work we'll ever do for maybe a bronze pencil." It was a ton of fun, but it was the same thing as the initial ad, where we had no idea that people enjoyed it so much until after the fact! [Laughter.] We really didn't know until we got back to work the next day. We just didn't know as it was going on. We didn't know that people were talking about it. That it was getting so much attention.

We were basically locked in a tiny little set with Isaiah and just typing as fast as we could for two days. That was even more shocking! I'll never forget the next day coming into the agency. People were being so kind and congratula-tory and then we were going online and seeing the buzz the campaign had gotten. It was flattering and humbling, but more than all of that, it was wildly, wildly surprising.

Tuten: Tell me: what's your favorite work that was never, ever produced?

Kallman: That was never produced? Oh my God. I think every creative has like a handful that come to mind immediately. Hopefully Craig or I will be able to use the really good ideas again ... for some other client down the road.

Tuten: So that's what you want to do? You want to write TV commercial scripts instead of ads?

Kallman: Yeah. A couple were bigger, event-style things. Those are the types of ideas that would be shot down for reasons beyond creativity—like for their expense. Sometimes the client loves an idea, but the expense of executing the idea ultimately kills the idea. The realities of expense always come into play. Still, there's not a creative in the world—there's not a *good* creative in the world—who doesn't have, like, five ads that pop straight to the top of their mind. Actually, that are always on their mind, that they love—that they keep on their mind as the best things ever that never got made.

Tuten: You worked so closely with Craig. Do you miss him? I was wonder-ing if you did because he's someone you worked so closely with.

Kallman: Of course I do. I MISS CRAIG. Put that in the book really bold. It's rare for anyone to have partners for five or six years at any level. And Craig was my first real partner. We were fortunate enough to produce a ton of work, and good work. When I think about it, it was like we spent forever together. We basically lived together in LA the whole time we were at Chiat New York. And especially our three years in Portland, I think I spent over a year and a half of it with him in LA, so—yeah. I miss my friend.

Tuten: Do you ever feel like you need to just call him up and just run through some ideas with him?

Kallman: Actually, the first ideas that I CD'ed [creatively directed] at Gerry's place, at Barton F. Graf 9000—it was like two days before the presentation and I sent him the work. Obviously, I wish I could do that every time. I was so excited about it, and a little bit nervous since it was my first work as a creative director.

It was the first time in my life that I was getting to make a call like that. I got to make the final decision. I was just excited to hear his opinion about what he thought of the work. Would he say, "Oh, it sucks. Is there only one good script out of all of these?" and that kind of thing. Obviously, I always trust that guy's opinion.

Tuten: But just the one time?

Kallman: That's the only time. It was right before my first presentation. It was half nervousness, half excitement, half "where's Craig?" [Laughter.]

Tuten: Some people might have thought that you and he would open your own shop together.

Kallman: Oh God! That would have been fun. I'm having a lot of fun now, too. I wish Craig came out here with us, with Gerry. Portland was a fabulous time.

Tuten: What things in the industry surprise you most?

Kallman: What doesn't surprise me? You know what doesn't surprise me are people's acceptance and excitement and enthusiasm and focus on all things digital. But what blows my mind is a lot of the enthusiastic people are saying, "This is a great new world and a whole new skill set to learn"—[to the exclusion of traditional forms of advertising].

Think about it. When the radio was developed, print ads did not disappear. When television was introduced, radio ads did not disappear. It's the same with television today. Whichever media being used, it's just another skill set, another tool to learn. I didn't work in advertising when these other media forms were introduced, so I don't really know how the industry reacted when TV came along. But I'm pretty sure that they didn't say "Hey, we have this great new medium. Forget everything you know about how to use the old ones because they are dead now."

I feel like people should be excited about new media and wanting to learn about working on digital, social, and interactive as much as possible, but that doesn't have to mean abandoning the skills needed to execute a print ad or a thirty-second TV commercial because no matter what anyone's good at or likes doing, I'll bet my life that in ten years I will still be watching live sports on TV every night, and those live sports will still have timeouts and there will still be television commercials or advertisements of some sort. So the whole excitement and rage about digital advertising and interactive advertising, it surprises me how separate it is in some people's minds. Do you know what I mean? And even the fact that the One Club has the One Show and then the next night has the One Show Interactive. To me, that's bizarre. They're all ads. They're all competing creativity.

Tuten: They're all one.

Kallman: In advertising, I think it's kind of appalling that there's two different awards shows for interactive and non-interactive work. I think it should be the same show. It seems to be a bit of rivalry or whatever. People who do one thing think the other isn't relevant. That's always been confusing to me.

Tuten: If you had a magic, fairy wand and you could change one thing about advertising, what would it be? Is that what it would be?

Kallman: Well, I would change people's mindset. There will be more and more digital and interactive advertising in the future. I'm sure there will be. And, other mediums might digress some, but "traditional advertising" on TV isn't dead just because there's something new to learn and advertise with, if that makes sense. So, yeah, that mindset has always been really confusing to me. It just doesn't make sense.

Tuten: Eric, if you were going to write an autobiography, what would it be called?

Kallman: "I Was Born at a Young Age." That would be the first line. That would be the first line of the first chapter. I don't know [laughter]. I don't think I would write an autobiography. I'm actually afraid to answer your question because I feel like it could come off like I'm a real a-hole. I work a lot. Maybe that would be the same thing. What would my wife call the book? "My Husband Works a Lot."

Tuten: "Just Keep Working."

Kallman: Yeah, yeah. "I Worked a Lot: The Life of Eric Kallman."

Tuten: So in all of the long hours that you work, what's your favorite beverage Kallman, Eric: beverage of choice to keep you going?

Kallman: I can't do the coffee too late because that's just crazy even though I do. I was a big, big Diet Coke man forever, and then I started working with Gerry. Gerry loves Coke Zero. Like he has a deep-rooted passion for it, and I was like, "Really?" And then I made a big, a big life choice. So now I'm a Coke Zero guy. Caffeine works.

Tuten: It does. Is there a brand that you're longing to produce work for?

Kallman: One that hasn't had famous ads done for it yet?

Tuten: Or maybe that has had famous ads, but you just want to work on that work or build that brand.

Kallman: When I was coming out of school, the first Skittles campaign, the first of the new work that was done by Gerry Graf had just come out. And I was like, "Oh my gosh, that is what I want to do." And if you ever look at my early portfolio, my student portfolio was almost like a Skittles ad for everything. It was like a Skittles ad for shoe polish, a Skittles PSA [public service announcement] about don't hurt your children. Everything I did was maybe along those lines, that tone, that style. And so basically I am a schmuck who was lucky enough to get my way in to the business and get to work on stuff I wanted to work on right away. Lucky.

Coming out of school I was like, "I want to work on that campaign, I want to work on that campaign." And then I was lucky enough to work on that campaign. Since then, I'm a big believer of working for people whose work you like, not necessarily on a certain product or at a certain agency. Does that make sense?

If you're lucky enough to get to work with the people whose work you respect and like the most, you'll learn the most. And I think you'll probably have the greatest chance that they'll like your work the most, too, if that makes sense. When I finished ad school, I looked for a job, and I was a little anal. And I made an A, B, C, and D list of all the agencies that I wanted to work for, with like the A list being, "I would love to work there," and then B, C, D. Well, when I mailed out my portfolio, I mailed it out to the A list first and two weeks later to the B list and then one week later to the C list. Like that, in my mind, I'm thinking that it would maybe get it in front of the people I wanted to work for the most the earliest. I would let them decide if they like my work or not and could use my services or not first.

And here's my long-winded point because everything I've had to say has been long-winded today. I thought for sure that the D list, my last choice of places, would be the people who might actually offer me a job. And I thought my A-list people would be the people who liked my work the least because, in my mind, they were the best people.

As it turns out, advertising is really not about being the best or worst. The whole industry is subjective. If you work for someone whose work you like the most, there's the greatest chance that they like your work or style or work or tone the most as well. In finding that match of views and interests, you'll not only learn the most, you'll get the most work produced. You'll also be working for the people who you like the most. So the biggest, surprising thing when I came out of school was that I got the strongest response to my book from the people that I wanted to work for the most, and not just in one instance. I got to talk to the four or five people whose work I admired the most, I got the jobs I wanted the most at the agencies I respected the most. I was lucky. I got to work with people like Craig and Gerry from the very beginning.

Tuten: You are. You were lucky. And you still are, but hardworking, too.

Kallman: I'm very lucky, yes. I'll be the first to tell you that, but, yeah, I work hard, too. Yeah, I work hard. Luck and hard work.

Craig Allen

Creative Director
Wieden+Kennedy

Craig Allen is a creative director at Wieden+Kennedy (www.wk.com) in Portland, Oregon. He earned fame and recognition as an art director/copywriter, working for the last several years with partner Eric Kallman on accounts such as Old Spice's "The Man Your Man Could Smell Like." Allen's early work in the industry was at TBWA/Chiat/Day in New York, where he (with Kallman) became known for their innovative work for Skittles. In 2010, Allen and Kallman were named among Creativity magazine's top 50 creatives in the industry.

Tracy Tuten: How did you come to be in advertising? Did you grow up wanting to work in the field?

Craig Allen: No, I didn't grow up wanting to be in advertising. Actually, I think I grew up wanting to draw comic books or maybe be a rock star! [Laughter.] When I think back, those dreams quickly faded due to personal talent problems. It turns out whether you want to be an illustrator or a rock star, personal talent is required! But, no, seriously, I went to school at University of Texas at Austin. I went to art school there. I had two concentrations. One focus was in ceramics, surprisingly enough, and the other in photography. About halfway through school, I realized I had the urge to design product packaging. I was drawn to it. I didn't know I wanted to do advertising, but I knew I wanted to do something, so I took the Introduction to Advertising course at UT–Austin on a whim. From there, I just kept going. I ended up double-majoring in studio art and advertising. But still, even after the double major, I really didn't know what I wanted to do.

Tuten: You had some clue though—you knew to double major. Some people find out well after school.

Allen: I know. Yeah, luckily, I didn't graduate and then find out. Thankfully UT–Austin had a great advertising program.

UT–Austin happened to have one of the best undergraduate advertising programs around. I didn't choose to go there for advertising. I just kind of lucked out. Plus, I actually graduated with a book.[1] That is pretty rare in advertising. Usually, you have to go to graduate school or a portfolio school to finish your book, so I was lucky in that I went right out of undergraduate school straight into advertising. I think I was twenty-three. A lot of people go to portfolio centers and programs designed to help you get your book together. By the time they hit the market, they are twenty-six, twenty-seven.

Honestly, I think no one has any idea what they're doing when they start advertising. When I started, in many ways, I started fresh, like an open book. I think that was good. I actually went straight to Chiat/Day in New York. I accepted a role in the Young Bloods program—a six-month internship. At the end of the six months, they hired a bunch of us on. And then I worked there for five years.

Tuten: You worked at TBWA/Chiat/Day and now Wieden+Kennedy. That's not bad coming straight out of undergrad.

Allen: Yeah, I've only had two jobs. I've just happened to have lucked into working for very smart people, you know. At Chiat, I was able to work under Gerry Graff, Ian Reichenthal, and Scott Vitrone. I think they are some of the best scriptwriters in advertising today. I kind of just lucked into them. You know what they did for me? Through blood, sweat, and tears, they taught me how to write TV spots. I lucked into advertising and then I lucked into Chiat. Chiat was evolving around me. It evolved into a very super-creative shop.

Tuten: You sound very pro-Chiat!

Allen: Yeah, I know. I think that's my downfall. I'm probably a little too loyal. But seriously, it's just like I said: I've just been lucky to fall into these great places. I don't know if there are many better places to work other than Chiat New York and Wieden+Kennedy in Portland. I think I'm the luckiest guy in advertising.

---

[1] Portfolios are sometimes referred to as books; for a creative, a book is akin to a résumé illustrating his or her own work and scope of capabilities. Many aspiring creatives go to a portfolio school in order to finish a book. It's unusual for an undergraduate student to graduate with a book of any consequence.

Tuten: What's it been like losing your partner? Since Eric Kallman has gone to work at Gerry Graf's new shop in New York?

Allen: You know, it's always a little bit difficult when you're changing. I miss working with Eric for sure. The hardest thing in advertising, I think, is finding somebody you can work with because it's a very weird process. You have to be open. When you work with someone new, you're opening yourself up and then you're asking the other person if they think what you created is funny. It's hard to find partners.[2] I've only had two partners, I think, or maybe three at most, in my whole career. When I find somebody that I like and I'm comfortable working with, I tend to stick with them as long as possible. It's easier than bouncing around from partner to partner. Once you get a copacetic feel for how two people work together, it can be so valuable. Eric was my last partner. It was so fun working with him. We're still good friends. I'm really excited for him at Gerry's place, and I think he'll do great things there. But, you know, he moved away from town, and anytime you lose a friend, well, it just sucks. Hopefully we'll get to work together again someday.

Tuten: The two of you worked together a long time.

Allen: Yeah, It was a great run and I'm thankful for it. It seems like to me there are not a lot of fantastic people in the business. When you find someone great, you ought to stick with them as long as you can. There were no hard feelings or anything, luckily, with Eric. For us, it was just simply that he wanted to move back to New York and I didn't.

Tuten: Do you have a new partner?

Allen: Actually, the creative director on Old Spice is now my partner, so one of the guys moved off to a different brand. I'm working with another creative director who also worked on Old Spice, so he already knows the brand. Becoming a creative director is a totally different job than writing ads. It's much more management, which I'm kind of learning now. But with this new person, new for me, it's great that he already knows the brand. Everything runs more smoothly.

Tuten: You are doing some creative directing now? How is that different from your role before?

Allen: It's totally different from before. Before someone would say, "Here's the brief. Come up with some good ads." Now, as a creative director, it's

---

[2] Creatives typically team up. A copywriter and an art director, when teamed over time, refer to themselves as partners.

"Here's the brief. Is the brief okay? Who should we put on this brief?" And then we begin trying to match the right team to the brief, and get great ads out of the team.

Tuten: What is that like? Moving from a creative team to directing other creatives? Is it scary?

Allen: Yeah, of course, it's scary. I think any time there's change, it's scary, but it's kind of exciting, you know? Just change to me is exciting. I hate repetition, so it's kind of nice. It's a new challenge, and I feel like I'm just starting over in my career. It's an amazing feeling to know that I'm doing something now that I've never done before. In this new job, it's kind of like starting from scratch with no work behind me. It's been challenging just because it's a new job. Plus I really enjoy writing and making ads. I miss spending time making the work, for sure, because obviously I don't do as much of it now as a creative director. Some days I feel like I spend the day not really knowing what to do, while other people come up with the ads and then ask me if I like them. It's been definitely challenging for me, but I'm getting the hang of it now, I think.

Tuten: Does it feel as though you are mentoring the creatives? Or is it more like managing them?

Allen: I don't know if I'd call it mentoring, but it's also different from managing. We have a bunch of senior people here, but everybody has their own kind of style and tone of voice. We each bring something to the table. It is very interesting to see how my style and tone meshes with that of the creatives I work with, especially as I try to teach them whatever I can. They're learning what I like as well. You could say we're kind of learning each other. It is a fun process.

But, besides that, there is definitely mentoring. Luckily, at Wieden, there just aren't any bad people in the building. We are always working with good people. For the young people, we are working with them, molding them, teaching them, just as I was molded as I developed.

Tuten: You are passing along the lessons you learned from your own mentors and past creative directors?

Allen: Yeah, exactly. I'm trying to remember all the good lessons and then teach the younger creatives as if the lessons were my own. That way I seem smarter [laughter]. Actually, at the end of the day, even reviewing these lessons is a benefit to me. It might be the best thing.

Tuten: What is a typical day like for you?

Allen: You know, that's what I love about advertising. No two days are the same, which works really well for me. I really like a hectic work environment.

I thrive on it and that's pretty much the state of the advertising business all the time.

Tuten: How do you stay up-to-date on what's happening in the industry? All of the things you need to know to be current?

Allen: If I have a recipe for success—if that even exists—I read a lot of ESPN and Longhorn football blogs, then I follow that up with celebrity news web sites for some reason. I'm not proud of that. And I also like funny viral videos. I try to do this every day. I come in and catch up on what's going on. I don't watch a lot of TV, but my wife watches a lot. For me, just living and being outside and getting out a lot matters for soaking up what's current. I try to keep in tune with as much stuff as I can, but I by no means watch a ton of television. I hate reality television, so that's probably the main reason.

Tuten: Do you have a ritual that's important to your ability to create? Something you use when you are ideating?[3]

Allen: As far as how I create, I wish what I did sounded "cooler" but sadly, my process is just sitting in complete quiet until I think of a good idea. When Eric and I would go into concepting sessions, everybody would always say it looked like we were sad or fighting with each other. For our sessions, we would basically just sit in a room, staring at each other in complete silence until we had something funny to say. I wish it were cooler. I'd love to tell you that we just turned on some good rock music and played ping-pong to get our creative juices flowing, but that doesn't work for me as well.

Yeah, for me, concepting means sitting there in a quiet space and going through everything in my head. When I was younger, this process took much longer than it does now. As you get older and more experienced, it becomes easier to run through the ideas and shoot holes in them on your own. Before we even share concepts, we can be running through things in our head, thinking "Ahh, that's not good because of this or that." Even as a team, there's a lot of pruning that can happen before we share with each other.

Tuten: What's the process like? How do you share and review ideas in a session? Are you recording yourselves so you can play back what you said?

Allen: No, but we usually have some kind of pad of paper. We'll think and think and when we finally have something to share, I'll say it or he'll say it, and then we'll laugh. If we laugh, then we write that down, and then we'll go

---

[3] Ideation is the term used in the industry for the phase of the creative process focused on the development of concepts and ideas.

to the next thing. We try not to dwell too much, especially in the beginning of the process. To dwell too much on any individual idea in the concepting stage limits what we are able to come up with. And concepting is just more about quantity. Later, we'll come back and revisit the ideas that made it down on paper. Usually, at that stage there will be three or four ideas that stick out and we'll say, "Okay, there's something here." But the beginning of the creative process is all just about getting it down and getting through the bad ideas. This is one of the key lessons I share with my creatives now. I tell them: the first round or two is just writing all the stuff that you probably shouldn't be writing.

Tuten: You have to pick all the low-hanging fruit and then purge it to get to the good stuff?

Allen: Exactly. And it's not easy. When you are working, there will be ideas thrown out in concepting that you like. It's funny. You'll be tempted by some of those ideas. But if you take a break from the work, get some distance, and then a few days later, even a week later, come back to the ideas, and you'll say, "Oh, that was horrible."

Tuten: Do you leave spare time to distance yourself from the work? Systematically plan in the time to be able to step away and then come back to see if the idea still resonates?

Allen: It depends on the project, but with Eric, we would always do "the overnight test." If there was something that we were really excited about, we'd end on that idea and then we would go home, and try not to keep thinking about it overnight. When we came back in the morning, we could better evaluate the idea. A lot of times, we'd come back the morning after, and I would be like, "Oh, man, this is not as good as I remember it being." Or sometimes it is good. It can go both ways. That's why the overnight test is an important one. At least do the overnight test. If there's more time, that's fine too, but you may have a couple of weeks to concept, but you may have less. Sometimes a week, sometimes two days.

Tuten: In your role as creative director, are you helping people sift through the good and the bad? Or are they doing their own purging before the concepts are shown to you?

Allen: I hope that the teams have already cleared through the bad themselves. As a creative, I would always evaluate and throw out work myself so that I could be certain that the ideas I was bringing before my creative directors were good before I showed the work. We always try to tell them, "Bring your best stuff. Don't bring, like, five hundred scripts that you know aren't good. Bring the stuff that you know is great." In our standard process, we have a couple check-ins for each assignment. This gives us time to push people to do more with their ideas or set work aside for a while if that's what is needed. We can encourage them and say, "Keep going," and try to push the work forward. As I was developing, I learned that doing a lot of work is simply the best way to go. Repetition—writing, writing, writing—produces the best work. That's how I kind of learned. It's like just beating the good scripts out of yourself.

Tuten: Beating the scripts out?

Allen: Yeah, a mental mind beating.

Tuten: You are talented at humor especially. How do you know when something is going to be funny? Especially funny to a lot of people.

Allen: You know, it's so weird—advertising is so weird, and pop culture is about one hundred bajillion times weirder. I wish I could understand pop culture. To pretend I understand pop culture would be a massive overstatement. But I see stuff all the time and think to myself, "Really? That's what's popular? Oh, man, I do not get it." I think everybody does that to some extent, in response to some things. Then you can see other stuff and you're like, "That's hilarious." At the end of the day, we just always try to write the best stuff we can and make ourselves laugh.

Usually, if I'm laughing, something is working. I'm pretty hard on myself and pretty hard on everybody else around me. I push to come up with good stuff. If we're laughing, there's a good point. At least we like it, and from there, it's a leap of faith. You just put the work out there and you kind of hope for the best.

I think anytime you start out writing for pop culture, you're in trouble. You can't set out to be funny on a grand scale. You can't begin writing with the notion of let's write something that will go viral on the internet. We never wrote any ads from the perspective of, "I think this would do really well on the internet." You just write and when you look back at the work and think, "This is really funny," you move forward. Then you try to go to a good director and you try to shoot the best film you can and come out the other side with something you think is funny and put it out there. For every ad that I've had that's been successful, I've had three or four that I thought were just as funny that weren't successful at all.

You think every idea you come up with is great because you came up with them. That's the nature of advertising. And I think that's true of everything creative. So there have been spots that I did earlier in my career that were successful enough, but I was like, "Oh, this one's going to do just fantastic."

And you put it out there and people are like, "That's weird. I don't like it." I just don't think there's any way to tell. I will say that for any of our most successful spots, they came from a stack of ten to twelve scripts. And we like them. We like *all* of them. We've never presented a script and been like, "This is the one. This one is going to really ignite pop culture on fire." That has simply never happened. For the successful spots, we probably liked those scripts no more or less than the next three behind it. They would have all made us laugh. Some scripts you really like and you hope that they will be produced and be successful. But, it's just funny because you never really know what's going to catch on or how people are going to react.

Tuten: Do you usually test scripts to decide which one to produce?

Allen: It's different for every account. You know, I've been lucky that we haven't tested much for the accounts I've worked on in my career. I haven't done a lot of testing. Sometimes we do testing afterwards, which is great because you can use the film. If you are testing with a storyboard, you're trying to explain to the people involved, "On paper, this doesn't look that funny, but we swear it's going to be really funny when we shoot it." You know, they're kind of taking a leap of faith when you can actually shoot it and come to them and say, "See? It is funny." And then they actually think it's funny. In testing, people always react better when you have finished spots as opposed to little drawings that come one after another with voiceover on top of them. I've worked with clients that test a lot, and I've worked with clients that don't test as much.

I'm sure there are benefits to testing, but I find that the best work comes from not having to test before because the participants are reacting to something that's not made. It's not a true test. For instance, take the Skittles "beard" spot, for instance.[4] The message is very subtle. On paper, it's just a drawing of a beard feeding a woman Skittles. When the idea is depicted on paper, I can't imagine it would test very well. At best, people might say, "That's weird." But once you see it fully executed, you're like, "Oh, that's actually not as weird as I thought. It's funny." So, overall, testing afterward is much more beneficial than testing before, I think.

Tuten: How can you know what's going to be perceived as funny? Especially if you aren't testing.

Allen: That's an interesting question. Everybody has a different sense of humor. We can present stuff that makes us laugh. We may think it's hilarious.

---

[4] Readers can see this spot at http://creativity-online.com/work/skittles-beard/7205.

But then we'll go present it to our creative directors and they're not laughing. When we leave, we're thinking, "How did they not think that's funny?" It's just that advertising is probably the most subjective business you can be in outside of art or music. It's just so subjective. During my first job at Chiat, we had some of the hardest creative directors to please, Scott, Ian, and Gerry. We wrote *so* many scripts. Round after round after round after round of scripts to come up with one spot. But that was a great first job because by the end of it, I had learned a really valuable lesson. You can't be too precious with the ads. That's what I learned and I was lucky to learn it early on.

We have creatives that come in all the time with one script, and they're just so passionate about it. If as a creative director, I don't respond to the script in the way they thought I would, they will be crushed. It'll take them a day or two to recover. That's the worst thing one can do for developing the creative process. That's how people get stuck. At Chiat, I learned to move. You develop a set of scripts and you just know that the creative directors are going to go through them like, "No, yes, no, no, no, yes, no," and, "Okay, next one." Of course, you're a little hurt because you put your soul into creating something and you believed it was really funny. But you cannot be too precious with the ads. You have to learn to move on. If the ads become too precious, well—it'll be hard.

That said, I'm still very passionate about my work and my ideas. When things don't sell that I wish would sell, I'm upset. But you can't let it ruin your whole day. You can't let that disappointment stifle what could come next.

Tuten: Do you find that as a creative director you are mostly working with ideas based on humor?

Allen: I do work mostly with humor, but I like to think that I'm good at other things as well. And I've worked on other brands that are maybe not as humorous. I like to challenge myself. I'd like to do something that's maybe not funny at all. It's good as a creative to step outside your comfort zone every now and again, even though it's scary and terrifying. But it's also exciting.

Though, here's the thing. No matter what kind of concept I'm working with, I always try to think that *story is king*. Whether it's humor or some other focus, I always try to include an element of story in the script. That's where this work gets really fun—to be able to tell a story in thirty or forty-five or sixty seconds. The story is what people respond to. Even though it seems like I'm always working with humor, I'm really working with storytelling. You know, I would love to do more with long-form scripts. I've dabbled in longer-form work, and I would like to do more. It's super scary because it's longer, but that's why it's so exciting to me.

Tuten: Are you thinking of television programming or movies?

Allen: Every creative has screenplay ideas and, you work on those whenever you get a chance. I've been collaborating on a TV pilot with Eric and a director that we work with often. When we can, we've been working on it. But, unfortunately, advertising keeps us so busy it's hard to just focus fully on doing one thing.

Tuten: What other challenges are you facing in your career now?

Allen: A recent challenge for me has just been producing work for new global markets, as boring as that sounds. Seriously, I try to sound smart whenever possible [laughter]. It's just that going into these new markets is so hard. I haven't been to a lot of these places. I may not have experience with the culture. Can you imagine trying to come up with something that is funny to the entire world? It is very challenging and a relatively new twist in advertising. Before we only wrote advertising for North America and we knew our sense of humor, our sense of culture, and what people tended to like. You can take something that worked great here and take it into some other country and it may not make sense to them at all. I feel like North America really likes subtlety in advertising, especially when it comes to humor. But in a lot of other countries, they just don't get it. That's been the hardest thing for me. I'm still learning it, learning how to make a good, funny global ad. But I'll tell you, making an ad that is funny to the entire world is very challenging, if not almost impossible.

Tuten: Are you doing things to help you learn other cultures? To be able to incorporate cultural understanding into your work?

Allen: It's a challenge. Not only do you have to deal with different cultures, but there are even different languages within those cultures. A lot of my humor is very dialogue-based. Nuances in dialogue may not translate across fifteen different languages. Instead of focusing on the dialogue, it may mean using more visual humor. Global advertising definitely means developing for a more visual market because the work has got to transfer to so many places. It's challenging, but it is also interesting. It makes us do work that we probably wouldn't have done otherwise.

Sometimes it means shooting one spot several different times in different countries. For many of our accounts, the scripts are dialogue-heavy. People don't respond well to dubbed ads, so that means creating many different voiceovers. It's just a weird game. A very expensive game. There are many times when you just don't know the culture well enough to guess if the people in that culture will get the meaning of the message. I run into it all the time. There'll be a joke about something and I present it to the client and depending upon whether the context applies to their experiences, the ad may not make sense to them. Sometimes it's simply that humor doesn't translate at all. Some cultures are just serious cultures. North America is becoming a smaller market. The world market comparatively is becoming more important and it becomes more critical for brands to speak with a global message. It affects our work.

Tuten: Is testing more important then, when the advertising is being made for a global market?

Allen: Yes, it is. In a North American market, there's less risk that what you find funny won't be to the target audience. But with global, you make something you think is funny and then you have to test it. And you may have to test it in several different markets. Sometimes a product is new in country A, but in country B it's been around forever. There are so many issues you may be dealing with. We try to take trips over to experience the cultures we are targeting. Whatever [the country or region] the work is for, we try to go there and immerse ourselves in the culture so we can understand at least a little bit, but ultimately, you only know a culture by living in it for a long period of time. There are certain things that are just impossible for us to know.

Tuten: What a great benefit of the job—to experience so many different places. To learn so much about different cultures.

Allen: Right. Yeah, totally. The travel can be great. We're just about to begin tours of several different places, but so far I've been to Morocco, Paris, Thailand, London, and Sweden. I missed a China trip, which would have been really cool. But there are more places coming up soon. Everything feels really foreign to me because I've never been to these places. I've never been to Russia or South America. Part of me thinks that at our core, people are the same and we will think the same things are funny. To a point, I think I'm right, but there are just so many things that do not translate.

Tuten: How are you managing technology? Do you have creative technologists on your teams?

Allen: Well, as far as technology goes, luckily Wieden+Kennedy hired some of the best digital technologists. They keep us up-to-date. Some people seem to assume that if you aren't a digital native, then you can't do digital. That's just not true. Good ideas are good ideas. The question is, where do you put those ideas? How do you execute those ideas? Our job is to develop the ideas and then we can work with the digital technologists to ask what's possible or what could be done with the idea that we hadn't yet imagined. We ask them questions like, "Will this make the internet explode by accident?"

Most of the time, we'll ask a question and the answer will be "Actually, that's very possible," or a lot of the times, "That's not possible at all, but you could do [blank] instead."

The relationship with technology is collaborative. If you combine a great creative mind and a great digital mind, the digital mind will know executional possibilities that the creative may not have heard of, but the digital mind may not have the practice of disciplined creative for developing stories. You asked me about keeping up with industry news. The technologists keep up with the latest advances and that's not something creatives dedicate time to doing.

What you have to remember is that a good idea is still going to be a good idea. It's just finding out where it fits best. A lot of times we've written a campaign thinking it's going to be TV, and we realize, "Actually, this is really cool. It's a completely digital campaign." And, starting from maybe digital thinking as opposed to TV or maybe TV as opposed to digital—I think switching up the potential media focus keeps the campaigns different from one another as well.

Tuten: Is this tied to the Wieden+Kennedy philosophy? Focusing on the ideas? Some shops tend to be known for digital, or print, or TV. Is Wieden all about the idea?

Allen: The philosophy here is pretty tremendous in that the focus really is on the idea. I mean, every agency is saying, you know, "Ideas come first," but here they actually do. It's refreshing, especially as a creative, to experience a culture where ideas are meant to thrive above all else.

Every agency will say the ideas are the top priority but it doesn't always happen. Why does it happen here? I think it's probably because this agency is independent. Most agencies are part of a big holding company and there will always be someone above that a creative must answer to. At an independent agency, there just aren't as many people to satisfy as the idea makes its way through the process. The big men in suits hiding in the clouds don't exist here. Here Dan [Wieden] sits upstairs, and at the end of the day, he can make the final call without a lot of repercussions.

One of the sayings here is "fail harder."[5] "Don't be afraid to fail" is an important philosophy here. For me, it's kind of amazing because there aren't many businesses where failing is actually encouraged. Especially when you're coming up with work, if you are afraid of failing, you become so afraid of screw-

---

[5]At the Wieden+Kennedy Portland office, a wall of 100,000 pushpins spells out the words "Fail Harder." One red pushpin lives among the 99,999 others.

ing up, so afraid of someone yelling at you, that the work is stifled. You can come up with a lot better work and innovative work when you're not afraid. When you are free of the fear of failing. There are many times where somebody doesn't agree with a path an idea is taking and the creative team will be nervous. Here it's more likely that we'll end up saying, "You know, let's just go for it."

If you're doing any kind of creative work the right way, you're always a little bit scared and you're always kind of forging ahead and doing things that make you a little bit nervous. If you're not, you're probably not doing anything good. One thing we do to kind of test the boundaries is to use our account team for research. We go in and we present the account folks an ad. If they just laugh and say, "That's good," it scares us. We must not have pushed the boundaries. We played it too safe. But when we go in and the account people say, "Oh, no," and they start acting like they are actually nervous that we might present the work to the client, that's when we know we've done something pretty interesting. When they react with a kind of confused terror, that's good work.

Tuten: Have they figured out that their words of affirmation are the opposite for you? Do they know you really want to extract terror? [Laughter.]

Allen: Yeah, I think they do. One time we told them. We said, "If you guys don't say 'please tell us you aren't pitching this,' then we know we haven't done a good job." And you can tell if they're faking it or whatever [laughter].

No, you can tell. If you do it right, their reaction is just like, "Oh my gosh, can we even do that?" Well, I feel like when you're asking the question, "Can we even do that in any medium?" it's probably good, especially in today's world, where everything's a piece of entertainment and you're going online with TV spots, and you're competing against sites where comedians write funny videos. You should always be scaring yourself a little bit.

Tuten: Is pushing yourself beyond what's comfortable something that comes naturally to you or did you learn it?

Allen: You know, I probably did learn it, but I didn't realize I was learning it through my experiences. I've had creative directors and executive creative directors who didn't like anything that wasn't completely crazy. Over time, I guess I learned to write work that way and I also learned to assess my work on my own. Part of that assessment is knowing the work needs to beat something else. I think I honor that philosophy, but I didn't realize I had it, that it was a part of me, until I got to a new place and wasn't working for those bosses anymore.

Tuten: Are you doing the same for those teams you direct now?

Allen: Yeah, I think so. I tell the creatives here all the time, "I want you to scare me. I want you to do something that makes me ask, 'How did they think of that?'"

Tuten: Do you think about opening your own shop some day?

Allen? That's the dream, right? I think that's supposed to be the dream at least. But, no, for me, I have two first names, so I don't know if that's going to work, you know, as a name for a shop. [Laughter.] I'll have to get more clever, I guess. Right now I'm just happy learning this new role, just honing in. There are a lot of good creative directors here, and I'm learning from them and the ECDs [executive creative directors] and everybody. But, I have no idea what the future holds. If the future does present the opening of an agency for me, I will have a lot of business-name concepting to do to say the least [laughter].

Tuten: No ideas?

Allen: Really, I don't know. I'll have to think of one. I feel like it should be funny-sounding and slightly confusing. I don't know if there's a name that could capture what I'd want. Maybe there is. There are acronyms for everything, so maybe I could think of an acronym that would say what I wanted.

Tuten: *Mad Men* is a popular drama now. Do you see any clear similarities or differences in advertising then and now?

Allen: *Mad Men* is actually one of the few TV shows I watch. I think it's pretty good. I wish some of the things portrayed in *Mad Men* were still the same in the industry. I wish we all still dressed really suavely and drank Scotch. I'm not much of a cigarette smoker, but I think that looks cool as well.

Tuten: You could carry one as a prop.

Allen: Exactly and just gesture with it [laughter].

It's funny but people always ask that question nowadays. A lot of people ask us how close that show is to real advertising. We actually met Jon Hamm at the Emmys last year. We asked him, "Can we take a picture with you?" and he kind of looked at us a little weird. So I said, "We're in advertising," and he laughed. He was like, "Okay, let's do this." He even asked us how close the show was to real advertising. [I said,] "I'm sure it was really close to advertising in the sixties."

The aspect of the show that just makes me laugh is how segregated the teams are. There are copywriters working with copywriters and art directors working with art directors, but the copywriters and the art directors don't work together. The copywriter writes words, and they take it down the hall, and the art director makes it look pretty. Obviously today, art directors and copywriters work together, but even more so, there is a blurring of the lines. Technically I am an art director, but I write just as much as a copywriter, if not more. And my partners, who are technically copywriters, do just as much art direction as writing. When you can do both jobs, you are a kind of a hybrid creative. I think the days are gone when you can just be a really great designer and then hope that somebody will come up with ideas and you can just put them down in a fanciful way. I think that's gone.

But that's what we see on *Mad Men*. The art director sitting around with his markers, waiting for the ad to come in and then draw the ad up. There was no collaboration then and when you can collaborate on all aspects of an ad, the work is so much better. Titles have become a little bit meaningless, I think. And there are a lot of titles. There are digital strategists and nontraditional creative, and art directors, and copywriters, and all kinds of things. And I just think all these titles are kind of funny. Frankly, we should just all be called "creatives."

Tuten: In school, we still tend to teach creatives to pick a side—art direction or copywriting.

Allen: Exactly. I think that if you say, "I'm only one thing," you might be in a bit of trouble, especially as advertising keeps changing. I think you've got to be able to do a little bit of everything. I like to call myself an art writer.

Tuten: Do you have a better title for your role as creative director?

Allen: No, I haven't come up with a creative director one yet.

Tuten: If you open your own shop, you can dismiss with the titles. Or change them.

Allen: There you go. If I ever have an agency, we'll have art writers and copy directors. And smart business people instead of accounts people.

Tuten: Do you interact with accounts much?

Allen: To make good work, you have to have smart, good, account people. I've been lucky to have good account people, and I've heard stories about how bad account people can be. I'm not afraid of our account people here or at my last agency. I like being able to walk in the room and share ideas with them, and for them to have some input. It never feels like it's us against them. We're all in it together. That's when we make the best work.

Tuten: What's next for you? Career wise?

Allen: Well, maybe I should go back to trying to draw comic books or be a rock star.

Tuten: Given the recognition you've earned for your work, like being one of *Creativity*'s Top Most Creative, some would say you are a rock star.

Allen: Oh, thank you for saying that. Right now this role as creative director is an interesting new thing for me. It's made advertising a lot more interesting recently. I'm not doing the same role. Instead, I have to learn how to be a creative director. It's a new challenge and it's fun. I would still love to write some long-format scripts, if possible. If I can ever find some time. And, we're having our first child in November, so that's going to be a fun game.

Tuten: Congratulations!

Allen: Thank you. So now I'm becoming king of putting things together and I'm also packing away all the cool things that I like. I told somebody the other day it's like a bad episode of *Two and a Half Men*, where I'm literally packing up my golf clubs, and guitars, and amplifiers and taking them down to a storage unit so that I can fit in baby toys.

Tuten: That's what bigger homes are for!

Allen: Yeah, I guess that's true. That's what we need to do: just get a new, big house. Seriously though, that's probably the next step.

Oh, and I did have one thing I was going to say, one last point that I want to make. If we have time? I actually wrote myself a note on my hand to remember to tell you. The note says, "Don't avoid traditional media."

Tuten: What do you mean by that?

Allen: A clear trend I've seen in advertising today is that everybody is so hungry to do digital work that they run away from traditional media. They run to digital work. I think that is a mistake. It seems that people are avoiding traditional media just because it seems old, when actually traditional media can still be very effective. What we have to do is figure out how traditional can support digital and how digital can support traditional. The answer is not to run away from traditional when traditional still offers a lot of value. The best campaigns I've seen at award shows have had a bit of everything—all kinds of media—traditional and digital. Given that the best incorporates a mix of media, it's funny for the industry to turn its back on traditional media.

We just did a campaign where we used TV to set up the digital idea. Television was the activation point. I think that's a good way to do it. Usually people would say, "We don't need to do TV." But TV's still pretty effective, and it's a good tool to use instead of completely going in favor of digital. It's just finding how they can work together.

Tuten: Are your clients focused on digital? Are they excluding traditional or will they listen to your advice on media strategy?

Allen: We have great clients. I've always worked with great clients, and that's another key ingredient. You need good account people and you need great clients that trust you. Going into a client pitch, we've done complete presentations, all digital. We've also done digital presentations where we start with the preface, "I know this is a digital presentation, but we want to start with a billboard," you know? They're always okay with these suggestions as long as you can back it up and the strategy is based on good, sound reasoning. I like to think all clients would be open to it as long as it makes sense, but maybe that's wishful thinking.

Tuten: Is the focus on digital due to budget constraints?

Allen: Digital budgets are getting so big these days. I would say that they're almost as big as our traditional budgets. It's funny that some clients are a little behind and may not be aware of the costs of putting together a shiny digital campaign. But more clients are ready to invest money in digital and understand that for it to be really good, it needs budget too. The digital experience is getting a little bit more fancy. I don't want to avoid digital, but it's important that we figure out how to leverage old and new media. They all have value.

That's it. That's all I had written on my hand: don't avoid traditional media.

Tuten: Craig, thank you for talking with me today. I've learned a lot.

Allen: Great, yeah, and if you find any places to insert jokes to make me funnier or any places that words might make me seem more handsome, just feel free to add those [laughter].

Ryan O'Hara Theisen and Jonathan Rosen

Founders

Lucky Branded Entertainment

Ryan O'Hara Theisen began his creative endeavors in photojournalism with various newspapers and magazines. His curiosities then pulled him into advertising, where he worked as a full-time and freelance creative for award-winning traditional and digital agencies like McKinney, R/GA, Wieden+Kennedy, and BBDO. He has worked on global brands such as Nike, Audi, Starbucks, HBO, Smirnoff, and Heineken. O'Hara Theisen then attended Duke University's Center for Documentary Studies and eventually moved on to a directing program at New York University (NYU), where he met his sidekick Jonathan Rosen. O'Hara Theisen's work has garnered him awards from the Cannes International Advertising Festival, the One Show, the One Show Interactive, the International Andys, and the London International Advertising Awards. He's also been profiled in Communication Arts, Contagious Magazine, the New York Times, CNN, and NPR's The State of Things.

Three continents, five countries, one deportation, and a dual-residency later, **Jon Rosen** *has been The International Man of Advertising—all in search of the freshest ideas. Jon developed his success at award-winning traditional agencies such as Leagas Delaney/London, Fallon/New York, Wieden+Kennedy/Amsterdam, and Publicis Mojo/Sydney, where he worked on global brands such as Nike, Adidas, Diesel, Powerade, Gor-Tex, and Coca-Cola. He began directing, and this new love ultimately led him back home to the media epicenter of New York, where he met his future business partner and wingman, Ryan O'Hara Theisen.*

The duo's love for ideas and production, mixed with their appetite for the evolving world of branded content, created the foundation for Lucky Branded Entertainment (luckyny.com). Lucky is a hybrid—half agency/half production company that writes, directs, and produces viral films and branded content. The New York City–based company has created and produced films for clients like Nike, Diesel, Google, Speedo, and Gucci. Lucky's unique business model allows the team to keep clients ahead of the curve without burning a hole in their pockets.

Tracy Tuten: Why don't you just start by giving us an overview of Lucky Branded Entertainment and the role that branded entertainment[1] plays in advertising.

Jonathan Rosen: Okay. We've been going full-throttle over the last couple of weeks. We started Lucky as sort of a viral company. Ryan and I both came from traditional creative shops. Most of my career has been overseas, and Ryan's been mostly in North Carolina and New York. We met in film school. We both started film school for the same reason—because we were both kind of burned out from traditional advertising. We did the summer directors program at NYU and probably worked harder than we've ever worked in the industry before. And that's saying a lot considering how much we had worked in the industry.

But the work was so fulfilling because film school was helping us to realize our passion. Film school was amazing. During that time, we made some great films, and I went back to Australia. Then, sometime later, Ryan sends an e-mail to our whole film class, saying "Does anyone feel like they're not doing what they're supposed to be doing?" It caught me totally off guard, but

---

[1] Branded entertainment is made with the direct financial support of a brand to communicate the brand's message to an audience. It is different than "product placement." Instead, the brand plays a role in the production of a video, movie, television program, or game, and so on; any form of entertainment may be developed by and for a brand's communication purposes. Rather than an audience watching a television program with commercials shown during breaks, for example, the program itself is funded and produced by the brand.

at the same time, this message came at the right time for me to act. A week later, I was on my way back to New York, and I called Ryan and said, "Ryan, let's start a new type of company."

Little did I know that Ryan had just taken a new job at R/GA. He had negotiated everything he wanted. It was a sweet position for him, but still, he said, "Let's do it."

I was like, "Wait, have some time to think about it. You know, relax."

He had more to lose at that point. He's like, "No, you don't understand. We've got to make this happen now if we're going to do it."

The next thing you know, we're off and running and we thought we were going to just specialize in viral films. But actually, as we've been progressing, the industry's been changing. And the calls we've been getting are wider. While most of our work is creating online videos, some virals, many documentaries, we're doing other forms of film, too. We recently even shot a TV pilot for Teach for America that we're about to shop.

Ryan O'Hara Theisen: To give you the simplest view of what we stand for—to "capture our motto"—we consider ourselves a creative agency and film production company combined into one. We typically approach brands directly or we'll collaborate with another advertising agency that represents the brand. In those cases, when we partner with another agency, we'll work with them from the point of developing strategy, taking whatever research they have. And if they don't have research findings to inform the work, helping them develop the research to get to the insights that will then lead us to the concept.

We then work on developing the concept and handling execution, which for us usually means a video-led campaign. But, you know, a video-led campaign might be what comes out of our concepting, but not always. Sometimes that's not the right answer for the project at hand. But that's what we do best—focus on the video-led campaign world. If we're handling that, when it comes to execution, it's producing and directing those films and then helping to strategize the seeding and placement of the videos as well as develop any digital and social support the campaign requires. A lot of times we've been getting into more traditional TV and print because those media support the needs of the campaign. Primarily, most of our work lives online and most of it is in the video world. Above all, everything we do is storytelling-led. It's all storytelling.

Tuten: I like the way you said that, "all storytelling." A focus on the story really gives you a lot of options as you move forward as a company.

O'Hara Theisen: Yeah, it does. And like Jon said, we started with the shortest format. A lot of viral films are still in the thirty-second to one-minute range, especially the successful ones used for branding. We had two key reasons that got us most excited for starting a company, both of which focused on the end goal of short film. First, if you want to play in this space as a client, you need to be really brave. Why? Because if you're going to make a commercial and put it online, it's going to go nowhere fast.

We all know our time is precious, and especially online there's just so much competition. If a client wants to play in this space, they need to be ready to do something different than a traditional commercial hosted online. We felt that this is a missing expertise to some extent in the industry.

Second, for us as directors who are growing our reels, this company gave us the chance to work on breakthrough content and to do "brave work." There's that phrase again—brave work.

It's a win-win, but the thing is when you play a motto out like that, sticking to a niche, we started to realize that viral films, and even viral series, are not the type of the things that represent high budgets. Nor do they always represent, you know, a long-term kind of brand message for clients or a brand. What you're left with is the kind of projects that may focus on a launch, or may help to reinvigorate a brand that's lost energy. Viral projects are powerful setups for a brand launch or product launch, or to give energy to a brand that's sort of fallen by the wayside. A viral film might be just right for these kinds of situations. But, realistically, these opportunities, limited by such parameters, well, they don't exactly represent a lot of revenue potential in terms of growing a company.

Tuten: Jon mentioned that even in the brief period of time that you've been working in branded entertainment, working with your own agency, the industry has been changing a lot. In what ways has the industry changed?

Rosen: It's still changing a lot. It's changing all the time. We actually just hired an outside consultant to help us define that change. We're in the process of defining the changes and what they could mean for us. One thing is that in the sphere of branded entertainment, just in this brief time since we've entered the market, the phrase "branded entertainment" has become a buzzword. Now there are parties from many different sectors getting into this space and competing for business.

You have your traditional agencies that have opened up little entertainment divisions. You have the TV networks that are now going to the brands and saying, "Hey, we've got writers. We've got production companies. We can work with you to make a show where your product is fully integrated in the script."

Then you've got the people who are hobbyists who are making content, user-generated content, and making content first. They build a reputation on creativity and speed, and now brands are going to them and saying, "Hey, can you make something for us?"

And there's the media companies, who formerly wouldn't touch any sort of creative development or production, but now they're offering clients value-added packages where a client can buy X amount of media and the media companies include the offer to create programming and online videos as part of the deal.

God, there are so many forms of competition in this field now. There's even CAA[2] and the talent agencies.

O'Hara Theisen: They have a lot of brand relationships, too.

Rosen: Totally, so they started an agency within CAA that puts these deals together and puts writers on certain jobs and gets products placed in scripts. The landscape is changing rapidly and everyone is trying to figure out the magic solution.

O'Hara Theisen: And to Jon's point, the branded entertainment space has changed so much. From the standpoint of competition, there's just so many more hungry entities, powerful, large entities that are part of the old media model and the old advertising model. They're jumping at this opportunity. They're jumping from a hungry perspective. They need to figure out ways to stay alive, and they see this work as a way for them to stay relevant and current.

There is even competition on a consumer level, in the form of user-generated content. We're always hearing stats like "Forty-eight hours of video content is uploaded to YouTube every minute." We cheer when we hear those kinds of numbers, but then you think about the competition for attention that added content represents. We compete against every bit of content from every source for those precious moments and views a consumer can allocate to content. We need people to consume the content, pay attention to it, and even engage in a conversation around the content. The more content is in the space, the more difficult it becomes to garner that level of attention and engagement.

Because the market is more competitive, I would say the production budgets and the creative development budgets are all over the place. We've seen budgets start to grow and be a little healthier, but we also see that clients don't have a realistic view of what it takes to produce a strong piece. Much of it depends upon the sophistication level of the client. If we are working

---

[2] Creative Artists Agency, a leading talent and literary agency.

with a brand that's done a lot of work in the past and they're used to paying TV production budgets, they understand the importance of strategy and planning and creating from a holistic point of view. They understand why it's important to spend time developing a concept.

Likewise, they understand that it takes time to produce the work, and so they might come to the table with realistic budgets. But, at the same time, it goes without saying that there are some brands, in fact major brands—let's say, for instance, soft drink brands and other major players—which might come to you and say they want all of that effort, planning, research, concepting, production, and still, and they are willing to pay you a totally unrealistic budget like $15,000. At this stage, at least, there's no real agreed-upon numbers or standards in the industry. Everything is still new. Everyone is looking for opportunities, including the clients.

Tuten: When you consider the notion of branded entertainment—and so far, branded entertainment has been primarily video-led—do you see this content form going beyond video, and if so, where?

O'Hara Theisen: Well, one of the things we think about is the media context for video. For many people, when you say "video," they think of just online. You know, as Rosen has mentioned, we've started to get more into television development. We're exploring longer formats, including thirty-minute shows, hour-long shows, and feature films. Those are entertainment forms for film and video. But gaming always represents an enormous branding opportunity. With a game, the brand is able to create an experience within a game.

We always recommend to our clients that they video-seed campaigns. Even if the campaign goal doesn't include the desire for a video to go viral, we always recommend that the client set aside money for a video-seeding budget because of the competition that exists for the consumers' eyes. One thing we've started to see from seeding is the use of online games as the seed.

One group came to us recently and presented on their use of garnering views by working with online games, and especially Facebook games. Some of the games that are out there offer the gamer the opportunity to either pay real money to move forward to the next level or they're allowed to watch one of three, branded videos. The consumer picks between which of the three that they want to see, so there's a little choice involved. By watching the video, then they're allowed to continue playing the game at the next level without paying for the opportunity. In a sense, this is also branded entertainment. You could say it's taking a commercial and throwing it into a game, but I would say for those campaigns to be successful, people still have to be offering true entertainment and not just heavy selling of the product represented in the video.

Rosen: Yeah, in a sense, the concept [of branded entertainment] has really existed for a long time now. There are certain examples in the advertising industry's past such as BMW films, or even well before that, P&G soap operas. We kind of look at it as a philosophy. We don't believe that old-school advertising—where the point is selling something and selling with a hard sell "buy, buy now!" approach—works anymore. Consumers are too savvy for that approach to be meaningful and effective.

The way we view things, the best approach is to "gift" consumers something, and in this case, we are gifting them with entertainment. That's the philosophy of branded entertainment. Just as a digital shop with great technology gifts consumers with useful and cool tools and apps the consumers can use, we also gift people with something that's useful to them, in this case, entertainment. The marketing-savvy aspect is that the consumers welcome the gift because of its value and they take the gift with them. Since the gift is imbued with a brand, the brand has an opportunity to then build a relationship with the consumer.

Tuten: We hear so often now that marketing is content marketing, but the content has to offer value. I think the challenge for everyone now is "how can we give something of value?"

O'Hara Theisen: Yeah, definitely.

Tuten: You spoke earlier about video seeding. Will you share with me a little bit about what that means?

O'Hara Theisen: Video seeding is something where basically we take the video or the series of videos that we created and then we strategically ensure that the most people possible interact with the video. We set up a plan using online influencers to ensure the interaction. The online influencers might be a few influential bloggers. They might be people who have video social-sharing sites. If you consider seeding from the perspective of paid versus earned media,[3] seeding straddles both.

We prefer to utilize organic-earned media sites, but ultimately you may need to pay someone or pay groups of people to consider using your content. You

---

[3] Earned media refers to brand coverage, publicity, word-of-mouth communication, and buzz. Earned media is brand-related messaging; the brand does not pay for it.

can reach them directly or you might be paying "seeders" who have connections with online influencers. These seeders work with bloggers and web
sites. Some bloggers are very ethical and concerned about their own reputation and the value of their web site. They blog for their fans. They may say,
"I will not take any money. I only want content that's really cool because my
money is my reputation. And I make my money off ads on my site and other
things like that." Those people are picky bloggers, and the value to them is
to be able to highlight new, sensational content, rather than funding. Other
bloggers are more open to accepting some sort of payments to host and
promote your content.

The really good seeding groups have amazing connections. They have
influence, but at the same time, we've found that they also need to be
more than just about blogger outreach because that really only allows you
to get a certain amount of views. After that, you need to look into other
things to promote the content. This might be when an online game integra-
tion, possibly on Facebook, comes into play to help hit the kind of numbers
desired.

Tuten: What kind of numbers, views, are we talking about for these
campaigns?

Rosen: It might be five hundred thousand for one client, or a million for
another. The content only has value to the client if it is seen and experienced. You need serious amounts of viewers and people coming across the
content. That's why we activate the content with these other tools, like seeding, and other channels where people are coming in in large numbers.

Tuten: This kind of strategy, seeding in particular, is something that you
would propose to your client as you're working through their objectives for
the campaign?

O'Hara Theisen: No, not generally. Honestly, when we originally started
Lucky, the plan was to have our own seeding arm within a year and a half.
However, we found that clients are still at a place where they don't fully
understand seeding. Even though we feel it's hugely important and we spend
a lot of time trying to educate clients about why seeding is valuable and how
it works, they don't always set aside that money for seeding.

To influence a client to fund a seeding strategy requires a whole other level
of pitch. It means the client going back to their boss, or to the CMO [chief
marketing officer], or to the president, and educating that person who
controls the budget about the meaning of seeding. For us, we've chosen to
pull in seeding groups that we trust rather than develop our own seeding

capability. We're still working together with our seeding groups and our clients to develop sound seeding strategies.

We use different groups now, because one group of seeders may be perfect for one project, by virtue of the connections they have. Meanwhile someone else might be great for another project because of the nature of those connections. Of course, every seeding group will tell you they are right for any project. But we've had experiences with different groups where, regionally, some of them are better. Or, topic-wise, another seeder might be better. So, for instance, if you're trying to reach stay-at-home moms, you will know that there are certain kinds of blogs that make sense for this audience. You'll want to work with a seeder who has connections with those specific opinion leaders. Not all seeders will have the ability to pull off that level of specificity in the sphere of influence.

Tuten: Do you think that you'll end up adding the seeding arm to your agency at some point?

O'Hara Theisen: I don't know. Honestly, we really care about it a lot. From a strategic, smart business point of view, I think it makes a lot of sense. But at the same time, as we plan for our business model, seeding isn't entering our conversations as offering the best path for us in terms of sustaining our business. Right now, I would say we will probably pick partners rather than invest in this division in house. We'll pick the right partner for the right job all along the way. There's also a sense that the market is still too young for us to invest in as a core capability. But for the right company, the company who is really able to crack it, seeding represents a major business potential.

Tuten: You said that you both met in film school, but you had been working in advertising before that time. Is that right?

Rosen: Correct.

Tuten: So what led you to advertising as a profession? Did you grow up wanting to work in the industry?

Rosen: For me, one of my first jobs in high school was working at a sneaker store. I was able to witness the great Nike and Michael Jordan spots and their influence over people coming in, wanting to buy Michael Jordans. That was probably the first time that I actually got excited about advertising being a possible profession for me. But at that time, I really thought I was going to go into the music business. I did some internships at places like Epic Records, and Sony, and a few others, and quickly realized music wasn't the creative field I needed.

By this time, I had also started to dream about going to film school. My parents got divorced during this stage of my life and the financial concerns around the divorce made me worry that film was a little too unpredictable financially. With these influences—the music industry lacking the creative outlet I wanted, film seeming to lack stability, and my understanding of the need to make financially-sound choices—the answer came back to advertising. In advertising, I could combine all of these passions. I could combine my love for film, music, pop culture, and history.

O'Hara Theisen: And I guess for me, I started out more with a love for photography. In college, I worked as a photojournalist for four years. I really planned on doing photojournalism for my life's work. But then I took a couple of advertising classes my senior year of college. I was also taking some design courses just for fun. What happened is that this introduction to advertising and design introduced me to the world of art direction. It seemed cool and interesting.

I decided on a plan: "Oh, maybe I'll just go kind of go into the creative side of advertising for a few years, and then I'll have my darkroom downstairs and I can kind of play off both worlds." What really ended up happening was that I went to ad school. Both fields, photojournalism and art direction, really require a lot of work to hone your skills and practice your craft. You have to dedicate a lot of energy into building your abilities. Eventually, you become attractive enough for a company to take you on. For example, for photojournalism, I wanted to work for *National Geographic*. I knew I was going to have to continue to study to land a place at a magazine that could eventually be a stepping stone to *National Geographic*. I recognized that this was a long road ahead. I thought advertising would be a shorter road. I knew I would still need to work on my skills, but I saw a more direct path from ad school to an agency.

I went to ad school for two years, and all the while I was slowly becoming more and more passionate about advertising. Then five or six years went by and I realized I hadn't touched my camera literally in five years. That was a wake-up call for me. So I enrolled in some documentary film courses at Duke, down in North Carolina, and that's what sort of sparked my return to pictures. Except then the pictures were motion pictures.

Tuten: Does it seem surreal now to realize—like do you ever just think during the day, "Wow. We have our own agency."? You're both very young to already be at this stage.

Rosen: Yeah, it's been definitely a roller coaster. I don't think even if someone told us ahead of time everything that was going to happen, everything that was before us, we'd have believed it was possible. I don't know someone could get what it means to do this until you actually experience it all.

A lot of our time has been in building and managing the agency. We are doing things now that when we worked in traditional agencies, we were always protected by the large resources available at those agencies. When we worked in large shops, we could just be "creatives." Now, Ryan and I are the product of our own agency. If we're not creating, we're not growing our business. That's a hard pill to swallow at times. It means every minute, every task we take on, there's the understanding that we're playing with resources that we need to succeed.

At a large agency, you just don't have that sense of accountability about day-to-day life. We have to be resource-savvy. At the same time, being a small company, we don't always have enough manpower to do all the jobs that we need to do to get the work done. And then the company isn't moving forward. Sometimes you get stuck chasing your tail.

O'Hara Theisen: We definitely have moments. When we moved into our new office a year ago, it was a pretty incredible feeling. It still feels great to go to work. It feels different to come to work here, at our place, than it did to go and make a good salary or a day rate somewhere else. Working and earning felt good, but now our life is really about our work. Especially when you compare our life now to time spent as a freelancer. When you are free-lancing—at least in New York—you're really mostly doing the work to make enough money to live, or enough money to live a good life. As a freelancer, you are rarely able to produce the work you develop.

To Rosen's point, it is surreal to look back and know that we made something happen. We have a vision and we have seen that vision come to life. At the same time, our roles can be overwhelming from the day-to-day management and operational side of things. I don't want to label it "the good and the bad," but there is definitely an element of the good and the challenging.

Rosen: With that being said, I don't think we could go back and work for someone again.

Tuten: Is that because of the experience of being in charge, and having the authority to choose your priorities, or because of the burnout you mentioned at the start of our interview?

Rosen: It's probably a little combination of those two. I think we both have other interests outside of advertising. And we may pursue those down the road. This agency is our shot at doing work our way. The industry has done things a certain way for a long time. There's a risk of getting sucked into the vortex of the old ways of doing things. This is a constant challenge for us. We remind ourselves, "Okay, we want to do it differently. We want to do it our way." And, working with clients who've done it the old way, we have to remind ourselves and educate them. I think where we are right now is a good place to be. I know, too, that we are not the only shop trying to figure out how to do things differently. A lot of other shops are trying to figure this out as well.

Tuten: What's a typical day like for the two of you, especially given that you play creative roles and also roles as managers and leaders?

Rosen: Well, when we first get into the office, we get a really big, iced latte and I get an egg sandwich. O'Hara Theisen does more healthy choices every once in a while [laughter].

O'Hara Theisen: I try to do oatmeal, yeah. We usually get in anywhere from like nine-thirty to ten, and then kind of see what e-mails have come through. I actually check e-mails when I get up at eight. I check e-mails while I am getting ready so I know what's happening or if something came up we need to deal with the moment we enter the office. Then we are in meetings, either in person or on the phone, and trying to set up new business opportunities.

At any given time, we'll have one or two projects actively in progress, so each day there'll be time set aside during the day to dive into those. This usually means leaving the office for a while to go and get something accomplished. This could be anything. It might be casting later in the day, and we may have people come into the agency or we may be going to a casting agency and picking out people for an upcoming video we will be shooting. It's fun. We have a mix anywhere from strategy to conceptual development to projects that are in preproduction. We manage post-production right on site, so we might have another project that's in the editing process. It keeps our day-to-day life really interesting because there are different projects in different stages of the production time line. Our brains need to be able to shift around a lot and yet still be focused when it's on any given activity.

Rosen: We have to work at being efficient in the creative development process. When you are a full-time writer on something, you really have a lot more time. Back in the day, we used to complain that the planners would have so much time on the brief and then the creatives would only get a week to work from the brief. Looking back, that seems like so much time dedicated to individual tasks in the creative process. Now owning our own company, we have to be more efficient than that because of all the other duties that we're working on day-to-day. And we are doing that successfully.

We can pound out really good work in a shorter amount of time, so that's definitely different.

Tuten: Do you have any rituals that are important to how you gear up for working creatively?

Rosen: I personally work better outside of the office when I work creatively. Ryan may differ. I work better at a café or a park or something like that. It just depends on the assignment. But for me to get out of the work environment, it really frees me up creatively. When I'm in the work mode, I don't want to be distracted by everything else, like e-mails and so on. For me, that's best. But for O'Hara Theisen, I think it's different.

O'Hara Theisen: Everyone has to find their own best way of working. I like being here at the office. I don't know why that is. But you start to figure out, like Jon was saying, the way your brain works best. And for me, maybe it's just because there might be other things, like I feel I need to be ready to jump back on, but that's sort of the way I work. And then I would say on the production side, I like to be super, super, super prepared, so I put a lot of time into preproduction, and that way I feel a lot more relaxed on the shoot day. This extra focus lets me feel like I can focus on the directing side of things. There are so many logistics that go into directing and shooting.

Meanwhile, I might also be dealing with the clients, be it an agency partner or brand manager on the set. As a smaller production company, we're not working with a one- or two-million-dollar TV budget. We might be directing, and then called away to manage clients during the shoot. That's why we like always have all our ducks in a row so the shoot goes as seamlessly well as possible.

Tuten: How big is your staff now?

O'Hara Theisen: We're at six people, six staff members.

Tuten: Do you have to use freelancers, too? Or do the six of you manage all those roles?

O'Hara Theisen: You know, that's a great question. When creative development picks up, we'll bring on other creative teams. We've brought on media planners, strategic planners, and even some digital media specialists when the right project called for it. For us, our success is really important because that's all we really have as a smaller company. Every client opportunity that we have has to go really, really well because it is such a small world and referrals are huge. We always try to overdeliver and always impress. Sometimes that might mean we are not getting to hold on to the amount of revenue that we want because we chose to forgo that to build a relationship.

As far as the production side goes, the model works the same way. But I would say it's more natural in the production world to call in teams by the project because a lot of times a production company might only be a few executive producers, like a business manager, and, you know, that can be an entire production company. And meanwhile, they might have one shoot that's got two hundred people on it.

O'Hara Theisen: We're that same way. Like we definitely will go from let's say four of us who are focusing on one production to—when a shoot happens, we've had all the way up to like seventy people working for us.

Production is so fast. You might get a call on a Tuesday and then on a Friday or a Saturday, you're shooting something and there's twenty-five people standing around you, working together, and somehow, you know, it's like this dance that gets pulled off.

Tuten: I read an article several years back about Mick Jagger, and it was talking about how when the Rolling Stones are on the road, that's what their business is like. They go from five people and a small recording staff to two hundred–plus people to create the show.

O'Hara Theisen: Yeah, exactly. I think for any kind of big production you need to be able to expand. Another thing we're always doing is we're always meeting with crew, cinematographers, and great producers here in New York. We do this because two things happen. One is that people will be booked, so when your job comes along, even though you always love working with person A, they're booked on something else so you need to have a pool of people you can turn to. Second is that people move up the ladder, you know? They might end up becoming too expensive for you for certain projects, so you've got to always be out there meeting new people. In some ways this is like advertising, but in some ways not like advertising. The production side of things has a lot more trust in it.

As a production company owner, you need to be able to put a lot of trust in other people's eyes. With an agency, sure, you might hire a group to help you with concepting or things like that and they might not nail the work. Then in the end it's up to you to pull the work through. But with production, it's usually a lot of money going into one or two days and there's so many things that can go wrong, from the weather to the actors to accidents like an electrical fire on set. We've even been robbed during a shoot.

O'Hara Theisen: You really are putting a lot of trust and a lot of money into people's hands that you may know from referrals and networking. It works because this is a small, trusting kind of community.

Tuten: Do you have a favorite campaign, one that has special meaning to the two of you that you've produced at Lucky?

Rosen: The Teach for America TV pilot that we're about to sell is a special one for us. It's actually not on our web site, but we could send you a link to take you further.

Tuten: That would be great.

Rosen: That was a project that we worked on for a year, and we pretty much didn't make any money on it. Obviously, we have high hopes for it to sell to networks. Basically, Teach for America came to us. Actually, I think it pitted the work against two other production companies. Our bid was one of the highest, but still really low in the grand scheme of things. Teach for America liked our treatment the best. From that day on, we worked for a year developing this project.

Basically it's a documentary-style reality show where we take a master teacher into an inner-city classroom where a struggling teacher has lost control of the classroom. The struggling teacher is overwhelmed, and the master teacher helps transform the struggling teacher, and thus transforms the classroom. If this kind of work occurred on a large scale, the implication is that in the end, the educational system could be transformed. To work on a project that is as lofty as that is in terms of potential impact in the world, well it's a really awesome project to be part of.

Tuten: That sounds like reality television for good instead of evil.

Both: Yes.

O'Hara Theisen: Yeah, Jon has mentioned we're just starting the selling process. Even in our preliminary talks with people, with network executives, that's the challenge. The tendency is for network executives to want to add cheap drama to it.

We are trying to approach the project from a documentary sensibility. We want to let the reality of the situation tell the story. In reality television, all the hours the world has spent watching *Real Housewives* and things like that, has made reality television a little cookie-cutter. That's the reality mindset of television audiences now. That's what we're up against right now, trying to find the right network, the one that will believe in the format.

Tuten: That's a challenge.

O'Hara Theisen: Definitely.

Tuten: This brings me to a question related to challenges. Imagine that you have a magic, fairy wand and if you wave it, you can change one thing about the industry that you hate. What would you change?

Rosen: I would change advertising.

Tuten: In what way?

Rosen: I would get rid of it. [Laughter.]

I mean, we're seeing, not only in branded entertainment, but even in these sorts of social events and social projects, the industry is changing a lot. Here I am, an old advertising guy. I can't stand watching commercials. I fast-forward everything on the DVR. People have a choice now whether to watch, whether to consume advertising or not. For me, if all advertising were removed, I wouldn't miss it.

But I guess you're asking this question from the perspective of someone who makes advertising, what I would do to change it. Actually, this is a bigger philosophical question. I'm lucky that I can share how we're approaching the industry and where Lucky is going because it represents what we believe in for the industry.

I think if we could make things first that would represent a positive change. A Hollywood production company comes up with the idea of the script. They develop the script concept before they find funding, and before they make the work. In the advertising world, we have to wait for those opportunities to show up on our lap from our clients, or in our case half the time, from other agencies. With that waiting, we're missing so many other opportunities. It feels like in our world we should be creating those opportunities. One of the ways moving forward that we'd love to explore is to actually make the work, develop the work first, and then find clients to attach to the work later. Obviously, right now, this approach is definitely a bit cost-prohibitive. But when we can shift to that approach, to that model completely, that's when I'll be fully happy in the industry.

Tuten: Then you'll be an artist.

Rosen: That's funny that you should say that. Yes, that's been my mantra for the last eight months. If I could be an artist in everything I do, whether it's my bank account, whether it's how I plan my vacations, I would be a very happy boy.

Tuten: What about you, Ryan?

O'Hara Theisen: I don't know. As Jon was saying everything, I was trying to think about it. Geez, what would I change about advertising? I don't know. I think I'm stumped on that a little bit. Sometimes I feel the industry doesn't accept new ideas quickly enough. There's a frustration—you know, this is from a smaller company so you have to consider who we compete against: large agencies that are part of holding companies.

Tuten: Right.

O'Hara Theisen: Those holding companies really manage a lot of the largest relationships with brands, and for us, those represent the opportunities for us to do great work because there's a better budget there to support projects. Not that money always means good ideas, but money does mean resources to help your idea grow and have the best kind of chance in the beginning.

For me, I think there's a frustration that as much as the world is changing from a media and a technology point of view, and advertising supposedly could lead changes, communicating is very slow to change because of these archaic models. I wish we could tear that all down and work on a level where things are a lot more fluid and reactive. I think we would be seeing a lot more interesting work that way. Instead, there are a lot of people at the top levels who are protecting their jobs, and so they slow the progress of new models down.

Tuten: At least to the extent that you control your agency and your decisions, you've embraced what you want form the industry at Lucky.

O'Hara Theisen: Yeah. I think that's a major, major reason why we did it. I mean, it's so funny because, you know, in a lot of ways things have not changed much at all. We get called in for consulting jobs and we're in those environments. Sometimes you're totally impressed and you have great surprises as to cool, innovative things going on at agencies, but I would say for the most part, a lot of times you're kind of like, "Really? This is what you're having us do? Like, you know, this seems like the same exact kind of job we would have done four years ago." And then you're promising the client that this is going to be effective, and I know you really want it to be, but why aren't you just opening up to a whole other way to look at this?

Tuten: I know you both are running short on time today and will need to go. But before we wrap, I'm curious, how did you guys come up with the name "Lucky"?

Rosen: It started with the May meeting we had three years ago. This was when I came back from Australia. Ryan said yes to starting a company, and that night I went to a concert alone. The concert was The Verve, and they have this song called "Lucky Man." I was thinking how we're really lucky to be able to move out of the industry and start a company that would combine our conceptual passion with our new love of filmmaking.

It's funny because I wasn't really that serious about it, but I just wanted to throw it at Ryan. I was like, "Oh, what do you think of this name, Lucky?"

He's like, "That's it."

I'm like, "Give it some time. Think about it." It was sort of like what happened when I said, "Do you want to start a company?" I wasn't prepared to commit to the name, and Ryan was ready right away. We checked out the uses of the name. Lucky Man, Lucky Brand jeans, and then when we Googled "lucky"—five hundred Chinese restaurants show up.

Tuten: [Laughter.]

Rosen: But ultimately lucky is a mantra in a way. We're happy-go-lucky kind of guys to begin with.

O'Hara Theisen: And it's also got a mischievous kind of confidence to it. And that's something that we always try to keep alive here, whether it's parties on April Fools' Day and we're having a little bit of fun, whatever we're doing. We're kind of sticking to this personality that we agreed was ours from the beginning. There's something we want to be and achieve here, something different than the old, stodgy model of the advertising industry, which seems afraid or unwilling to change. Lucky still feels like the right name, you know?

Tuten: It fits perfectly with the mission of entertainment.

O'Hara Theisen: Yeah, definitely. It fit really, really well with viral in the beginning, you know?

Tuten: Because you're lucky if it launches, lucky if it spreads?

O'Hara Theisen: Yeah, there is at least a little bit of luck in every project. You can put all the strategy and seeding and do it, but you need just a little good luck as well.

Tuten: Definitely. Any last thoughts from the two of you?

Rosen: No. If you want to throw out one last question?

Tuten: What do you still dream of accomplishing?

Rosen: Definitely making a feature film, for sure.

O'Hara Theisen: I agree. For me, it might actually be a documentary film, but feature-length.

Tuten: And would it be branded?

Rosen: I'm not sure. We'll find out.

Tuten: If the opportunity presents itself?

O'Hara Theisen: Yeah, if the opportunity's there. I mean, obviously, we don't think advertising's gross, considering we're pretty passionate about it from our roots. I think if the right brand allows you to tell the pure story you want to tell, then for sure, we'd brand the film. But, there is sort of marriage that needs to come together for that kind of relationship to work well, as we know.

Rosen: Lucky's based off of this Madison Avenue-meets-Hollywood sort of love affair. They need each other pretty badly, so hopefully, our feature films and documentaries will be right in the middle of all that.

John Zhao

Independent Filmmaker

John Zhao is a Korean/Chinese–American independent filmmaker. Born in China, he spent his childhood with his grandfather, an acclaimed calligrapher who sparked John's everlasting love for art and poetry. John went to the cinema for the first time in Germany; he was a young boy, but decided that day he'd start making films.

While growing up in America, John spent this time riding skateboards and taking heavy interest in scuba diving and studying the behavior of sharks. He studied marine biology before transferring to Virginia Commonwealth University (VCU) for its esteemed creative advertising program. During this time, he frequently visited China to teach and travel.

John's first ad stint was an internship at Wieden+Kennedy the year before graduating. At age 23, during his first year in New York City, he successfully wrote, produced, and directed his first feature, Days Gone By, *with rogue tactics and few resources. (Learn more about the film at www.johnxzhao.com.) John is currently developing several more features while freelancing in advertising and film production projects in New York City.*

Tracy Tuten: How did you get started? Did you grow up knowing you'd work in advertising?

John Zhao: Well, indirectly. I knew that I wanted to be a filmmaker since I was a kid. It was later that I realized I could take skills I gained from being a filmmaker and apply it to projects in ad agencies as well. Advertising could provide a steady career for me that was also related to my love of film. I was living in Germany, actually, when I realized I loved film. I was born and raised in China and then I went to Germany as a young boy. That's when I went to my first movie theater. Ever since then—I think I was seven years old—I just wanted to make films. And I think I wrote my first feature film when I was like twelve or something. It was a really terrible horror movie. I just found it in my basement the other day. But, if you look back into my childhood, there's evidence that this is what I wanted to do for the rest of my life.

Now, advertising is something I knew nothing about until I got to college. I didn't want to go to film school because my favorite filmmakers never went to film school. They just picked up a camera and made their first films. I figured film school was expensive. If I had the money to do that, then I would just make my own film, too. I also seriously considered spending my college years as an English and history major because literature and the humanities were important to me as a storyteller, but I realized I could do a ton of that on my own as well. When I saw that the strength of VCU's communication program was in their creative advertising courses, that's when I realized that if I wanted to make films, I would also have to be able to advertise them, to market them, so that's what made me choose advertising initially.

I'm the only child in my family, so it also convinced my folks that I wasn't just going to spend four years learning how to "tell stories," you know? Even though that's all I wanted to do with my life. They were more supportive knowing I'd be able to get a job out of school. Also, I knew I wasn't the best businessman. I knew I had ideas, but film is a pricey venture and I had no clue how I'd deal with getting my creative work into the marketplace. So I felt like an ad agency would be a fast-paced place to start and learn. Surprisingly, the creative advertising program opened up my mind a lot. It wasn't so much about making ads or selling something, but more about learning how to be specific with your message, collaborate with strangers, and be a faster thinker. Everyone in the program became very close with each other. So I started out with these two separate things, but they turned out going hand in hand. Yeah, it was a fun couple of years.

When I think of film, this thing I was after since I was a child, I was always unsure how or what I'd do to support it. Even full-time filmmakers do other things to make a living. They direct commercials, write screenplays, wait tables, they do whatever it takes because being able to make feature films isn't a career—it's a privilege, and your so-called career can end any day. So for me, having found and extracted the hard skills in something I love to do and being able to apply it to another part of society is a very lucky thing I've been able to do between films.

Tuten: How did this unfold from the time you were in college?

Zhao: I interned while finishing my undergrad degree. After I graduated, I did some freelancing. Soon I decided to make my first feature film and moved to New York. While I was editing the film and telling people about it, it helped me find a full-time position in a new branded entertainment company. So it's been a kind of straddle between advertising and filmmaking, then discovering a place where I can I juggle the two.

Tuten: Most people starting out in the field would target a traditional agency and work with a mix of media. You've targeted film and especially branded entertainment early on. Did you eschew traditional agencies?

Zhao: I was really enjoying working in a traditional agency, and I loved working with the partners that I had. But during that time, I wanted to get out of the office and onto a film set. Even prior to graduation, I was spending my free time on film shoots so I missed the physicality of that a lot. I felt like if I could find people who would let me apply my conceptual skills in advertising to film production, I would be able to create a more distinct line of work, if that makes any sense.

Tuten: You started with film on your own. You did your own writing, filming, editing?

Zhao: Yeah, I mean, that's the way you *should* start these days. It's easy to get someone else to do the dirty work, but as a first-time director, you should know what it feels like produce, to write, to edit, to cook meals for your cast and crew. The technology these days really allows you to do a lot and very quickly. Almost as fast as you can think of something. While I was still in Richmond, going to school, I'd spend as much time working in plays, being a production assistant on commercials, music videos, anything really. Even in a small town I was able to do that and it taught me a lot of stuff.

Then by the time I was able to have some time and mostly have the courage to make my first feature, I thought the best thing to do would be to do everything—that included writing, producing, shooting film, editing, directing. I felt like, "Okay, the technology is available for me to do it all." It would [also] obviously save a lot of money.

And the third point, and probably the most important, is that I would be able to learn everything and figure out what aspect am I good at and what aspect of filmmaking I am not good at. I knew that by handling each step of the film, it would be fun, but I would also learn firsthand what I wish I had more help on. I knew that would inform my work on the next film. I would develop a new model of working. I'll know where I should reach out for more help and so on. That was my philosophy when I started making my first feature.

Tuten: Beyond that, your work is focused on film whether you are making feature films, shorts, or commercials. Are there other synergies between your work in advertising and your film making?

Zhao: VCU has a great advertising program. It really hits the most important aspects of the work. You're working with different partners, and you learn how to work with people and how to find a point where the team can agree on the creative direction of the concept. Coming out of that program, I knew how to come up with ideas very quickly and work under deadlines—you know, pulling all-nighters. All the things that I learned in advertising school have also taught me how to be a good director. These are the same key qualities needed to direct film.

I wasn't aware of it at the time, but it turns out that film directing is very similar. You're working with different actors, and each actor is a different person. You have to know how to talk to each actor a different way. And you have to be aware that they're coming from a different background. And you have to be receptive to any ideas that they come up with because filmmaking is a collaboration. It's not about writing a script and then me telling people what I want them to do. That never makes a good film.

You should always be collaborative, receptive—and it's a high-stress job. You know, it's like every day you have so many hours of daylight, for example, to shoot a certain scene and you have to get all of it done and also be aware that there are going to be technical issues that fall in your way. I hope that answers your question.

Tuten: You speak passionately about the work, about each aspect. Things that others might consider just another chore on the list of things that have to happen in creating the work.

Zhao: I see all the steps in creating something from writing to shooting to editing, as all one motion, in both advertising and filmmaking. Sure, we need to designate jobs to organize the machine, but I really get disappointed when someone doesn't go the extra mile because it's not part of their job description. It's very common for me to have to rewrite an entire scene while shooting, or begin producing while writing, so it's all part of the same motion for me.

For me, though, in making my feature film, I had some challenges in terms of getting everything done in a way that was consistent with my vision. Typically, it's useful to have more than one camera running on a scene, but I couldn't do that because I simply didn't have the resources to hire another cinematographer. These limitations got in the way of my directing at times, because I was playing other roles.

Sometimes during the process, I felt like there was a glass wall every time I had a camera in my hands. I felt like there was a glass wall blocking my relationship between me and the actors because I was more invested in the technicalities or the framing or how things looked and how things would cut together in the end, and the colors and, you know, very technical things. For me, it was a tug of war between the left brain and the right brain, which is working with actors, getting the best performances, and being able to tell the story in a meaningful way. The next time I work on a feature film, I would definitely love to have a cinematographer and a producing partner to help me organize the whole shoot a little better.

Tuten: Was it a detriment that you didn't go to film school? How do you learn what aspects should be represented in film if you didn't go to film school to learn the process?

Zhao: I have a lot of film school friends and I think it's a great place to learn technical things. It's a great place to meet like-minded people, but I think it's super important for filmmakers to be inspired outside of film. And I think that I get a lot of my ideas and inspiration from life. I get better ideas from walking around Brooklyn or just traveling than if I were to sit down at my computer and watch a ton of movies. I think talking to people and being connected with people is super important.

And I want to make a film school if I wind up making enough films and having enough to teach from those experiences—this is going to sound weird—but I want to make a film school where we don't even watch any films during the time we're at the film school. You're going to learn, you're going to study literature, you're going to study music, and you're going to be inspired by other things, and then in the end, you're going to learn how to make a film by making a film. I don't think it's an academic thing. It's more of a physical process. And that goes with advertising, too. I don't really want to keep my head too high in the sky ever.

One scary thing I realize is that the more comfortable or secure I feel in my life, I tend to be less creative. Like during the whole time prior to making my film, I was in university or I was interning or freelancing at a large agency. You live pretty comfortably in an agency. Offices are hip, you get a desk, you get to travel. I was eating well and everything. And then I dumped all of my savings, which when you start out really isn't much at all, into making a film. But suddenly, I felt very creative because I had to find ways around those financial difficulties in creative ways. I couldn't throw money at problems. It was very physical because I had to run all over the place to find things. It was great to be able to work with very creative, successful people at an ad agency, but it was also very refreshing to be like a street-level creative where I was talking to people at diners, bowling alleys, or what-have-you to see if I could film there or get their stories.

I even cast some people in my film who weren't actors. Like if one location was a pharmacy, I would actually cast a pharmacist there and learn about their life and know where they came from and things like that. I think that's super important to stay connected with people outside of your industry because in the end, you are in the business of connecting with people. Being in that twentieth-story corner office is actually detrimental to creativity. I would rather come up with my best ideas in a diner at three in the morning while I'm talking to my waiter or something like that. I feel more connected to people and I guess I'll end at that. That's a big thing for me, to keep my life polarized where I can work in an office space and work with bigger budgets but also never get my head too high in the sky.

Tuten: Would you say that's the philosophy that guides your work?

Zhao: Yes, that's my philosophy for the rest of my life. And also make films and maybe start a film school and continue to work in advertising because I think it's fun and it's great practice, especially in branded entertainment. It's great practice for me as a filmmaker.

Tuten: Overall are you happy with how the film turned out? Do you feel that it met its purpose in your life?

Zhao: Yeah, definitely. I think the first feature someone produces, it's something you can't expect too much out of. You just have to do it all on your own, stay focused on telling the story you want to tell and get it out there and then get some feedback. Then you grow. The experience feeds future work. I don't think a person really becomes "a filmmaker" until the second feature, or maybe even the third.

It's weird because I didn't expect this film to really go anywhere. I knew I liked it, but I knew this year's Sundance alone had like five thousand film submissions, which is crazy. Eight hundred films would get submitted back in the nineties. So when I made my first feature, I [thought], "Wow, this will just get lost in the clutter. Like this is kind of my self-taught film-school and that's all it will be." But it's getting into festivals, and I couldn't ask for more, so at the same time, I just don't know what to expect because I just wasn't prepared for it. Basically, I've screened it in New York a couple of times and it went over well with the audiences, so I'm just more curious now to see what will happen at the festival in London. Since it's an international festival, I'm curious [about] what a more international audience is going to think of it.

I thought making the film was the hardest part. I'm realizing this stuff is the part where I actually need the most help, the most people involved. Right now I don't have that. I don't have a team that's behind this film. I'm just flying solo. So, really, I'm just doing everything I can. It's a learning process.

My advertising skills come in handy. I'm able to put together press kits for example—just knowing how to design a good press kit and website pretty standard for film makers. And things like that, how to present the film. What I'm missing with this film is what a strategic or seeding expert would do at an agency. They'd organize and time the campaign release. Like I would organize and time festivals and distribution.

Tuten: How did you fund the work?

Zhao: It wasn't anything formal. I self-funded it by saving up money from my day job and I took the sacrifice by being basically homeless and living out of a suitcase for a while, couch-surfing, and pouring all my resources into the film.

Tuten: How do you stay current in the roles you play—whether it's writing or directing or filming?

Zhao: That's a good question. You know how I said I was trying to figure out what I'm good at and what roles I like taking on the most during my first film? For filmmakers now, especially when you consider how easy it is to pick up a camera and go out and shoot a film, there's just no excuse to not practice and do your homework. You can see this truth every day online with the films posted on YouTube and the prevalence of UGC [user-generated content] in ad campaigns. The technological resources are there for almost anyone with the talent to jump in and create film work, video work.

Actually, I am really in the mood to do a couple of short films, just very quickly. I'm thinking about, starting this fall, doing some short films with friends and actor friends that I've made up here, and that will keep me in good practice while I finish writing the feature scripts. I really want to package the scripts this time with the proper business plan, and pitch it and get some financing behind the production. It's not really about money, it's just that the stories—they require more resources for me to actually realize them the way I want, so I might be living out of a car again, but either way it's going to require more money on the production side.

Tuten: As you do this film work, will you be able to maintain your advertising career, too? Will you have to sacrifice it for the feature filmmaking?

Zhao: When I was still in school, my first experience at a larger agency was at Wieden. That was in Portland, Oregon. I left and came to New York specifically because I wanted to take the risk of making a feature film. I felt that New York was the place to try. Whether I failed or succeeded at it, I wanted to take the risk now. Later on in life there will come a time when I really need to make a living. I needed to try this path before the day that I really have to worry about earning money to live.

So during that time, actually, when I first came to New York, I wasn't working in advertising. I was just doing random, odd jobs. Sometimes they'd be freelance, but sometimes something completely different. When I was shooting, in 2010, I had the most jobs that I've ever had in one year compared to the rest of my life. Some of it involved freelance work that I was getting from recruiters where I was lucky enough I could work from home and schedule things around the work. That was during preproduction when I was writing. But for the most part, it was scrappy. I was meeting a bartender down the street that would let me take a gig at the bar for like two or three weeks, and they would be night shifts so that during the daytime I had time to shoot. And then I would find my next thing.

Somehow, day by day, week by week, I was able to make it work. Eventually there was a three-month period, where I needed to just focus on the film, and I was able to get by. Living on people's couches obviously saves you a lot of money.

I don't want to come off like I'm complaining. I was really blessed. The time I'm describing, it was the most crazy, intense, fun year of my life. I would do it again in a heartbeat.

But to really answer your question, I think there are a lot of students that wind up in ad schools, on the creative side, who want to be a copywriter or art director as their day job and then paint, write novels, or make music at night. The honest truth, it's not impossible, but it's very difficult. I really don't know any filmmakers who had a lifelong career as a copywriter, for example. But I think it's possible to switch back and forth between both. There's no right or wrong, but for me, I thought that before I could help other agencies and brands have something to say creatively, I needed to do something to see if I had something to say personally. Staying focused on one thing at a time helped me try different things in a short amount of time rather than trying to be everything at once.

Tuten: Now that the film is out and you are writing the next two scripts, you are back in advertising full-time. But still working with video.

Zhao: Yeah, definitely. I'm really blessed to have chosen advertising and film as two interests that I have. I feel like the more I work and the more I'm growing up, the more I feel like they go hand in hand, just because what I know from one thing definitely has helped the other. These days, I really love watching some of my favorite filmmakers who started out before this whole branded entertainment thing, take on their short films and other projects, funded by brands, and still make something that's uniquely them. There's definitely more of a dance going on between the two worlds.

In an artistic sense, whether film or advertising, it's all about finding a distinct voice. It doesn't matter whether it's for a brand or simply for a story. The key is to find something that's very, very distinct, very unique, that hasn't been said before, and that resonates with an audience.

But then you have to pitch it. Pitching a film is just like pitching a campaign to the clients. You're pitching a film to the actors, and the crew, and your producers. It's a very similar mindset. In the pitching, you're testing out whether the idea works. What doesn't work? Who do you want to work with? You're getting feedback. And then once you find what you're looking for, then you have to produce it. Once you've finished creating the work, you know, it's still not the end of the story. Then you have to see if the idea resonates with the audience.

Tuten: Usually in advertising, there's a leap of faith at that stage, especially if there hasn't been testing. But you know there will be media support to get the story in front of the audience. Is that the same or different for film?

Zhao: I think the biggest lesson I learned in making this film was that once you finish making the film, that's only half the battle. You have to market it. You have to put it through festivals. You have to find an audience. Those things can take more money and time than making the film! I didn't know that before I made *Days Gone By*. I thought eighty percent of the battle was just getting the thing done. In a way, advertising is the same. You have to have a strategy as to how to time the release of certain pieces of your campaign. Just like a film, you have to do that, too. You have to build a world around this story that you're telling and time it in a very efficient way and reach an audience.

Tuten: In what other ways is your film work similar to your day job in advertising?

Zhao: The job I have now is with a relatively new company totally dedicated to branded film work. Obviously all of us began in more traditional agencies, but we are all film lovers and we see how film can tell a brand's story. The agency is quite small. With such a small group of us, we all have to wear many, many hats in order to get our work done. There, my main focus is writing. Most of my time is writing scripts. With every project that I've done, the work always starts out with writing, but then depending on what the project is and how it goes, I'm always branching off into various roles, especially during execution.

Primarily we are creating videos that are intended to be viral. Sometimes we will produce a series of viral videos in a short time. Especially in those cases we really have to split up the work in terms of directing them. Sometimes we have two different shoots in one day, and there's just not enough people to hold down all those shoots. I'm finding myself producing a music video here, directing a viral there. Sometimes I'm editing them. It's definitely a good balance between my advertising and filmmaking skills, and keeps my skills honed across the work. Still, I'd say I spend most of the time writing and putting together pitches—everything that happens with a traditional ad campaign up until the point of execution—and then I switch into my filmmaker mode.

Tuten: Do you think this will be the focus of your career in advertising? Branded entertainment? Or do you think you'll return to a traditional agency now that you've figured out the process for film and how it can co-exist with your career?

Zhao: Branded entertainment, or being able to take my film production knowledge and apply it to ad gigs, came at a great time for me. After I finished my first film, I was a bit hesitant about whether a traditional ad agency would even ever hire me again! I finished undergrad and didn't have a huge portfolio like some of these bigger portfolio grad school guys. I was just beginning to work at agencies when I left to make a film. Then with that, it's like—wow, two years went by working on that film. Some might disagree, but I don't know if a feature film shows well in a traditional portfolio for agency work. It's kind of a weird thing to stick in a book.

So as I wrapped up the film, I was wondering what my next step [would] be. And then I landed this opportunity and it seemed to encapsulate both things that I live for. It's just the right place for me to be, especially now.

This is an important lesson for people getting started in their careers: to be open to feeding your passion and not just locking yourself into a set career path because that's the path that is most common or most understood. I feel like my generation should be open to more unusual paths and not just lock themselves in one career mode. They should be receptive to all these other things that are connecting with the ad industry.

There are so many roles to be played in branding. There are so many opportunities. I'm even reluctant to use the word "career" anymore. I feel like people my age especially are going to have several careers throughout their lives and maybe two or three careers at the same time. The choices should be more about going where you feel like you can be most useful and most talented and a place where you can grow and really give the world as much as you can rather than just pigeonholing yourself into something that the industry has said is the right path and being stuck in there forever. I think it's good to explore.

Tuten: Would you say that branded entertainment is more advertising or more about film?

Zhao: If I had to give a percentage, it's probably like a seventy percent to thirty percent ratio, advertising versus film. The thing is branded entertainment does begin with the same motives, the same goals, the same ideals as traditional advertising. But the model is about finding a new way to reach an audience. We know as an industry that traditional modes of communication are not as effective as they once were, whether that's because of the form, or the fragmentation in media, or whatever.

I try to be a good audience. That's how I inform my work. I try to watch what's out there. I try to enjoy films, and art, and commercials, and everything as much as anyone else would. Today I would rather watch a really fun, little, short film or a music video on YouTube than sit in front of the television screen and watch a TV spot. When someone passes me a viral video that's hilarious, or it moves me in some way, or it surprises me, that leaves a much bigger impact in my mind than say a print ad these days.

I've grown up around all the other traditional media and to my way of thinking, they have become just background noise for me. I know that my interpretation is the same as others in the market. I represent the audience in many cases and if I recognize advertising as background noise, others are, too. And having branded entertainment seems capable of breaking through those barriers a little more effectively. From the perspective of the brand, you're able to tell stories in a way that you weren't able to before.

I'll give you an extreme example. My film's sound designer is French and he was nice enough to let me crash with him at the Cannes Film Festival last year. I had a brief chat with one of the Oscar-winning producers of *The Cove*—this really moving documentary about the murdering of dolphins by fishermen. Save it for a sunny day, it's pretty depressing.

But anyways, getting back to the point. The producer is an avid scuba diver and he went on to direct a 30-minute documentary called *The Deepest Dive* about the bathyscaphe *Trieste* that dove to the deepest known part of the Earth's oceans in 1960. During this dive, Rolex attached one of their prototype watches to the outside, and it emerged and survived. It was that durable. So naturally to make this film, it was supported by Rolex and produced by JWT [J. Walter Thompson], who does a lot of work with them and has their own production house, JW2. Even though the film is about this historic event—and I think it wound up broadcasting on National Geographic—I found that the little tibit about the watch that survived in Rolex's overall involvement of this film left a much more natural and interesting impression with me than if I saw some glossy cheesed-out TV spot during the commercial break.

Tuten: How do you go about writing a viral video or a short film that's branded? Is there a creative brief just as there would be for a more traditional advertising project?

Zhao: That's a good question. Yes, there is a brief. It's just executed differently. I often start concepting for my projects in the same ways that I would concept for a print ad, or a TV spot, or any communication intended for traditional media. I begin that way and I get that out of my system by writing all those ideas down. After, I realize that the viral world is a different medium. Many times viral videos, to be specific, need to have something that will make the audience pass it around. They need something that's super punchy. That something special needs to be a specific little quirk, to be of the brand rather than something encapsulating the whole campaign. It's often a little joke, or a little whistle, or something like that that really grabs your attention.

So oftentimes, I begin as I would traditionally, but when I get all those little ideas out of my system from writing a traditional ad campaign, I will grab my partner, my art director partner, and we will just turn off our art director/ copywriter roles and grab a camera and go out and start shooting things. You know, we will start doodling or we will start improvising and telling jokes, until we find that thing that makes us laugh. And that's how we do it. With viral films, it's important to find something quirky.

Tuten: How can you know what will be quirky enough to go viral? How do you know when you've hit upon that special something that triggers the spread of a piece of entertainment?

Zhao: I don't think anyone really ever knows. You just have your instincts. Basically I think the idea of a viral video, or the appeal of it is they are naturally unintentional or voyeuristic—the videos of cats jumping in boxes or a friend catching on fire, those get a million hits and stuff. So when you're trying to achieve that spontaneity on purpose you have to be in a certain state of mind.

You have to surprise yourself. There's this quote from Robert Frost. He said, "No surprise in the writer, no surprise in the reader." You have to surprise yourself first and then that will surprise the audience. That's more important than ever with branded entertainment and viral films because for the video to be effective, it needs to be something that really resonates with people. Whether it's shocking or funny, it has to be so spontaneous and so out of the blue that it grabs your attention.

Tuten: Do you have a favorite campaign? Something meaningful to you?

Zhao: Off the top of my head, those Old Spice virals Tim [Heidecker] and Eric [Wareheim] directed were just phenomenal to me. Their sense of humor is just so visceral and really I think it redefines what comedy can be today. It's the kind of stuff I'd laugh at and joke around about with my friends since I was a kid—this kind of absurdist sensibility. I think they're totally artists in themselves, and in a way, "anti-commercial." So, like, to see a mainstream brand like Old Spice and an agency like Wieden be open to something that wild gave me more hope for working on ad gigs. That I can be myself. Like Tim and Eric!

As far as something I worked on goes, we did a series of virals for Google called demoslams. As we all know, Google has tons of different technologies and new ones coming out. From what exists already from Gmail to "Gchat" to the way the search engine works, basically Google wanted to create a unique viral for each service. So, for example, for Google Translate we came up with a viral that documents these three kids who are obsessed with kung fu films. Of course, they're American kids and they don't speak Chinese. They use Google Translate to redub what they film into Chinese. For each technology, we basically made these fun demonstrations. The reason why I enjoyed working on these is because everything moved so fast. Literally, we were pitching our ideas one day and the next week we had it approved and we were shooting like ten videos in a two-week period. That's fantastic for me as a filmmaker because I didn't feel like anything was stalled. I felt like everything was very spontaneous, and that's the vibe and the energy that I like to work in. Especially in making viral videos, you need to be very spontaneous. Everything needs to feel slightly scrappy and that's how you get all those surprising ideas. Even during our shoot, we were improvising with the actors.

During that two-week period, I was able to go from writing to pitching and then the next week we were looking for the cast already and we were building sets and we were shooting. We were coming up with more new ideas on the set. That's great practice for me. Amazing. A wonderful opportunity to have.

Tuten: The fast pace is important to you. The ability to plan and execute quickly.

Zhao: I think so. I always knew filmmaking—here I'm talking about traditional, narrative filmmaking for cinema—can be a long process. You hear about these great films that come out, like *The Tree of Life* or *Blue Valentine* that take a decade to just develop. So working in advertising, I think I could be synergistic. It balances out the time component of filmmaking for me.

I needed something that would balance out the time commitment to film and also provide a creative outlet for me in between projects. But, then again, you'd think that advertising is always fast, but there are so many pitches that take a long time. Where I work, we are set up to be a one-stop shop for branded entertainment. We are the ad agency and production agency all under one house.

But even with that, you still find situations where the process seems extended. One thing we like to do where I work is take on more personal projects, to keep ourselves sharp. I produced and edited a music video for a musician friend of ours, who's on his way to release his album and other great things. Because the budget was so low, we did it very quickly and it turned out wonderfully. But because the musician's manager had a specific way that they wanted to plan the record release and video, timeline and all that, it's been months and we're just releasing it this spring. We shot it last summer. Sometimes you can work very fast but there's other things you can't control.

I also find it enjoyable and fulfilling to work with a small team. I started out in agencies where there would be 400 people running around. Communication is key. With a small team, communicating on creative tasks is much easier. I can come up with ideas much more efficiently and faster.

Tuten: Your plan is to stay with a small agency then.

Zhao: Yeah. I prefer a nimble work environment. I guess I went from one opposite to the other, going from a large agency to what now is probably the smallest work environment one could have. Between those two polar opposites I would definitely choose a small team because I like working with people that I feel are family. It's not that I don't like bigger agencies or more people. It's more that I like working with people I have a history with, and at bigger agencies, you're put on a project with a group of people, and once that's done, you might be switching to a completely new set of people. That can be great, but I like making those really long, personal connections with people. I like to know my partners. I like to know what goes on in my partner's private life.

Less people also means fewer walls to hop over to get my ideas launched. Though it does, in part, depend on the scale of the campaign. Obviously, if I was working on a huge Nike campaign, I would rather work in a big agency where I have all the support and I'm working on a piece of a bigger whole. But when you're working on one documentary project, or one music video, or one viral video, I think it's good to keep it focused like that and not have too many cooks in the kitchen.

I'm really not opposed to working at a traditional agency again. I just prefer working with a group of people that I know really well. The day goes by in a much more productive fashion.

Tuten: Do you have advice for people who are getting their start in advertising now?

Zhao: Thinking back, to get a gig in advertising out of school I wanted to do work to impress people. To do things the "right way," whatever that meant. I guess I wanted to get hired! [Laughter.] Now I think my 20s are more about figuring out what kind of work I can create that others might lack the sensibilities to, and why I'm doing the things I do, as opposed to just how to get it done. All that's a lifelong journey but, I think I do feel I'm beginning to have a deeper sense of what kind of stories I'm good at telling and what kind of projects I'd be better concepting for.

Everyone is unique, but it's hard to stay that way when you have pressures to conform to an industry or when any kind of group thinking is involved. Even in a huge agency it's important to not fall into a role where you become an advertising machine. Once you begin to develop your aesthetic and what kinds of ideas you feel like you have a talent in coming up for, you can gravitate towards those more and in turn create better work. Because as a creative you're like a tastemaker, or a filter for all the ideas floating around in the air.

Yeah, I think being nimble, and I think being spontaneous and a little bit scrappy maybe helps create great things. And that also comes from my experience as a filmmaker. I think it's good not to be too precious about things. I know people are going to kill me for saying that because you're always supposed to review your work and things like that, but I think there's a point where, you know, there are twelve different opinions. The audience is going to look at something very differently [than you].

When you start out, you want to just work. You want to impress others. And in a way it's good to learn the rules first before you try to bend them. But I wish more people had told me that eventually, the stuff that you make to impress yourself will probably impress others as well, so I'd be a little more of a risk taker from the get go.

These days, I try to come up with ideas and then make sure that I'm happy with them, first of all, and that my partner's happy with them, before I just let it out and unleash it into the world. For instance, I try to go out there and I purposely listen to music, and see art and things and films that are outside of my personal taste. Those kinds of activities keep me in balance and keep me in check on what's out there, how others may view concepts. The more

I work, the more I feel it's important to gravitate towards being a differentiated creative. A creative who is focused on certain things or good at writing certain kinds of concepts. Not to pigeonhole myself, but to be good at something specific so when there's a project that comes around, I will know whether I can match well with it instead of just saying, "Oh, I'm just a creative. I do well at everything."

Tuten: You're saying young creatives should be true to their own sense of identity in developing their work.

Zhao: Yeah, you know, you come out of school and then you are trying to get the first job. That's an important step because it's those early experiences that will help you learn what you like and don't like. But sometimes people will feel that you shouldn't question things because you haven't had any experience yet. We have to remember even when we are new to an experience that we have a voice. We have a mind. And the sooner you can identify your gift, that certain thing that belongs to you, then you'll begin to find those projects, and find them earlier in your career.

The advertising world can be subject to slow response times and the tediousness can be frustrating for young creatives. I am a young creative and it might be a little immature of me to say this. Probably a lot of young creatives feel this way. We just want to jump in and get a lot of work done and get it produced. Still, I know there are a lot of reasons why it takes time to approve things.

There was this one campaign or TV spot that I was working on, writing. I think it took like a year or something, or a year and a half before I ever saw it. It was just so much back and forth. I just know there's got to be a better way of communicating ideas or a better system of approval. Sometimes, I feel like filmmaking is great for me, especially in the way that I make films, where I'm working with a tiny crew. It's very refreshing because I'm just with a group of actors and a sound guy. It's very tiny and we're getting a lot of work done, as opposed to if I'm working on an advertising campaign. I'm dealing with clients that could be a huge team of people as well as other agencies that we might be working with at the time. It's just a lot of things that might stall the energy and the creativity.

In making viral films, I think it's important to have spontaneous energy and mindset every time I walk into my office. And if there's something stalling it that leads me astray a little bit. So I wish there were a way to like speed up the process.

Tuten: Do you have something you think you really wish you had known before? Questions of your own?

Zhao: The questions I still have are mainly about the business itself, in both advertising and film, just where it's going and how to reach audiences. Personally, I think there's too much content out there. There is too much clutter. Often, I watch virals posted on an advertising blog or somewhere else online, but I often question whether all the money that is poured into it and all the effort to produce the work that the agency did with the client— I wonder sometimes if it even resonates with people. Does it matter? Did it make a difference? How can a message really get across to people when there's just so much stuff out there? That's my biggest question, how do I as a creative not only come up with new ideas, but figure out ways of reaching an audience in a better way? How can I speak to my audience without simply putting more stuff into this ocean of clutter? I think that's the most critical question for me as a filmmaker and as a person in advertising.

When you create something, you create these works not just for yourself, but also because you want people to experience something. You don't want the audience to go numb because the whole landscape is so cluttered. I really think it's so easy to go through, say, 20 years of work and have only two or three campaigns or one film that actually resonates with its audiences's memories. So it's like, how do we focus that?

It doesn't need to necessarily be everyone. Obviously, films are just as targeted as ad campaigns, but, you know, when you create you want the work to reach and influence an audience and not get lost.

Tuten: Things change so fast in this industry. How do you stay current with new technology and the latest advances?

Zhao: I meet documentary filmmakers who work on their films often for a much longer time than a lot of independent feature filmmakers because of the amount of research required for a documentary. Especially if you're doing a piece on someone's life, it takes time to film and document life changes. The good documentary filmmakers are always so on point about using the latest technology and writing business plans to market their film. By the time they finish their film, whatever technology they used is going to be old technology because it's from five or four years ago, and the same with the business plan that they used. It is constantly changing. The same is true with advertising. The years between the nineties and the 2000s represented crazy, crazy change. It just makes you wonder: if that's just one decade of change, then what's going to happen in the next decade, you know?

I remember one of the partners at Wieden, John Jay, whom I admire a lot, was giving a talk about creativity to these visiting Japanese students. In it, one of the questions he asked was, "Why do truly creative people dislike change?" As he was talking about that, it hit me personally. I feel like

filmmaking has, more or less, the same hierarchy of studio and crew structures for most of the time it's been around. But if you look at the ad industry, it's so much more accommodating to changing things up. Messing with
the structures, you know? So, I start to wonder a lot about how the film
industry could follow that kind of flexibility. Even working in a specific and, I
suppose, new area of advertising—we still wind up doing things in a certain
way, and we get comfortable doing things a certain way, but that could shift
anytime. It's pretty exciting I think.

Tuten: Some people in the industry might say that there needs to be a
process of multiple levels of approval and refinement from other creatives.
You've talked a lot about getting work out, speed, creating quickly. You focus
on agility. In this project, there are people who are on one side of this con-
tinuum and then others on the opposite side.

Zhao: Yeah. I once read about a social experiment done with a school. I forget which school ran the experiment. The school took an art class and split
the class in half. There were maybe twenty people in the class. The first half,
their job was to come up with pottery. They made one piece every week.
That was their goal—to produce every single week. The other half spent
their entire year making one perfect piece of pottery. They all sent their
work anonymously into a competition. The surprising thing was that no one
in the half that spent the year perfecting one amazing piece of pottery was
selected in the competition. But the people who made things every week,
several were actually selected in the competition. Their work turned out to
be more beautiful and more human. Why? They released it at a time where
it was still full of life, before they killed it—before they killed their own ideas
through tons of editing.

And, again, I know it's very hard for me to say this in the advertising world
because when you create advertising, you are creating something that a
brand relies on. You are creating work that, when people see it, will affect
their impressions of the company. It's not just like me as a filmmaker, I'm
telling a story. You are reaching a broader spectrum, and it's hard to not want
to gravitate towards that. But to hone real creativity, it's good to just pound
out ideas instead of spending the whole day writing the perfect TV spot and
spending a whole week like sitting around writing this one idea and trying
to cut it down and rebuild it. In the end, it's not that it doesn't matter, but I
think you're taking the life out of a lot of things by doing that.

Tuten: What's next for you, John?

Zhao: I just hope I can keep making feature films. In between those, I want
to put my creativity in anything else that magnifies my storytelling skills—
and lately it's been advertising and music videos. I just enjoy making things

and also figuring out, as I said earlier, the infrastructure. Or being part of the dialogue of figuring out better ways to meet audiences. And being more effective and not wasting things and cluttering things.

I'm very minimalistic. If you walked into my room, [you'd see] I have a very small book collection, a very small DVD collection, my computer, and some clothes. I like it when things can be seen in a tangible way, and I feel like the landscape is the opposite of that in some ways. If I can make films and help the industry, both in advertising and film, find the audiences better and maybe build new structures, then I'm a pretty happy guy.

And I guess one last thing: in the end, if I learn enough from working in this throughout my life, I would like to build a film school some time later on in my life. If things click. That's a faraway dream of mine, but I would love to set up some one-year film camp, where I can offer an experience for kids that's very inspirational, and I can teach kids how to make films.

Ellen Steinberg
Jim Russell

Group Creative Director/EVP
Chief Innovation Officer
McKinney

Ellen Steinberg is group creative director and executive vice president at McKinney in Durham, NC (mckinney.com). She joined McKinney in 2006 after serving as co-creative head of Fallon New York. Steinberg's work has won virtually every major creative award and covers such iconic brands as Sherwin-Williams, Russell Beam, Miller Lite, Nikon, and Sports Illustrated. She has served as a juror for Communication Arts competitions and the One Show. Steinberg is a graduate of the University of Delaware. She is also a yoga instructor and a justice of the peace.

Jim Russell is chief innovation officer at McKinney, where he's worked since 2003. He joined McKinney after work at Circle.com in Boston, following work on the online launch of the MINI Cooper. The campaign was named Most Innovative Marketing Campaign of the Year by Business 2.0. Russell helped reinvent McKinney by fully integrating digital into its existing disciplines, rather than holding digital as a separate business unit. As a result, 90 percent of McKinney's front-line staff is active in creating and managing integrated digital efforts, including online advertising, online CRM (customer relationship management), social media, *interactive brand experience, mobile, and site design. Russell began his career at Accenture, first working in artificial intelligence and later for Accenture's Center for Strategic Technology in Palo Alto. He is a graduate of the University of Wisconsin at Madison.*

Tracy Tuten: What led you to advertising as a profession? Did you grow up wanting to work in the field?

Ellen Steinberg: I'll start. My father was a commercial artist. I grew up around a lot of graphic design and the kind of advertising that was more like writing a headline that rhymed, and doing the illustration. I have to say, growing up with it, I never looked at advertising and thought, "I want to do that." I actually went so far as to target occupations completely different from advertising. I always had the fine-artist gene, though when it came time for school, I actually applied to a school for accounting. I was good at math and I really had no idea what I wanted to do. By the time I got accepted, I was taking an accounting course my senior year in high school, and about a month into it—actually, it was probably more like an hour into it—I thought, "There's no way in hell I could do this for a living."

I actually stumbled upon what I would say is now my career [during] my freshman year at the University of Delaware. I had heard really cool things about this hot department called visual communications, which was in the art department. Word was that the department was very hard to get into, and there was a really crazy professor who taught in the program. The professor was giving a talk one night and I attended. It was a one- or two-hour presentation, and the professor showed student work.

One of the slides showed a spread, a print ad for Scotts Lawn Care. It was the first slide up there. I actually remember this slide. It was a line drawing of a house sitting on a horizon line, and it was repeated on the left side and the right side. And on the left side was a green crayon scratch on the ground, and it said, "Green with Scotts." And then the exact same chicken scratch was in the sky on the right, and it said, "Green with envy." And I looked at it, and I went, "I want to do that." And that's how it happened. That's why I'm here. It was actually the perfect solution for me, because I could use art and I could also solve problems. I found it really just fascinating.

Tuten: Ellen, was your first job out of college in advertising?

Steinberg: It was. I ended up being in the visual communications program, which was a three-year program undergrad, and I developed a portfolio, and I went straight up to New York, and found a job.

Tuten: And stayed in the business ever since?

Steinberg: Yeah, just about. I've had brief hiatuses here and there. I free-lanced for about seven years, but it's twenty-one years that I'm in the business, I'm horrified to say.

Tuten: And the improv, justice of the peace, and yoga work—that's all on the side?

Steinberg: Yes, yes [laughter]. Jim has a very different story than mine.

Tuten: Jim, tell us about your story.

Jim Russell: Okay. I've always enjoyed creative media, whether it's music or film or good advertising, from the time I was a kid and into college. But in college, I was a psychology major and then picked up a computer science degree as well. I was a double major. I did that because I was really interested in artificial intelligence. I loved the idea of trying to teach computers how to do things that humans do well.

Straight out of school, I worked at Andersen Consulting, which is now Accenture, as one of their small group of AI consultants. AI consultants go to their different clients around North America and build different AI systems to help the clients with underwriting, and this and that. I did that for a while and I really liked it.

This is where serendipity comes into play. Andersen opened up an applied R&D center in Silicon Valley, a bike ride from the Stanford campus in Palo Alto. I moved there in '93. Half my job was still sort of building demos and doing technology stuff, but the other half was focused on a business center for different clients of Accenture. One day Citgo would be in, and the next day it would be the *New York Times*, and the next day would be a company like Volvo. All of these clients had different problems, and what we were basically doing was building the business center. It was really a sort of marketing center. We built these demos, and if all was going well, the chief information officer would point to what was being shown on the screens and say to his or her underlings, "I want to build one of those. How quickly can you make it happen?"

That was really what caught me first—using technology for storytelling to get people to do what you want them to do. That's a crass way of saying it, but that's what we were doing at the time. So I did that and I realized I was sort of a square peg in a round hole in traditional technology consulting, even at that R&D center. Slowly but surely, the next job was helping executives at Intel with their keynote addresses and speeches and building the demos around that. And then the next job over was at an online agency, so even though I have been working for about twenty-three, twenty-four years, I've only been In advertising since 2000, so for about eleven years now.

Tuten: What was it that made it clear that advertising was a place that you could belong and make a difference?

Russell: I didn't know that actually. Once I got over to the online agency, from the work I was doing before, it just felt like such a good fit. Every problem you're trying to solve has creativity at the center of it, but it's grounded in some form of technology. I'm not a creative. I don't work in the creative department, like Ellen does. I'm a little bit different. I'm sort of half-strategist, half-thinking about what's next in the world of innovation. My focus is on how technology can be applied within the realm of marketing. So for me, I can apply all those skills, but in a very creative way and in a very emotional way. You know the best doorway into influencing somebody to love the brand is not through their mind, but through their heart. Trying to figure that out was and is really interesting to me.

Tuten: You both have really different roles at McKinney, but you're both, at heart, creatives. Tell me about what a typical day is like for both of you and also how it is that you both end up working on the client work. How do you feed into the client work that's coming out of McKinney?

Steinberg: I'm a group creative director, so I'm basically a creative director for several accounts. That means a typical day for me is either kicking off a project, or I'm reviewing the work of one or two teams. I always say that I go in there and I kill as much work as I can. But I'm just trying to make sure that whatever we're doing feels really original and fresh. Those are my internal responsibilities, making sure that we have great work that actually is solving a problem and is not just, I would say, art for art's sake. Creatively solving the problem.

The second part of my job is dealing with the clients and trying to sell work to them, which is incredibly challenging. You know, with good work there's usually some risk involved. I always joke that it's kind of like we're more like lawyers because we're trying to argue someone into something when we understand why it's good, but they don't come from the same world. I think *we* all get that, and it's trying to respectfully and intelligently present a case of why this work is good and could be effective.

Tuten: Does the sales side come naturally for you?

Steinberg: God, no. You know, if anything, I've learned after being a manager now for several years that the best thing I can do is just speak from my heart. It's kind of like what Jim was just saying. I find the best thing I can do is form a relationship with clients so they know I'm a friend. They know I'm a supporter, and then I just really give my honest two cents on what I feel would be good for them. I find that when I can just be myself and—if they choose something that I don't believe in—to just ask, "Do you *really* want to do that?" They'll actually listen to me. But it's a fine art. It's as much of a dance as learning how to do the creative itself.

Tuten: Was there anything that you had to do to prepare yourself for that part of your job?

Steinberg: Yeah, the ten years prior to that. I think it's one of those things, and I watch it in younger creatives—that the more you do it, the better you become at it. You start to learn what the pitfalls are. You start to learn to better set up what you're trying to solve without just going to the executional device. I think for me, at least, it was just doing the work and getting in front of clients and learning from my own mistakes. And also, I have to say, every time I watch a good presenter, I sit and I watch them, and I just take notes.

Tuten: I think we all can improve on our presentation skills by watching people who are better.

Steinberg: Absolutely.

Tuten: Jim, talk to me about your typical day.

Russell: My role here at McKinney has really shifted in the past year. We got so good at practicing the craft of digital. I just got a report that a bunch of people who reported to me who were interactive strategists were being disbanded and being moved to where they needed to be. They are being moved into creative or planning. We got so good at doing digital, and now we live in a postdigital world. It shouldn't be thought of as something special or unique. Since then, it's been really fun. I get to work on what I want to work on. Part of that is looking at what we should be paying attention to—what's coming down the pipe six to eight months from now. It used to be eighteen months, twenty-four months, but things are moving so quickly.

The other thing is in pitches, just making sure our digital ideas are really good, so that's where creativity still comes into play with what I'm doing. And then the last part is just thinking about how we can work internally to come up with more leading ideas faster for all our clients and for ourselves.

Tuten: Can you tell us something that's coming down the pike technology-wise?

Russell: That we're working on or just overall?

Tuten: Just overall. Something exciting that I can't even imagine yet.

Russell: Geez, there are quite a few. I think we're going to get to the point in the world pretty soon where we're going to have bandwidth that's like twenty to thirty times more than what we have right now. The experiment that Google's doing in Kansas City is an example. When this happens, and again, this is not far off, communication such as PowerPoint, Skype, and basic videoconferencing that we see now as being standard practice will seem incredibly primitive. I don't want to go all the way to say there will be holograms that we'll look at and communicate via gesture, but certainly, from the perspective of what is possible when one can transmit large amounts of data, we'll begin to see these possibilities to be true. For some capabilities, we're already there.

The crux is that we'll have to figure out a different way to invite people into the world in which we wish to communicate. We'll have enormous technologies able to support how our brands wish to present themselves and impact the lives of their target consumers. But how do you engage the consumers in this context? How do you invite them to your world when their own world is competing with you?

Tuten: And do you have any answers that you can share?

Russell: One critical point is that we can't consider ideas as solely a message anymore. The message has always been the core, but we can never again focus on messaging *to* consumers or talking *at* them. If there isn't some natural conversational part, where we're inviting them to participate with the brand or co-create with the brand, it's probably not a good idea. The idea that we're focused on probably isn't worthwhile.

Tuten: What rituals do you both have? Things that help you work creatively or work productively?

Steinberg: I'll explain, but keep in mind that I'm describing my creative rituals more from when I was actually coming up with ideas on my own, rather than my work now as a creative director. Now, my work is largely managing. But on my own, so much for me is figuring out what the problem is and letting it just sort of simmer overnight. I rarely like to just jump in and start concepting. I like to let the problem or opportunity sink in a little bit. I come from an art background, so my approach is primarily visual. I always like to start from that angle, even if it is just purely a routine method of getting into the concepting. Of course, I want the resulting ideas to be smart and resonate, but it can be fun and worthwhile to approach ideation from different angles. Especially if you're in a visual medium.

And then another important aspect for me, as far as creativity and creating go, comes from a Buddhist learning. It's to really honor when it's not working. It's the whole square peg/round hole phenomenon. There comes a point where, if you just have to force it, it's better to stop and come back to the issue at another time. I've learned now that the creative process shouldn't be that hard. This is true with managing, too—it just shouldn't be that hard. So it's being able to not be attached, to be able to walk away and just throw the cards up in the air, and try something completely different. You really do have to practice the art of nonattachment, because it's easy to cling and go, "No, this is it. This is my baby. I want to see it grow up." But it's far better to say, "Ehh, yeah, that was just not meant to be," and just let it go.

I also think it's important to be able to walk away in general, cleanse the air, have a life. That's something I always try to invite people that are working for me to do whenever I can tell they're stressed out in their minds. I tell them to walk away for a little bit.

Tuten: How do you draw that line between when you should protect an idea that you think is really good and when you should throw the cards up in the air and let things end as they may?

Steinberg: I definitely encourage people to try to figure it out. It isn't always intuitively obvious when you should give up and when you should hold your ground. Sometimes I struggle to figure this out. I mean, I won't be as attached to a concept as my creatives are. I keep saying this word "honoring," but I think you also have to honor when you first see an idea and it resonates with you, and you think, "Oh!" That reaction came from somewhere, so I feel like [you should] really give it its due, give it its due chance of being. Try it twenty different ways, but then, okay, twenty is enough. If it doesn't work at twenty ways, it isn't working, so let it go.

You know, it's a real fine art. I think you know when, in the beginning, you look at the work and go, "Ehh, maybe. Play with it and see if it develops into anything." Those are easier to let go of because they never really had that fully convincing first spark.

Tuten: But the other ones, you can?

Steinberg: But the other ones, I feel like you've got to give it its due shot, play with it, but then, you know, after a while, if it's not working . . . It's all relative to how much time you have, but if you try for a couple of days and it's just not developing, then let it go.

Tuten: Are you as involved in client work as you'd like to be?

Steinberg: I am. There's part of me that misses creating from the bottom up. I feel like I've become sort of a third or fourth partner with my creative team, where I'm definitely adding to the idea or helping shape it. And I get a lot of fulfillment now from directing the project and helping steer the creatives down a path where they can keep blossoming and the work can keep blossoming. That's really fulfilling for different reasons, and I do feel like I still am able to help put my own personal mark on work.

Tuten: That's good. Jim, what about you? Tell me about the rituals that are important to you.

Russell: I don't know [laughter]. I guess for me, the ritual is to not take myself too seriously. It's kind of important. Again, I'm not creating the ideas necessarily. I'm often justifying the ideas as to whether they can work digitally. With digital, you can make a fact-based argument for why something would work, and often that's my role. I don't know. I think with me and my field, often it's the lateral move of an idea from another industry that gets transferred over to the category you're working in or something else like that that's really important. And that's something that is not going to come to you a half an hour after a briefing happens.

Or even the next day. Everybody in advertising says they don't have enough time. But, I don't think the advertising industry is unique in feeling pressure to solve problems with a deadline.

Often we are told to come back with ideas within four or five business days of a client telling us what they want solved. And that's just the way business works. Maybe lightning will happen during that time, maybe not. Often you just need more time to marinate on the idea, and understand where the hidden connections are, and what's the right way to express the idea and find the idea.

Steinberg: And, actually, sometimes the best gift is when an idea dies. For whatever reason, you find out, "Oh, it's not quite the brief we wanted," or "Someone did this idea a few years ago," or "The client just doesn't like it." Sometimes that's the best gift because, more often than not, with the thinking that you already have and all the stewing, you can come back and actually do something even better. I see that all the time. You have a quick mourning period—and it has to be quick—but then you move on and do something even better.

Tuten: It's like football when you have twenty-four hours to worry about the loss and then you're on your way?

Steinberg: Yes, exactly that idea.

Tuten: Did you have mentors who helped you as you developed into your careers?

Russell: I don't think I had one, not in the traditional sense. The only person I could say served in this kind of role—and this still sticks with me—is the person who was CEO of Accenture at the time. This was in the mid-nineties. I was basically his technology lackey. I didn't fix his laptop, but I would show him new things. I was the first one to show him the Internet. His name was George Shaheen, and he then went on to found Webvan. I just remember, even with me being a twenty-something-year-old kid at that time, when I'd go into his office, he would tell his assistant that we were not to be interrupted. Here's a CEO of a multi-million-dollar company, one of the leading professional services firms in the world, but I'd have his undivided attention to show him what I had brought to the meeting. I say I don't consider that a traditional mentor because he wasn't advising or guiding me, but at the same time, I learned so much from that.

Actually, one thing I learned is to pay attention to the priority in front of you at the time. Rather than checking messages as they arrive, tweeting, and whatever else we call multitasking. The fact is, you don't get much done if everybody's trying to multitask.

Tuten: So do you emulate his behavior?

Russell: Wait. I have a tweet I have to read, so if you'll just give me a second here—I'm kidding. Go ahead [laughter].

Steinberg: Make sure that you get that.

Russell: What was your question?

Tuten: Do you emulate his behavior when you meet with people now?

Russell: I try to. When you said, "Who's your mentor?" that's the only example I can think of.

Tuten: That makes me sad that he's all you had.

Russell: Really?

Tuten: Yes.

Russell: Why?

Tuten: Just as I've done these interviews, some of the people—well, it's like they're tearing up thinking about the people who really made a difference putting them on their career path, and so I wish you had that, Jim.

Russell: I haven't been doing this for twenty-three years, right? My career has shifted. I'm not in the same industry where I started out. In fact, this is the longest I've been in any one industry. That's why this is fun for me. When this stops being fun, I'll go do something else.

Tuten: That's an important lesson. When it stops being fun, go do something else.

Russell: Yeah, maybe I'm a little bit different. I've always been that way.

Tuten: Ellen, what about you? A mentor?

Steinberg: There are people in my career who have taught me things along the way. But, technically, what's a mentor? Is it someone who teaches you along the way? I don't think there were people along the way who adopted me the way I think a mentor would, but I've had the privilege of working with some amazing people.

Actually, I'll back up to a professor in college who was incredibly instrumental in shaping my life and just being the catalyst for me to be who I am today. I always credit him. He really forced me to come out of my shell. He taught all of us super-important lessons about advertising that go beyond just creativity—but more about being open and sharing your work versus being private and competitive. And, you can see this in certain schools where people come out guarding their work. His point to us was you *want* to share because it's going to get better and why hold that back? But he also taught us about earning your way into places.

We would do a lot of field trips to New York when we were just in piddly old Newark, Delaware, showing them that we studied what they do and why we admire them, and never just cold-calling people. Really working hard, working without pay, offering to help in the office without pay just so you can breathe the air. He taught us a lot of invaluable information.

And then along the way, as a very young art director, I worked with people that really honed my craft. I thought I was a good designer and then they would be looking over my shoulder and telling me just how horsey everything looked. It was a while until I could actually spot that myself. So, my professor, and people in my early New York days, and then the people I worked with at Fallon in Minneapolis. I always say that when I had the chance to work at Fallon McElligott, that was me getting to work with people that I studied in school who were my heroes! These people were the most generous, open people, absolutely humble, and they really brought to life the things my professor had told us about in school. They all taught me to just be open, and that your work will grow from that.

Tuten: So you started off in New York, and then you went to Minneapolis, and now you're in North Carolina.

Steinberg: Yeah, and there was New York and Australia in between as well, yes.

Tuten: How was it you ended up moving to so many places?

Steinberg: I guess for creatives, we tend to get focused on the New York thing, but I really think, especially when you're young, people make hops every couple of years. So I did that. I think a big reason I sort of jumped all over the place is that I got to see just how different places worked. When I was freelance, that was great because I got to sample different agencies all over the country and just see how differently they work, what the culture was like, and so on. But me going out to Minneapolis—I would *never* have chosen that at the time. I was absolutely in love with New York, but I knew at the time that Fallon was just one of the best agencies in the world and it was such an honor to be invited to work there. There was no way I was turning that down. That started my jump off the island.

Tuten: And how long were you with Fallon?

Steinberg: I was with Fallon for five years in Minneapolis and then I was with them again in New York for a few years.

Tuten: That's a good experience.

Steinberg: And I freelanced for them in between.

Tuten: Do you have a favorite campaign?

Steinberg: That's a hard question for me. Here at McKinney?

Tuten: It might not be at McKinney. It might be something from your past, but something that you had a role in.

Steinberg: Hmm, hmm, hmm. You go, Jim.

Russell: Okay. There's one at McKinney or really one and a half I'd like to share. The cool thing about digital work is often you're doing stuff that's really on the cutting edge, and what we are putting into the world is more like improvisational than, you know, just producing ads and seeing what happens.

We created a campaign for a ringtone company sort of in the pre-iPhone era. They wanted to sell a lot of ringtones, so we invented this construct called "Not pheromones but pherotones," or ringtones that cause intense sexual attraction. We created a doctor, a professor, who was researching this term. She was a Danish doctor, and she was on tour in the college campuses in America. We crossed the line a little bit by putting a Wikipedia entry for pherotones. We had staged one of them. We created some low-end banner ads and stuff like that. It was just getting the conversation around to whether this was real or not, and then exposing that, "Oh my gosh. Pherotones do exist, and you can buy them at Oasys Mobile," and get these ringtones. The professor had office hours. People could chat and converse with her and IM.

This is all before the pre-social media days. We have all sorts of other tools as our disposal. It just was a blast seeing this take off and never knowing what was going to happen the next morning in terms of the discussions that were occurring and other stuff around this campaign.

Tuten: That sounds like a lot of fun.

Russell: The other one, the half, is that I was kind of blessed that when I joined advertising in 2000, I got to work on the launch of MINI in the United States. I was an account person at the time. It was a live campaign. It was amazing and I just thought all clients were going to be like that. The head of [communications at] MINI Cooper at the time, Kerri Martin, sat in the room and said, "Look, my only goal for us is to put out great work and be brand of the year. If we do that, I'll be happy." And, I didn't know. I thought they were all going to be like that.

Steinberg: Yeah.

Russell: To be told, "I just want great work. Do this," it was so nice. To work on a brand that was very powerful to begin with and be empowered to make the brand even stronger. Since then, I have known what it is to have client situations like that—and I've had them since then, too.

Tuten: Ellen, do you have one to tell?

Steinberg: This has always been a really hard question for me. There are certain projects that I've loved for different reasons. I almost feel like what's more interesting is just what shapes my favorites now. It's probably a product of being in the business over twenty years, but I feel like you can do cool TV and print and interesting, creative execution. You can keep doing that, I think, till the cows come home. I really love doing something that's more just a really innovative business-building idea these days. We're working on something now for Sherwin-Williams called Chip It! that's an online tool in their digital color tool collection that I just love because it's just so out of the box and really fun and engaging. Basically, it turns any online image into a palette of paint colors. And then you can save the colors with the picture, send it to a friend and even print it out. You know, take it to the store with you. It's nowhere near a traditional "ad," yet I think it will do a lot for Sherwin-Williams.

I think it's just kind of interesting how what moves me now is not what it was before. I used to love to do a really killer one-two punch print ad, like the good old days at Fallon. And, I still have appreciation for those types of things, but the world's just totally different now.

Tuten: Okay. Imagine that you have a magic, fairy wand and with it you can change one thing about advertising. What do you change?

Steinberg: Honestly, my wish is that every client would embrace risk. Because honestly, at the end of the day, while I do think superstar creatives are not easy to find, but there *are* a lot of really good ones out there. Finding a great CMO [chief marketing officer] that has an appetite to do something that's differentiating, that will get people's attention, that can be a challenge. To find clients that have an appetite for risk would be the biggest step for advertising.

Tuten: Have you had any of those ideal clients?

Steinberg: A couple times, yeah, a couple times I have. But a couple times out of twenty years, you know? I feel like, more often than not, a version of your idea gets through, but the version is not quite the way that you hoped for it to be. Or the campaign that you really thought would get people's attention, never remotely sees the light of day. To be brave is rare. And there's a game to this business. I truly feel like there's a game to how you succeed and, more often than not, clients land on the side of safety.

Tuten: Do you have an example of a client who embraced risk?

Russell: I think the span of even within the past five years, there's just a finer point of "I want return on my marketing investment." That means there's more testing. That means there's more analytics to try to uncover what return actually means. Sometimes what we do is so creative, showing storyboards to people or using intrinsically false ways to get feedback, like focus groups. The dynamics of focus groups don't do service to the work and what the work could do to move a brand.

So it's difficult, but at the same time I respect why they want to test things and why they want to understand potential outcomes. Media is a very different animal. I don't understand why clients want to place bets in safe media outlets in some cases.

Steinberg: It's that lack-of-risk thing.

Russell: Yeah, it's that lack-of-risk thing.

Tuten: So, Jim, is that the one thing you would change, too, or is your answer a little bit different?

Russell: I don't know. I can't think of anything I want to change necessarily. I'm just in a pragmatic mood.

Steinberg: I think the problem is focus groups. I think focus groups are just a subset of this overall lack of strength or lack of conviction to leap off a cliff. Man, if we could obliterate focus groups, that would be really great.

Russell: I think I have a more accurate left brain than Ellen does. Maybe. If I were a CMO, and let's say I had a $40, $50 million advertising budget. I'd say, "Look. I want the best possible creative work, but I want to work with you in ways we all agree on to test, and we can test this and have some degree of confidence that the consumers will love this work just as much as the ten of us in the room will." And now the tools in your tool kit for testing include brain scans, and other measurement technologies people can't even imagine, and what not. Any test has its flaws. You've just got to be smart about which ones you're doing to honor the creative process as opposed to sending people animatics and storyboards or something else and saying, "What did you think?" So, that's all.

Tuten: Jim, are you working on any of those innovations in measurement and testing?

Russell: There are other groups that do that more than I do, honestly. In our planning department, we do analytics. We are using more enlightened ways of testing now than the focus group.

Tuten: *Mad Men* has reinforced some of the ad industry's early stereotypes. Are any of those types that you see on the show still prevalent in the industry today?

Russell: I just think the common element is that this is hard work, and you want to blow off steam after work. The difference is this isn't the fifties anymore, or the early sixties, so you have a lot of more options to blow off steam. By that, I don't mean methadone and pain killers. No. No.

Tuten: We're not limited to Scotch.

Russell: Or Ecstasy. They didn't have that then. The main point is that you can exercise, do yoga, use meditation. A lot of people I know here, they go rock climbing before they come in to work. We work hard and we feel stress and we handle it in very different ways than what are shown in *Mad Men*. You need a release in some way. I don't think it has to be booze and womanizing.

Steinberg: I think the deadlines are still pretty prevalent. Of course, they had probably a month to come up with one print ad. There's always an ad that looks kind of suspect, but then after a night with some liquor and some hookers, they go, "All right, I'll run that print ad."

Tuten: When you look around the industry now, what surprises you most?

Steinberg: It's just so different now as far as turnaround times go. And also, I miss the good old days of presenting an idea in a thumbnail sketch. People expect it to be very blown out, very quickly. But, you know, bigger picture, it's because the world is just absolutely changing, so it's interesting to me just now. What is an ad, you know? Now there are stunts, there are online tools, there's a social media campaign. It's all advertising, so would I have predicted the business would be like this ten years ago even? No way. It's just a totally different game. I think for people like us that are a little bit older, it's breathing some life into it, breathing some fear into it, too, because you have to quickly learn what all the young kids know.

Tuten: What advice would you give to those young kids?

Steinberg: I'd still give them the advice that it's all about the great idea. You can do the coolest execution and make it look really sweet, but there needs to be something that I emotionally connect to.

Tuten: Jim, what about you? Advice?

Russell: The big advice from me for young people is "get used to failure and cherish that." Some of the best projects I worked on here at McKinney and elsewhere, some people would look at in terms of the results, whether it tipped to be viral and other silly things, and say, "That project was a failure." But I look at all of those projects as a learning experience. That's how you learn, right? I look at those projects and see skills I learned. Like how I learned to propagate a brand through Twitter, or how I learned to work with a team more effectively. The point is—these projects are not really failures. Instead, it's important to hug and cherish those things because nobody else will do that for you. Your batting average for getting an idea past someone like Ellen and on to a client might be one out of fifty ideas. Embrace what others would consider to be not succeeding.

Tuten: Are you systematic about it, so each time you have a failure, do you do a little analysis?

Russell: I do with my projects on the big things. I do try to have a debrief or an after-action type of report, where we get everybody in the room and [discuss] what worked, what didn't, what would we do differently the next time. I don't know. Maybe we should be more premeditative and do that for the small things here, too. Those certainly help.

Tuten: I love the idea of learning from the failures. It's such an important lesson.

Russell: The important point is for people to know the lesson: when you face failure, dust yourself off and go on.

Steinberg: Yeah. Get used to it.

Russell: Don't get attached to the failure, like, "Oh man, that really blew. I thought that was the best idea I ever thought of." You know, it's kind of what Ellen was saying before: you mourn the loss of something that didn't get sold and just dust yourself off.

Steinberg: Yeah, give yourself a compartmentalized amount of time. I get it. I get the loss people feel. You put a lot of work into it. You love it. You see all the right reasons for it to live, but at the end of the day, it died. For whatever reason, it's dead. Fine. You have thirty-six hours to mourn. But then pick yourself up and stop bitching about it [laughter].

Tuten: Ellen, I have a question specifically about you this time.

Steinberg: Okay.

Tuten: It's pretty unusual still to see a female leader in creative. Do you see that gender gap closing in creative departments in the future or what kind of advice would you have for women to be able to move up through the ranks of creative?

Steinberg: McKinney is pretty interesting because there are so many female creatives here. I have to say, I've never seen as many female creatives as we have here. It's funny. I am asked this question a lot, just what it's like to be a woman. I do think probably the industry doesn't see as many female managers because the women make a choice at some point. A lot of them choose to start families and get away from this exhausting career. I completely get that. But then there are others that stay. You know, there's a stay-at-home dad or whatever. But whatever the case, my advice for people, or my own experience at least, is I've never worked at a place where I'm aware that I'm a woman. Maybe I've been really lucky. I personally would not take that if I was at a place that would not let me voice my opinion because of my genitalia.

I encourage people to find an environment where you simply are finding that the people are recognizing you for your intelligence and your talents, and that's all that's there. That it doesn't matter if you're a female or a male. I've been really lucky that that's all I've had. But I don't believe in luck, so there's something that I'm putting out there and I'm finding the right people to play with.

Tuten: Did that just come naturally?

Steinberg: I guess somehow I've been inviting that in. I do know that if I was around an environment where it was a definitive boys' club and I was not invited in, that would not be okay with me. I would push my way in, or I would speak up, or I would, quite honestly, leave and say it's not worth it because I really think, especially as a creative, the best ideas should be rewarded. It doesn't matter where they're coming from.

Tuten: So what's ahead for you two? What are your next steps, dreams, and aspirations?

Steinberg: To get out of advertising!

Tuten: No! Seriously?

Steinberg: No, I don't know. Dreams and aspirations?

Tuten: If you weren't in advertising, where would you be?

Steinberg: I'd probably be a yoga instructor part of the time. I'd probably really be enjoying not working, quite honestly. I might be a yoga instructor in Vegas.

Tuten: Doing weddings on the side.

Steinberg: Yeah, doing weddings on the side. I do know I love creating, so I think I would get bored if I were doing absolutely nothing, but I would have to be in some environment where I could creatively problem solve. I think that's why advertising kind of keeps me around.

Tuten: It's got it all.

Russell: I think of one or two ads. Sometimes when I have to think too much, I wish I were a blackjack dealer in Vegas, and my job was nothing more than to just deal those cards. Keep the numbers in my head and see who wins and who loses. Probably the bloom would be off that rose in about two weeks, but, you know, it's cool for them. But I always like to be around stuff that's what's new and what's next, so working for a technology company or a startup that's using technology in an interesting way always is appealing to me.

Tuten: Do you ever think about having your own agency, either of you?

Steinberg: No. I have no interest in that.

Russell: No.

Tuten: How come?

Russell: Well, you know, interviewing—my beautiful interviewing skills to the contrary—I'm simply not a people person. I have a hard time when people say, "Hi, how are you?"

"I'm Jim Russell. I've been working hard for you, too." [Laughter.]

Steinberg: Running an agency, it's just so difficult. I've watched several friends go off and open their own agency, and it's absolutely stressful. If you're lucky, you have a client come in that can pay for your overhead and [you can] think of as your stepping stone. But it's so fragile these days, and to have that many people that I'm responsible for and—oh God. I don't know. It just stresses me out just thinking about it.

Index